EFFECTIVE PASTORS for a NEW CENTURY

Effective Pastors for a New Century

Helping Leaders Strategize for Success

James E. Means

Baker Books

A Division of Baker Book House Co.
Grand Rapids, Michigan 49516

Published by Baker Books,
a division of Baker Book House Company
P.O. Box 6287, Grand Rapids, Michigan 49516-6287

Printed in the United States of America

Library of Congress Cataloging-in-Publication Data

Means, James E.
    Effective pastors for a new century : helping leaders strategize for success / James E.
    Means
       p. cm.
    Includes bibliographical references.
    ISBN 0-8010-6302-7
    1. Clergy—Office. 2. Pastoral theology. 3. Christianity—21st century. I. Title.
BV660.2.N39   1993
253—dc20   93-2853

To Vernon C. Grounds
President Emeritus of Denver Seminary
my friend, confidant, and mentor
for nearly forty years

Contents

FOREWORD

Henry David Thoreau once wrote, "For every thousand hacking at the leaves of evil, there is one striking at the root." It is good to add the name Jim Means to those who are striking at the root of what is wrong with the church. Not only does Means address the real problems, he offers solutions that are finely honed for church life at the turn of the century. I especially appreciate his willingness to swim upstream against the flow of popular culture and its effects on the contemporary church. In a day when most are calling for less commitment, Means calls for high commitment. In a day of the market-driven church, he calls for a theologically-driven church. In a day when congregations and their artificially stimulated appetites are sovereign, Means tells us that only Scripture and God himself are sovereign. This work faithfully analyzes the current trends in our society that have negatively affected churches, and gives step-by-step methods to counteract those trends to create a more healthy, productive church with disciple-making at its heart.

J. I. Packer has said, "Every movement of ideas needs its own literature." Three cheers for Jim Means, who has now added another important piece of the literature necessary to take forward the disciplemaking agenda in the United States and then around the world. Thanks, Jim; keep up the good work.

Bill Hull

ACKNOWLEDGMENTS

The production of this book has necessitated the labor-intensive cooperation of numerous people—to whom I owe a debt of gratitude. First, I am thankful to the faculty and administration of Denver Seminary for granting me a long sabbatical, the essential time for research and writing. No practitioner of ministry works with people of greater integrity and spiritual vitality. Second, I am grateful to numerous students through the years—now serving in strategic places around the world—who have repeatedly challenged my thinking, sharpened my understanding of ministry, and inspired me to contribute to their lives as they have contributed to mine. Third, I express my appreciation to the library staff of Denver Seminary. They graciously and efficiently complied with every request I made of them—and I made quite a few. Fourth, I am profoundly indebted to my family, who encouraged me repeatedly when the task seemed intimidating, and especially I thank my treasured daughter, Kathy Mulhern, an editor and author in her own right, for her sacrificial service in reading and rereading my manuscript and for her many valuable insights and corrections. Without the loving assistance of all these special people, this book would have been impossible.

INTRODUCTION

If anyone sets his heart on being an overseer, he desires
a noble task.

Paul the apostle

American pastors stand at a crossroads. One path leads to
effective ministry, revitalization, and growth. The other road accommodates the value systems of a secularized culture and allows the
church to slide further toward the irrelevance and impotency that
has eviscerated Christianity elsewhere. The struggle for renewal
requires delicate balance, rigorous discipline, and unwavering perseverance. These do not come cheap, and many lack the will to pay
the price.

Athletes demonstrate the value and the difficulty of balance, discipline, and perseverance. Some teams have either a good offense
or a good defense, but few have both; they never win the World
Series or the Superbowl. Many Olympians run fast, but fade in the
stretch; they don't win many races. Some boxers hit hard, but can't
take a punch; they don't last long. Many athletes have tremendous
talent, but lack discipline; they never become champions.

Churches and their leaders contend with similar problems. The
exhausting task of balancing values, objectives, and resources to
achieve a worthy mission exceeds the discipline and perseverance
of many. The comfort that the flesh loves and the complacency that

God abhors form significant barriers to those aspiring to spiritual leadership. Many pastors simply surrender and settle down to the dull business of survival, but once they commit themselves to manage the status quo, stagnation and rot inevitably follow.

Churches can be organizationally superior but spiritually anemic. Some sustain unity but fail to celebrate diversity. They will tenaciously preserve approved dogma but lack cultural sensitivity and contextualization. Other churches create exciting meetings and pack people into pews but function poorly as hospitals for the spiritually sick. Many modern churches take pride in their relevance—particularly in music—but fail to realize they are communicating insipid or false doctrine. They utilize the paraphernalia of technology but fail to exercise the weapons of spiritual warfare.

Sometimes pastors begin their ministries with great energy and enthusiasm but quickly lose heart. Others strain toward the goal but lack discipline or never learn to rest properly. Some strike good blows but can't take the bruises of ministry. Many possess skill and confidence, but their unbridled arrogance eventually undoes them. More than a few have an excellent offense—they seem to do everything well—but lack a good defense, and they succumb to the staggering temptations associated with ministry. Some display wonderful gifts but lack character and training; they never achieve enduring success in ministry.

Humanity's real disease—rebellion against God—and all its symptoms can never be treated successfully by secular methods, techniques, and therapies. Sound theology and the spiritual authenticity of our leaders must be returned to the top of our agenda. Failure to teach balanced doctrine contributes to the weakness or ruin of many churches. Teaching of grace, assurance, and freedom in Christ without also teaching the holiness of God, the dangers of sin, and the disciplines of discipleship fosters a dangerous inclusivism and antinomianism, and always produces functionally weak churches. Sometimes lopsided theology—disguised heresy—generates statistical strength that masks impiety and impotency, and deceives leaders into thinking all is well. Success as judged by human standards bears little correspondence to God's evaluation.

The difficulties of congruence and consistency confront authors as well as pastors. My prayer is that the Holy Spirit will reinforce everything in this book that is true. I have attempted to balance six criteria of pastoral ministry:

> effective pastoral ministry hinges upon character and skill, but results depend upon the sovereign grace of God,
>
> pastors must be spiritually authentic, theologically faithful, and passionate for ministry, but none of these qualities excuse leadership incompetence, managerial sloth, or relational bungling,
>
> worthy pastors trust implicitly in the work of the Holy Spirit, the spiritual weapons of our warfare, and scriptural guidance—including prayer, preaching, and teaching—to accomplish their God-given agenda, but utilize the best contemporary ethical methods and technology,
>
> spiritual leaders think strategically and globally about the future, but demonstrate compassionate concern for individuals and pay excruciating attention to detail,
>
> effective pastors orient their churches to penetrate their community and world with the gospel, but obsessively concern themselves with discipling their members and equipping them for the work of the ministry,
>
> effective leaders work and pray for excellence in the missional, communal, and organizational dimensions of the church, and never rationalize neglect of one by attention to another.

This book builds upon these principles.

The celebration of a revitalized American church seems far off, but our vast opportunities and challenges are exceeded by an infinitely greater God. Hope rests in a fresh outpouring of the Holy Spirit, anointing pastors to do a good work. Our noble task balances pivotal doctrines and principles of ministerial excellence, perseveres through inevitable testing, and leads to effective service that concludes with a "Well done, good and faithful servant."

1

WHAT'S IT GOING TO TAKE?

You are already of consequence in the world if you are
known as a man [or woman] of strict integrity.

Grenville Kleiser

Success in pastoral ministry seems like an elusive dream
to many who begin ministry with hope but find their expectations
shattered by brutal realities. Ministerial fulfillment often seems to
be reserved for those blessed with charismatic personalities,
unusual skills, or extraordinary circumstances. Yet, effective ministry may be attained without exceptional talents. Most of the early
disciples were ordinary people who had uncommon devotion and
commitment.

Too many pastors err in thinking that change in other people or
a change in circumstance would foster success in their ministries.
Effectiveness relates to individual character and competence (and
God's sovereignty), not to spectacular gifts or advantageous circumstances. God rarely blesses the ministry of those with dubious character, questionable behavior, and unremarkable spirituality. God's

blessing normally rests upon those who have their moral, spiritual, and intellectual act together.

When Charles Colson challenged the leaders of the Prison Fellowship, he spoke of God's blessing and the open doors before them; then he asked, "How are we going to accomplish these tasks?" Immediately he corrected himself with the statement, "But that is the wrong question to ask. The important question is: What kind of people are we going to be?"[1] That question transcends everything else in Christian ministry. To look at oneself critically may be the hardest thing any minister must do, but ministry is the lengthened shadow of the minister. This statement harmonizes with the teaching of Jesus: "The good man brings good things out of the good stored up in him, and the evil man brings evil things out of the evil stored up in him" (Matt. 12:35).

The most compelling requisite in pastoral ministry is not new programs, bigger budgets, superior technology, state-of-the-art buildings, more talent, or better marketing, but leadership authenticity and competence. Churches often throw money at problems, add bureaucracy, utilize technology, maneuver politically, and employ a vast variety of techniques. However, our great need is for leaders, particularly clergy, anointed with the Spirit of God, equipped for every good work, consumed with holy vision and passion, and who say with integrity: "Follow my example, as I follow the example of Christ" (1 Cor. 11:1).

John Harris declares: "The inauthenticity of the clergy is the greatest weakness of organized religion."[2] Jesus reserved his severest rebuke for the Pharisees, who were plainly incompetent: "blind guides" who "shut the kingdom of heaven in men's faces" (Matt. 23:13). Few things hurt the church more than leaders who are learned but lifeless, politically powerful but spiritually impotent, fanatical about law but ignorant about grace.

The best leaders are nevertheless flawed. Sinful omissions and commissions corrupt every area of every life. God entrusts his treasure to "jars of clay to show that this all-surpassing power is from

---

1. *Fellowship Communications* (tape), Prison Fellowship Staff Conference, 1988, Washington, D.C.
2. John Harris, *Stress, Power and Ministry* (Washington, D.C.: Alban Institute, 1979), 3.

God and not from us" (2 Cor. 4:7). Yet, people inevitably evaluate the local church chiefly by the quality of its leaders. Further, effectiveness in pastoral ministry depends heavily on a few indispensable competencies, without which clergy ensure their own mediocrity or failure. Spiritual leaders cannot be perfect, but they must be authentic, ingenuous, and able representatives of and role models for the church.

Authentic leadership requires credibility, monogamy, temperance, self-control, hospitality, skill in teaching, maturity, judicious family management, and freedom from drunkenness, violence, quarrelling, and greediness (1 Tim. 3:2–7). Scripture forbids autocracy (1 Pet. 5:3) and commands servant hearts (Matt. 20:26). Leaders must be examples "in speech, in life, in love, in faith and in purity" (1 Tim. 4:12). The credibility of the church and gospel relate directly to authentic leadership; therefore God gave these stringent requirements for spiritual leaders. Just anyone will *not* do for elders and deacons in the fellowship of believers.

Fruitful ministry depends on *character* (1 Tim. 3:2) and the *requisite skills* (2 Tim. 3:17).

First, we will consider the character imperatives of pastoral ministry and, second, we will examine the requisite skills for ministry.

Character in Pastoral Ministry

Four character attributes are nonnegotiable in pastoral ministry: personal integrity, spiritual vitality, common sense, and a passion for ministry that arises out of love for people. Absence of even one trait hampers the efforts of otherwise gifted servants; without these traits, failure is inevitable.

Personal Integrity

Today's church problems often stem from a lack of integrity. The decade of the eighties has been labeled "Pearlygate," and in the face of so much clergy embarrassment and church dirty linen, *Time* magazine asked "What Ever Happened to Ethics?"[3] Secular society has never viewed clergy and the church in America with more cynicism and distrust. In our nation of declining morals we have jokes

3. *Time*, 25 May 1987.

about integrity: "The secret of success is integrity, and once you learn to fake that you've got it made!"

American Christianity has never experienced more clergy failure, scandal, brownout, burnout, dropout, firing, frustration, and disillusionment. Clergy status and esteem have steadily eroded for at least three generations, and the downward spiral accelerates. Warren Wiersbe observes our integrity crisis: "For nineteen centuries, the church has been telling the world to admit its sins, repent, and believe the gospel. Today, in the twilight of the twentieth century, the world is telling the church to face up to her sins, repent, *and start being the true church of that gospel.* . . . For some reason, our ministry doesn't match our message. Something is wrong with the church's integrity."[4]

"Integrity" comes from the Latin *integritas*, meaning soundness; hence, the quality or condition of being whole or undivided, complete; a basic congruence between external profession and internal reality. Integrity involves ethics, honesty, honor, principle, and morality; yet no individual word encompasses its breadth and depth. Integrity can be lost in a thousand ways, but gained in only one way: rigorous, unrelenting devotion to truth and honesty. A. W. Tozer came very close to describing the absence of integrity: "It appears that too many Christians want to enjoy the thrill of feeling right but are not willing to endure the inconvenience of being right."[5]

Integrity embraces uncommon devotion to truth, unyielding opposition to falseness, and unvarying commitment to ethics, morality, and virtue. Jesus recognized the integrity of Nathanael: "Here is a true Israelite, in whom there is nothing false" (John 1:47). No artful cunning, duplicity, or insidious deceit sullied Nathanael's character. Integrity forbids internal hypocrisy, suspicious maneuvering to gain advantageous impression, shrewd manipulation of the strings of power, adroit coaxing through flattery or promises, crass pragmatism at the expense of principle, or treating persons as objects to be used for self-aggrandizement.

4. Warren W. Wiersbe, *The Integrity Crisis* (Nashville: Oliver-Nelson Books, 1988), 17.

5. A. W. Tozer, *The Root of the Righteous* (Harrisburg, Penn.: Christian Publications, 1955), 52.

Integrity concerns itself with truth, not popularity. Our society idolizes happiness and materialistic success, and in playing to such natural desires, some preachers major in "prosperity theology" or the so-called success gospel. They pander to fleshly appetites and gain the praise of people, but in doing so they ignore basic principles of hermeneutics and gut the gospel of its demands. "The God of the 'success' preachers is not the God of the Bible or of the historic church. He is a manufactured god, an idol."[6] Paul declared, "We are not trying to please men but God, who tests our hearts. You know we never used flattery, nor did we put on a mask to cover up greed—God is our witness. We were not looking for praise from men, not from you or anyone else" (1 Thess. 2:4-6).

Capitulation to compromise for pragmatic purposes is epidemic, as Klaus Bockmuhl warned: "Successful evangelists in their institutes teach their lesser colleagues how to be successful by avoiding to speak about sin."[7] A driving zeal for integrity declares: "We have renounced secret and shameful ways; we do not use deception, nor do we distort the word of God. On the contrary, by setting forth the truth plainly we commend ourselves to every man's conscience in the sight of God" (2 Cor. 4:2). Devotion to the success syndrome creates a few church superstars, but destroys the integrity of many a preacher. Integrity prohibits the lowering of biblical standards to gain temporal or tangible advantage.

Lack of integrity disqualifies the most gifted individual. Without a basic congruence between the message and the messenger the candidate for ministry has nothing the church needs.

Spiritual Vitality

Spiritual vitality is knowing God and living under the authority of Scripture. Spiritually vital leaders demonstrate passion for ministry, contagious enthusiasm for Christ, and faithfulness in the spiritual disciplines. Can anything be more tragic than clergy who possess political savvy, managerial shrewdness, and entrepreneurial expertise, but have none of the savor of sainthood? Robert Murray

6. Wiersbe, *The Integrity Crisis*, 52.
7. Klaus Bockmuhl, "Christianity Has a Moral Backbone," *Christianity Today*, 6 Oct. 1978.

McCheyne said, "It is not great talents God blesses so much as great likeness to Jesus."[8]

Spiritual vitality means taking the message of the gospel seriously: love for and obedience to God. A daily practice of the presence of God—including personal worship, confession of sin, and intercessory prayer—gives reality and freshness to ministry. Mr. Standfast in Bunyan's *Pilgrim's Progress* speaks for spiritually vital pastors: "I have loved to hear my Lord spoken of; and wherever I have seen the print of his shoe in the earth, there I have coveted to set my foot too. His name has been to me as a civet-box; yea, sweeter than all perfumes."

Many of the church's ills reflect the prayerlessness, spiritual aridity, and inertia of the clergy. Helmut Thielicke asserts, "This is the point, it seems to me, where the secret distrust of Christian preaching is smoldering. Behind all the obvious and superficial criticisms . . . there is, I am convinced, this ultimate reservation, namely, that . . . the [minister] . . . is not really living in what he—so boringly— hands out. . . . The attractions by which his heart is moved seem to come from some other source."[9] A meaningful prayer life is essential to spiritual authenticity and effective ministry, as Saint Augustine suggested: "A preacher must labor to be heard with understanding, with willingness, and with obedience. Let him not doubt that he will effect this with fervent prayers more than with all the power of his oratory."[10] The static nature of the typical church often testifies to the weakness of clergy's personal relationship with God. Without the marks of deep spirituality—"righteousness, godliness, faith, love, endurance and gentleness" (1 Tim. 6:11)—no one should seek or retain church leadership.

Religious hucksters flourished in New Testament days, and Elmer Gantrys still prey upon the gullible, abuse good people's generosity, and exploit the church to satisfy their own ego. Always there "are false apostles, deceitful workmen, masquerading as apostles of Christ" (2 Cor. 11:13) who prostitute the sacred mission. George MacDonald suggests a scary truth: "A man may sink by such slow

8. Andrew A. Bonar, *Robert Murray McCheyne, Memoir and Remains* (London: Banner of Truth, 1966), 282.

9. Helmut Thielicke, *The Trouble with the Church* (Grand Rapids: Baker, 1965), 9.

10. Cited in Richard Baxter, *The Reformed Pastor* (Portland, Ore.: Multnomah, 1982), 17.

degrees that, long after he is a devil, he may go on being a good churchman . . . and thinking himself a good Christian [or a worthy pastor]."[11] Pastoral service often takes place in the muddy waters of excessive busyness, leading to tragic loss of perspective, cloudy vision, and insensitivity to the reality that personal relationship with and accountability to God cannot be subordinated to anything. Few things are more tragic than pastors who hang onto their credentials and pulpits, but who have long since lost spiritual legitimacy. Such burned-out relics have nothing to offer the people who come hungering for the Living Bread and longing for a word from an authentic person in touch with God.

All pastors must heed the counsel of William Perkins, a Puritan who put the matter bluntly: "Good words are vain where there is no good life. Let not Ministers think their golden words shall do so much good as their leaden lives shall do hurt."[12] John Calvin echoes the sentiment: "It were better for him [the preacher] to break his neck going up into the pulpit, if he does not take pains to be the first to follow God."[13]

Common Sense

Common sense seldom appears in a list of character traits to covet, perhaps because the generalities of common sense preclude carefully defined terms and circumscribed boundaries. Furthermore, common sense seems so mundane and unremarkable. Yet, in ministry, common sense transcends both genius and gifts.

What is common sense? The expression derives from a translation of the Latin *sensus communis* and the Greek *koinē aísthēsis* (ordinary insight). Sound practical judgment, independent of specialized knowledge or training, is the mark of true common sense. Paul asked God to give common sense to the saints at Philippi: "And this is my prayer: that your love may abound more and more in knowledge and depth of insight" (moral discrimination; Greek *aísthēsis*, Phil. 1:9). The verbal form (*aisthánomai*) means to perceive or understand (e.g., Luke 9:45). In the Septuagint the word

11. C. S. Lewis, ed., *George MacDonald, An Anthology* (New York: Macmillan, 1947), 102.
12. Cited by J. I. Packer in *A Quest for Godliness* (Wheaton: Crossway, 1990), 76.
13. Ibid., 76.

can be compared with wisdom (Prov. 1:7).[14] Our English words *insight, discernment, wisdom,* and *judgment* approach the idea of common sense, but none alone quite does justice to its meaning. The *American Heritage Dictionary* defines common sense as "native good judgment."

Common sense enables a leader to set proper priorities, order schedules wisely, choose better rather than worse alternatives, and recognize the relative value of differing matters. Common sense keeps a minister from making mountains out of molehills and vice versa. Clergy who lack common sense rarely succeed at anything worthwhile. Charles Spurgeon rightly commented that God occasionally spoke through a jackass (i.e., the story of Balaam, Num. 22:28–30), but that normally he does not.

Perhaps we can understand the indispensability of common sense by observing those who clearly lack it:

• A young pastor, suffering from the Rodney Dangerfield complex, figured that he was not receiving the respect he deserved. Therefore, his parishioners were instructed to rise when he stepped onto the platform in church services. Within weeks the church split and before long the pastor left the ministry altogether. He lacked the common sense to know that respect cannot be demanded or imposed; it can only be earned.

• A pastor took his church through a much-needed building program, but at each step he alienated members by insisting that his own preferences be enacted, even in issues of personal taste unrelated to the primary concerns of pastoral ministry. The pastor's ideas were irrevocably tied to his ego, prohibiting him from yielding to others, even in trivialities. He got his way on most things but made himself obnoxious, and his ministry ended shortly after the building was completed. He lacked the common sense to understand that preservation of relationships far outweighs in importance the color of carpet.

• A pastor was determined to exercise leadership, which to him meant controlling decisions made by every board or committee. He presented himself at every meeting and politicked tirelessly with the perceived power-brokers. He succeeded in domineering, but in doing so he neglected needy people and spent inadequate time in study.

14. See Gerhard Kittel and Gerhard Friedrich, eds., *Theological Dictionary of the New Testament*, abridged (Grand Rapids: Eerdmans, 1985), 29.

His preaching ministry revealed his low estimate of its worth. Before long, ministerial incompetence cost him his job. He lacked the understanding that successful leadership means self-denying service, modeling discipleship, spiritual direction, and substantive preaching-teaching, not authoritarian control.

• A pastor thought himself indispensable to the church (the junior messiah complex). He gave himself indiscriminately to anyone who made demands upon him, put in twelve- and fifteen-hour days, seldom took a day off, had his hand in everything, and burned out before he was forty. In addition, his children grew up without a father and his wife became bitter. He lacked the common sense to understand that ministry must be shared, good leadership requires training and delegation, and he who neglects his family "has denied the faith and is worse than an unbeliever" (1 Tim. 5:8). Defeated and broken, he left the ministry, a sad testimony to the destructive power of deficient common sense.

Some pastors never learn from their mistakes nor do they listen to the wise. Common sense, like other character attributes, cannot be easily taught. Experience and sound counsel can enhance common sense, but those lacking a basic reservoir of native good judgment do not profit from experience or listen to sound advice.

Passion for Ministry

Genuine love for God most readily expresses itself in love for people and passion for ministry. Without compassionate love, gifts mean little and even mountain-moving faith produces nothing of enduring value: "If I speak in the tongues of men and of angels, but have not love, I am only a resounding gong or a clanging cymbal . . ." (1 Cor. 13:1–3). Why some people enter ministry without this endowment mystifies the church.

Our current mentality and literature emphasize managerial exploits, pragmatic strategies, technological expertise, and an incredible array of pragmatic methodologies for building churches, but barely refers to the necessity of loving people deeply and passionately. As a result, many contemporary church members feel used rather than cared for.[15]

15. One recent book on evangelism contains no mention of the necessity of love or compassion for people. Methods, not motives, receive attention in contemporary religious thought.

The writings of the Reformers and the Puritans breathe the imperative of compassionate love, which must energize every facet of legitimate ministry. Richard Baxter speaks for a long line of these warmhearted, sensitive saints who seem to have faded into history: "The whole cause of our ministry must also be carried on in a tender love for our people. . . . We should be willing to have our name wiped out of the book of life for their sake, rather than allow them to perish and not be found in the Lamb's Book of Life. . . . When the people see, then, that you love them unfeignedly, they will hear what you say—they will bear what you ask—and they will follow you the more readily."[16] Similarly, Spurgeon exhorted the preachers of his day: "Love your fellowmen, and cry about them if you cannot bring them to Christ. If you cannot save them, you can weep over them. If you cannot give them a drop of cold water in hell, you can give them your heart's tears while they are still in this body."[17] Ministerial departure from such a mindset hurts the church and is to our shame.

Perhaps the scarcity of passion and compassion in ministry should not surprise us; Paul also testified to the exceptional spirit of Timothy: "I have no one else like him, who takes a genuine interest in your welfare" (Phil. 2:20).

Skills

In addition to character essentials, effectiveness in pastoral ministry depends heavily on a few carefully nurtured abilities. In order to make a significant difference in our world, those preparing for pastoral ministry must enlarge vision, develop talents, improve gifts, gain knowledge, and hone skills. No knowledge or ability substitutes for exemplary character, but neither do qualities of character make knowledge and ability unnecessary. Contempt for expertise leads to mediocrity or failure. Assuming the presence of worthy character attributes, superior training, development of skills, and discipline in learning generates greater success in ministry. God rarely blesses ministerial incompetence.

16. Baxter, *The Reformed Pastor*, 22.
17. Charles Spurgeon, *Metropolitan Tabernacle Pulpit*, vol. 59 (Pasadena, Tex.: Pilgrim Publications), 514.

What knowledge and skills are required for success in pastoral ministry? This question cannot be answered easily. Every geographical area has its unique mixture of culture, tradition, personality, and problems, making ministry a variable experience and some requisites for success changeable. Yet, despite widely varying circumstances, all pastoral leaders must cultivate *scriptural expertise, cultural sensitivity, relational aptitude, communication skills, and leadership ability.* Several of these fields interconnect (e.g., leadership is largely relational and communication skills), but pastoral success heavily depends on competence in these areas and deficiency in any one effectually cripples ministry. In particular situations, other skills and specialized knowledge may be crucial. In all circumstances, additional knowledge and other skills help overcome mediocrity. Pastors need not be walking encyclopedias or extraordinarily talented; yet, pastors impair themselves if they fail to read widely, learn all they can, and develop a wide range of skills.

Recognizing the danger of omission, we examine the handful of requisites for ministerial competence. These components represent the irreducible minimum for ministry and pastors must commit themselves to expertise in these universal imperatives.

Scriptural Expertise

Pastoral ministry consists chiefly in the diagnosis of spiritual disease and the prescription of biblical directives for cure. Therefore, effective ministry requires a lifetime love affair with Scripture, a love that produces a passion to know God's truth and thereby to know God. Failure to exegete Scripture accurately deprives the church of indispensable, God-given "antidotes against [our] faintings."[18] Without the ability to correctly handle the Bible, we have no bread to offer hungry people, no remedy for the poison of sin, and no fortification for the weak. Without sound theology, we have nothing to offer broken people except the paltry drivel of secularism and humanistic advice. Obviously then, Baxter's words about preaching deserve our attention: "Ignorance is almost every error . . . first light—then heat."[19]

18. Mr. Standfast's words in John Bunyan's *Pilgrim's Progress.*
19. Cited in Packer, *A Quest for Godliness,* 69.

All Scripture must be received and studied as the complete and coherent revelation of the will and purpose of God. Augustine remarked that just as there are shallows in Scripture where a lamb may wade, so there are depths in Scripture where an elephant may swim. The most learned biblical scholar still has much to discover in God's inexhaustible Word. No one knows enough; all must be lifetime students.

From the beginning, worthy pastors have wrestled with, determined their duty by, formed their worldview through, and derived their message from the Scriptures. The great pulpiteers of history seldom used the words *I think* in their sermons; their minds were occupied not with human thought, but with the truth of God. Authentic pastors heed Paul's counsel: "Preach the Word" (2 Tim. 4:2), for indeed, "all Scripture is God-breathed and is useful for teaching, rebuking, correcting, and training in righteousness, so that the man of God may be thoroughly equipped for every good work" (2 Tim. 3:16–17). When leaders do not know Scripture, their churches have nothing but inferior imitations of biblical shepherds.

Cultural Sensitivity

Chaotic mutations in society take place constantly. Urbanization, pluralism, materialism, scientific discovery, technological breakthroughs, media domination, and relativism indicate a changing world. We live in the age of microelectronics, instant world-wide communication, exploding technology, sophisticated weaponry, family breakdown, and information overload. Those who have travelled overseas realize the mind-boggling cultural differences in our world, but one needs only to travel across town to see cultural diversity. The urban church is almost always multicultural.

Pastors lead their churches in the penetration of their society with the gospel—an impossible task for those lacking cultural sensitivity. Cultural ignorance enfeebles ministerial efforts. The word *culture* identifies ideas, emotional responses, customs, traditions, and patterns of behavior shared by people in a given society. If pastors fail to discern and appreciate these things, they cannot relate the gospel effectively to their communities. Many modern pastors suffer from the basic irrelevance of cultural insensitivity.

Cultural insensitivity often causes city-bred pastors to flounder in rural areas and vice versa. American cities are melting pots of extraordinary diversity. Missionaries soon learn—sometimes painfully—that their cultural idiosyncrasies and preconceptions must be radically altered in order to work effectively on a foreign field. Paul realized the immense importance of cultural adaptation:

> To the Jews I became like a Jew, to win the Jews. To those under the law I became like one under the law (though I myself am not under the law), so as to win those under the law. To those not having the law I became like one not having the law (though I am not free from God's law but am under Christ's law), so as to win those not having the law. To the weak I became weak, to win the weak. I have become all things to all men so that by all possible means I might save some. [1 Cor. 9:20–22]

When Paul spoke at the meeting of the Areopagus (Acts 17), he revealed his cultural awareness by his adaptation—but not compromise—of the gospel message.

Pastoral training includes equipping students with tools for the study of any culture. We must figure out the cultural characteristics of our ministerial locale, draft a strategy for the penetration of the community with the gospel, muster resources, and lead churches toward effective ministry in their communities—whatever cultural traits and peculiarities we encounter. Such a colossal task demands the best trained leaders the church can produce. Cultural sagacity is a necessity in our pluralistic world.

Relational Aptitude

Competency in pastoral ministry necessitates the ability to develop and sustain friendships over a long period of time, skill in conflict management, and facility in making people feel important and instrumental in accomplishing worthwhile goals.

Excellence in ministry requires mutual warmth and concern throughout the church family, the love of which Jesus spoke: "By this all men will know that you are my disciples, if you love one another" (John 13:35). Some pastors maintain professional distance from their parishioners, but they never distinguish themselves as caring and loving ministers and seldom do their churches have much impact in their communities. Greatly blessed churches have transparent, personable, collegial, spiritual leaders. "The basis of life is people and how they relate to each other. Our success, fulfillment, and happiness depends upon our ability to relate effectively. The best way to become a person that others are drawn to is to develop qualities that we are attracted to in others."[20]

Pastoral ministry has everything to do with the building of group cohesiveness, a relational network of mutual trust and affection. John W. Gardner strikes the right note: "Leaders must not only forge bonds of trust between themselves and their constituents, they must create a climate of trust throughout the system over which they preside. Trust is not the only glue that holds a human group together, but when it dissolves, the capacity of the group to function effectively is seriously impaired."[21] The alienation of parishioners jeopardizes and eventually destroys the ministry of the most gifted servant. Broken clergy everywhere confirm that pastors cannot survive interpersonal estrangement. This truth deserves serious attention: building healthy relationships precedes effective, enduring ministry and failed relationships thwart effective ministry.

Pastors who fail in their ministries usually do so because of deteriorated relationships. Pastors may antagonize and alienate people by manipulative tactics, abrasive sermons, autocratic style, breaking confidence, or immature displays of emotion. The "one accord" of Scripture, and the many emphases on fellowship, unity, burden bearing, sharing, and encouragement testify to the significance of interpersonal relationships in the body of Christ. Seldom do pastors rise above the quality of their relationships.

Each pastor desperately needs colleagues in ministry—lots of them—and must cultivate friendships in order to accomplish ministry. Adversarial relationships devitalize and destroy any ministry. In his research, William Menninger discovered that 60 to 80 percent of people fired from their jobs in industry are discharged because of social incompetence. It has frequently been observed that lonely people live significantly shorter lives than the general

---

20. John C. Maxwell, *Be a People Person* (Wheaton: Victor, 1989), 9.

21. John W. Gardner, *The Heart of the Matter: Leader-Constituent Interaction* (Washington, D.C.: Independent Sector, 1986), 18.

population; and lonely ministers live exceedingly short pastoral lives. The tragic three-years-or-less cycle of pastoral turnover indicates interpersonal bumbling, among other things. Botched relationships abort many a promising ministry.

Friendship making is a learned skill.[22] In the past, many ministerial training schools have stressed theology, history, languages, educational theory, homiletics, and the like, but have done tragic injustice to the development of relational skills, as though such skills were unimportant or impossible to learn. Fortunately, today in our better schools, relational competence receives attention proportionate to its true value. Wise educational leaders know that failure in relationship means failure in ministry. Young people who desire effectiveness in future ministry should carefully examine a school's relational curricula in addition to its theological and biblical reputation. Additional consideration will be given to relationships later in this book.

Communication Skills

Communication is the art or skill of listening carefully and expressing oneself in such a way that one is readily and clearly understood. In no small measure, pastoral effectiveness depends on an ability to communicate. Pastors cannot build vital, meaningful relationships and cannot lead congregations competently unless they communicate well.

We must not think of communication as merely talking or writing. Many people talk plenty or write much, but communicate little. Pastors may preach long sermons, but convey nothing of substance or value. Rather, good communication involves carefully listening to others, responding to needs meaningfully and thoughtfully, framing the message in language or action clearly understood and willingly received by others, and accurately evaluating feedback, with appropriate alterations of the message to correct misunderstandings. Worthy pastors excel at these critical tasks of communication.

Communication, in many different forms, unites pastor and people in the common goals of Christianity: worship, edification,

---

22. This is the thesis of numerous books, among them the highly recommended *The Friendship Factor,* by Alan Loy McGinnis (Minneapolis: Augsburg, 1979).

fellowship, social concern, and evangelism. Without sound communication, worship declines into ritual, preaching degenerates into harangue, fellowship fades into gossipy get-togethers, social concern dwindles into welfarism, and evangelism collapses into intimidation.

Of particular importance in pastoral ministry is pulpit communication: preaching and teaching. Four crucial ingredients constitute good pulpit communication: accurate exegesis of Scripture leading to an important and clear message; application of the message to the listener; personal passion; and spiritual power, the anointing of the Holy Spirit. Without accurate exegesis, the preacher likely will proclaim a false, shallow, or obscure message, that which is not the vital truth of God. Paul sought clarity in preaching: "And pray for us, too, that God may open a door for our message, so that we may proclaim the mystery of Christ, for which I am in chains. Pray that I may proclaim it clearly, as I should" (Col. 4:3–4). Without application, few people will comprehend the relevance of the message. Without preacher passion, congregants remain unmoved and unenthusiastic. Without spiritual power, the most worthwhile message, given with great clarity, will fall on deaf ears. Effective preaching rests "not with wise and persuasive words, but with a demonstration of the Spirit's power, so that your faith might not rest on men's wisdom, but on God's power" (1 Cor. 2:4–5). In every case, the preacher must endeavor to be "a workman who does not need to be ashamed and who correctly handles the word of truth" (2 Tim. 2:15). It is difficult to overestimate the cumulative value of good preaching. More will be said about preaching later in this book.

Leadership Ability

Worthy pastors lead their congregations. Without leadership skills, no pastor excels in ministry. Without competent leadership, church success is marginal and short-lived. Spiritual leadership is the development of relationships with the people of a Christian institution or body in such a way that individuals and the group are enabled to formulate and achieve biblically compatible goals that meet real needs. By their ethical influence, spiritual leaders serve to motivate and enable others to achieve the purposes of God that otherwise would never be achieved. More often than not, any organization's success or failure is due directly to a leader's competence or incompetence.

Pastoral leadership includes organizational skills, critical thinking, analysis of problems, strategic envisioning, galvanizing a constituency, and enabling groups to achieve worthwhile objectives. Effective pastors promote growth in competence, responsibility, character, and leadership in members of their constituency. Leaders create the mood and lifestyle of the entire body. By their Spirit-enhanced powers of nonmanipulative, ethical influence, capable pastors promote a healthy, functioning, ministering body and enable the church to fulfill its mission in its global community.

In accomplishing such lofty ideals, spiritual leaders focus not on machinery, programs, or statistics, but on the fundamentals of value systems, reasons, philosophy, intrinsic truth, structures, objectives, designs, moods, emotions, and environments. Pastors must hone leadership proficiency or little will be accomplished in the local church except maintenance of the status quo. Many pastors adopt a managerial stance in the local church when they ought to take a leadership role, a role of vision and enablement.

Excellent spiritual leaders help the entire church constituency to reach the conclusion that each one is vitally important in the total scheme of things and in the plan of God. Thus, in leadership, the ministry of affirmation never rests; it goes to great lengths to reach every member. Good leaders create an environment in which personal sacrifice and hard work are enjoyable. The emphases of 1 Corinthians 12 loom large in pastoral ministry: the primacy of unity amidst diversity, the intrinsic value and giftedness of each member, mutual ministry within the body, and sharing of pain and honor, defeat and triumph.

Someone has observed that our attempts at managing a forest usually ruin it. Often, it seems, the same can be said of church leadership. Ignorance and incompetence in leadership create disaster, or at the very least, mediocrity and slow death.

A Final Word

The bottom line for effective ministry is given in the Great Commission: "Therefore go and make disciples of all nations, baptizing them in the name of the Father and of the Son and of the Holy

Spirit, and teaching them to obey everything I have commanded you" (Matt. 28:19–20). Our work is evaluated according to disciple-making standards, not according to the criteria of statistical or materialistic success. If people receive the Good News, unbelievers become disciples, disciples become spiritually mature, and the church grows toward a unified body of saints, then and only then pastors may be considered effective. The qualities of competence mean little if the fruit produced is anything other than disciples. Pastors bend their efforts toward the making of disciples.

Steps to a Successful Ministry

Pastors and those preparing for ministry must give serious attention to core skills without which ministry is likely to fail:

Carefully choose schools, courses, churches, and mentors according to the value they place upon integrity, spiritual vitality, common sense, love for people, scriptural expertise, cultural sensitivity, relational aptitude, communication skills, and leadership ability.

With the help of mature advisors, evaluate honestly your areas of strength and weakness in character, knowledge, and skill.

Design a prudently constructed program of education and training to strengthen areas of weakness, acquire the necessary knowledge, and hone the requisite skills necessary for ministerial wholeness and effectiveness.

Select a few gifted and mature disciples to hold you accountable in the areas of your study, reflection, and improvement.

Discipline yourself daily to progress in being, knowing, and doing what Scripture declares as essential for full ministerial fulfillment.

2

It's a Small (and Scary) World After All

The gradual changes of the '90s—
the result of three decades of ferment—
will hit with full force by 2000.

George Barna

The ancient words of Heraclitus seem more perceptive as we approach a new century: "All is flux, nothing stays still." Those living through the last few decades of this decaying century have seen more dramatic changes than anyone could have anticipated. Electrifying change shatters the status quo, challenges our faith, and carries with it powerful contradictions. The implications of our ever-changing environment on pastoral ministry can scarcely be overstated. Church leaders often fail to recognize changing conditions and, consequently, the church tends to play catch-up, a task increasingly hazardous in our frenetic world.

Never have opportunities for pastoral service been greater, but effectiveness requires understanding the context in which we minister, a context of pluralism, interconnectedness, and cultural upheaval.

The Global Village

Not long ago, what happened in South Africa, or China, or Eastern Europe had no bearing on pastoral ministry in Iowa, Montana, or California, except marginally, in a "foreign missions" sense. Indeed, a few generations ago, events around the world—politics in Japan, typhoons in Indonesia, drought in Africa, revolution in India—were not reported to the American frontier for months after the event, or ever, and nobody much cared. Two world wars and many smaller ones, instant communication, international economic interdependency, speedy travel, and a host of other factors have reduced our world to a global village. What happens to the American dollar in Tokyo affects the New York Stock Exchange and millions of investors within ten minutes.

The world's political drama dumbfounds our senses. Television documents daily dramas such as tearing down the Berlin wall, disintegrating Communism, dismantling of the Warsaw Pact, civil war, revolt, revolution, struggle for power in the former Soviet Union, the tortuous dying of apartheid in South Africa, the Palestinian quest for land and nationhood, bloody putdowns of democratic agitators in Beijing and a tyrant in the Persian Gulf—all, and more, within the last five years! The changes appear apocalyptic in scope. Americans sit in awe, mesmerized by televised reports of such upheaval, unable to grasp the significance of events too momentous and breathtaking to comprehend.

Despite the thawing of the Cold War, militarism continues to control the world's agenda, with $685 million spent on arms every twenty-four hours. America holds sufficient nuclear weapons to destroy the two hundred largest cities in the world thirty-seven times over, and we face the danger that the breakup of the Soviet Union may accelerate the proliferation of nuclear weapons in the Third World. Terrorism and political violence threaten hundreds of thousands of people annually. Oppressive regimes thwart freedom in many countries of the world, especially in China with its two billion people. More than fifteen million political refugees crowd makeshift camps in many places of our world.

Those in Christian ministry must realize that we live in a remarkably interrelated and interdependent world. Illustrations of this simple fact abound: A dictator who rapes Kuwait affects not only hundreds of thousands of Iraqi and Kuwaiti citizens, but also those of many other nations determined to stop him. Politics in Washington impinge upon the lifestyle of millions of Filipinos within days. Columbia's policy toward drug lords reflects quickly on the streets of New York. Japanese economics influences the decisions of many American manufacturers and investors. No sane pastoral ministry can develop with an ideology of individualism, isolationism, and self-sufficiency. Self-centeredness, greed, ignorance, prejudice, individualism, envy, malice, pollution, filth, pornography, immorality, and hate, wherever they occur on earth, brutalize and diminish all of us.

As never before, America needs pastors who see themselves as ministers in a global village. For today's spiritual leaders, nearsightedness may be a fatal flaw; apathy equals immorality. The world has invaded our back yards. The words of Jesus take on a new urgency: "I tell you, open your eyes and look at the fields! They are ripe for harvest" (John 4:35).

Economics

Church leaders can no longer avert their eyes from the true condition of the world's economy. More than two billion people are poor, hungry, and homeless. Many factors contribute to this obscene situation, including war, drought, exploitation, international debt, social upheaval, population explosion, shifting demographics, and so forth.

Consider the impact of international debt: "Millions of children have already died to repay debts to affluent nations. UNICEF blames the debt burden for the deaths of 500,000 children each year."[1] Resources that could be channeled to improve farming methods, utilize technology, and feed the poor instead flow to the

1. Michael P. Todaro, *Economic Development in the Third World* (New York: Longman, 1989), 414.

International Monetary Fund (IMF), provoking the worst economic crisis the world has known and "the poor, especially the children, have suffered the most. Forced to slash government programs dramatically, debtor nations have cut spending on human services like education, health care, and food subsidies."[2]

Frequent infection and malnutrition cause the deaths of 225,000 children each week. One of every three deaths in our world is a child under the age of five. Seventy million people exist on the threshold of starvation. Such conditions contribute to 150,000 voluntary abortions per day.[3]

Per capita income declines, while inflation soars in most South American, African, and Asian nations. Economic disaster devastates Eastern Europe and the countries that formerly made up the Soviet Union. In the Philippines, 60 percent of all the people are squatters, many more than that are poor, and 90 percent of the economic power is controlled by 5 percent of the people. In Manila, it is an awesome experience to stand near Smoky Mountain—so named because of the constant fires—and watch several thousand people pawing through garbage for their daily subsistence, while a few blocks away the walled-in and guarded mansions of the rich insulate the exploiters of the poor.

Some of the world's worst conditions, including massive malnutrition and starvation, exist in the sub-Saharan countries of Mali, Niger, Chad, Sudan, Ethiopia, and Somalia. More than one million Ethiopians starved to death in 1984–85, and presently another famine looms. The "pearl of Africa," Uganda, still bleeds from the devastation of immoral dictators who murdered hundreds of thousands of innocent people in the 1970s and 1980s. War has wasted Angola and Mozambique. Racial and tribal hatred add to the misery of South Africa. Millions of India's vast population live below the poverty line, many on the brink of starvation. Refugees, including tens of thousands of Palestinians, crowd temporary facilities in dozens of places in the Middle East.

2. Ronald J. Sider and Grant Power, "International Debt: In Whose Interest?" *Advocate, Evangelical For Social Action* 12, 10 (December 1990).

3. United Nations health agency report, *Reproductive Health, a Key to a Brighter Future,* 1992.

Organizations such as "Bread for the World," "World Relief," and "World Concern" cannot keep pace with the vast need of an exploding population and a dramatic escalation of poverty. The number and extent of desperate requests for aid has provoked "compassion fatigue" among donors.

The economic problems within America should not be underestimated. Thirty-three million Americans live below the poverty level and the gap between the rich and the poor becomes ever greater. The Associated Press reported (October 30, 1991) that one in ten Americans receives food stamps, with blacks and Hispanics below the poverty line in disproportionately high numbers. The middle class is shrinking, creating an economically polarized society. With a staggering ten-trillion-dollar debt, we live off our children's inheritance. The poor constitute the fastest growing segment of our population—and at a time when government benefits have been pruned. Thirteen million American children live in poverty, five hundred thousand of whom are homeless.[4]

Each pastor and church will have to determine the implications of these facts for their own constituencies. However, any pastor who fails to preach whole-life stewardship cannot possibly hope to maintain credibility in a world ravaged by poverty, hunger, and injustice. Any church that is indifferent or reluctant to engage in local action for global equity contradicts its calling to participate with God in the drama of human suffering. "He has showed you, O man, what is good; and what does the Lord require of you but to do justice, and to love kindness, and to walk humbly with your God?" (Mic. 6:8). Scripture everywhere condemns apathy: "Now then, listen, you wanton creature, lounging in your security and saying to yourself, 'I am, and there is none besides me . . .'" (Isa. 47:8). Indeed, "if a man shuts his ears to the cry of the poor, he too will cry out and not be answered" (Prov. 21:13). In God's reckoning, failure to minister to the hungry, thirsty, stranger, naked, sick, or prisoner means failure in ministry to Christ (Matt. 25:45).

The economic plight of the world and the vast numbers of poor, hungry, and homeless people directly affects middle- and upperclass American churches. Monopolizing resources for narcissistic

4. Jonathan Kozol, "The New Untouchables," *Newsweek,* special issue, 1990, 48-49.

concerns, the "edifice complex," and indifference to the open sores of the world's poor constitute an immorality and idiocy of the highest (or lowest) order.

Population Growth and Urbanization

Every two seconds, five more people enter the world than leave it, adding 3,600 people to the population daily. In the time of Christ there were 169 million people, but by the middle of the seventeenth century the population grew to 500 million. The billion mark was passed in 1830, the second billion by 1930, and the third billion by 1960. It only took fifteen years for the fourth billion to arrive and the projections now are for 6.3 billion population by the year 2000. Some predict that the total will stabilize at 10 billion by the middle of the next century, but others suggest a staggering 14 billion within another hundred years.[5] Ninety percent of the growth occurs in the poorest, least developed nations of the world.

A large percentage of the increasing population squeeze into and devitalize the resources of megalopolises. In the last fifty years 500 million people have moved to Mexico City, Manila, Shanghai, Beijing, Tokyo, and Calcutta. Almost 75 percent of the people in Calcutta and more than 50 percent of the people of Manila, Bogota, Caracas, and Lima live in slums, and these figures are representative of other world-class cities. Another 600 million will immigrate to these teeming urban centers before the year 2000. Seventeen million people already live in Mexico City and Manila, 13 million in Shanghai. Mexico City is projected to be the world's largest city with a staggering 31 million inhabitants by the year 2025 and Sao Paulo expects 25.8 million. Shanghai will mushroom to 22.7 million people.[6] Water, sanitation, and other services cannot possibly keep pace with the growth in cities, creating substandard living and serious health problems for untold millions. Cities are magnets, attracting those who hope for better employment and conditions. Most find deplorable circumstances in slums, astonishing pollution, and low-income jobs.

5. Statistics supplied by the World Resources Institute, Washington, D.C. Some estimate that the population could be as high as 30 billion by the year 2050.

6. United Nations, *Patterns of Urban and Rural Population Growth* (New York: United Nations).

The demographics of America are changing fast. Rural and urban population dwindles as suburban masses enlarge.[7] In 1920 almost 32 million people lived on farms in America, but by 1985 the number had shrunk to 5.4 million. Many displaced farmers have had to find jobs not to their liking or training in cities or towns. "We are now a suburban nation with an urban fringe and a rural fringe."[8]

Mobility characterizes American lifestyle—one of five households move yearly. The sunbelt states continue to mushroom, particularly the city suburbs, while the industrial states of the north struggle to maintain their population and their economy. The global urbanization movement includes American cities, with Miami, Atlanta, Houston, Dallas, Chicago, San Francisco, New York, Phoenix, San Diego, and Los Angeles leading the way. Life in the center of these gigantic megalopolises remains hard for many because of low income, drugs, crime, and the breakdown of the family.

Pluralism characterizes America as never before. New immigrants have changed the face of many cities, creating huge Chinese or Vietnamese communities, Polish enclaves, Hispanic neighborhoods, Italian boroughs, and so forth. In addition to legal immigrants, illegal newcomers swell our population yearly, perhaps by five hundred thousand. The Asian population in America increased twelve times faster than native-born citizens during the 1980s. The diversity in large American cities defies the imagination. Los Angeles includes more than one hundred first-generation language groups; in fact, Los Angeles is the world's second-largest Vietnamese city, Mexican city, Filipino city, Guatemalan city, Salvadoran city, and Korean city. Hollywood High School offers classes in thirty-six languages.[9] A great cross-cultural mission field exists in our back yard.

Single people and single-parent families now outnumber two-parent families. The old norm of two parents and two or three children per family died some years ago. Divorce and remarriage means that children living in a household often have different mothers or

7. Until 1920 most Americans lived in rural areas. In 1960 the country was divided equally between urban, suburban, and rural. The 1990 census revealed that the rural population was down to less than a quarter of the total.

8. William Schneider, "The Suburban Century Begins," *The Atlantic Monthly,* July 1992.

9. See Gordon Aeschliman, *Global Trends* (Downers Grove, Ill.: InterVarsity, 1990), 71.

fathers. The typical suburban church may have 50 percent or more of its people divorced or divorced and remarried; in the inner city the percentage is considerably higher, in some cases nearing 100 percent.

The diversity of languages, customs, family units, and lifestyles affect business, schools, manufacturing, government, and churches. Multilingual and multicultural churches, often with different congregations occupying the same structure, have become commonplace. Churches that broaden their vision and ministry to include ethnic minorities and subcultures will grow. "The health of the American Church will depend upon its ability to attract minorities to Jesus Christ, and to equip and activate them for ministry."[10]

The mass migration of people to the urban centers of the world will profoundly affect every person on earth. Pastoral ministry, as well as missionary strategy, must keep pace with the shocking ramifications of world urbanization. Churches, particularly in America, have an inglorious history of fleeing to the middle-class suburbs, leaving the vast inner cities with little witness to the power of Christ. Missionaries have not traditionally focused their ministries on large cities.

Ecological Disaster

The prospect of slow death by ecological extinction now haunts the human race. Our air, water, rain forests, ozone, and soil are being contaminated or destroyed at an unprecedented rate. "In its crudest form then the ecological crisis consists in the fact that the world has become top-heavy. The human world now dominates the natural world . . . as a result of its phenomenal recent growth in size and power. . . . We are threatening the structure of the natural world and therefore the structure of our human world as well."[11]

Few nations seem willing to curb polluting practices voluntarily, despite the avid efforts of a small core of concerned individuals. In the United States, some strict antipollution laws have helped, but still more than 150 million tons of pollutants pour into the air each year. The overwhelming majority of the world's nations have no

10. George Barna, *The Frog in the Kettle* (Ventura, Calif.: Regal, 1990), 194.
11. Rex Ambler, *Global Theology* (Philadelphia: Trinity Press International, 1990), 46.

enforceable regulations. The reprehensible pollution in the industrial areas of Eastern Europe have been documented graphically by many news magazines. What happened at Chernobyl a few years ago concentrated attention upon the awful possibilities of ecological disaster, but the furor died quickly.

Concern for the earth's environment grew throughout the 1960s, culminating on Earth Day, April 22, 1970. Since then there have been numerous attempts to generate interest in ecological concerns. A theology of ecology has been slow to appear. Henlee H. Barnette published *The Church and the Ecological Crisis* (Eerdmans, 1972) and included a chapter "Toward a Theology for Ecology." A number of books have appeared more recently suggesting a Christian response, including Loren Wilkinson (ed.), *Earthkeeping in the '90s* (Eerdmans), Lewis Regenstein, *Replenish the Earth* (Crossroad), Ian Bradley, *God Is Green: Ecology for Christians* (Doubleday/Image), and a collection of essays, *The Environment and the Christian: What Can We Learn from the New Testament?* (Baker).[12] Certainly, willful ignorance and indifference about our environment cannot be excused.

The earth's inhabitants need to be reminded that "ultimately there is an absolute limit to the ability of the earth to support or tolerate the process of industrial activity, and there is reason to believe that we are now moving toward that limit very rapidly."[13] All scientists agree that we have moved much closer to that limit than when Robert Heilbroner wrote those words twenty years ago.

Some scientists hold that the delicate balance between living things and the environment has already been radically upset, so much so that human existence on earth may be threatened within the next fifty years. Others label such doomsday prophets "ecomaniacs" who sensationalize and overdramatize the problems of the environment, but Lester Brown summarizes the viewpoint of many knowledgeable people: "Only a monumental effort can reverse the deterioration of the planet."[14]

12. See *Christianity Today,* "Ecoguilt," 20 July 1992, 57, for additional titles and information on a Christian response to the ecological crisis.
13. Robert L. Heilbroner, *An Inquiry into the Human Prospect* (New York: Norton, 1974), 47.
14. Lester R. Brown, ed., *State of the World* (New York: Norton, 1990), xv.

Moral Pollution

Environmental pollution, staggering in its implications, does not even approach the moral foulness of our society. The norms of morality have changed dramatically as the so-called sexual revolution sweeps the planet. The number of people living together outside of marriage or those sexually promiscuous in a nonresident sense—both opposite and same sex—has skyrocketed since World War II, and with virtually no social disapproval, even within many Christian circles. Militant "Gay Pride" week is observed in countless cities with parades, banners, and generally favorable publicity. Public opinion remains hostile to child abuse and to some perversions such as sadism and bestiality, but "soft pornography" has won acceptance as a harmless source of pleasure. Art galleries in prominent cities now exhibit photographs regarded as obscene only a few years ago.

Pornography is a billion-dollar industry worldwide, mostly controlled by organized crime. Thousands of children under the age of twelve participate every day in the production of "kiddy porn." It is doubtful that a child can be raised in much of the world without significant exposure to printed filth, sexually explicit films, and the corruption associated with them. "Pornography is everywhere and in every country. Once isolated in the decaying and industrial inner city, pornographic bookstores, movie theaters, and specialty shops now crowd the popular shopping centers of the world's most prominent cities. Explicit materials depicting every conceivable sexual act . . . are readily available in every nation, either legally or illegally. From Times Square in New York to the back alleys of Seoul, Korea, pornography is easily accessible to all people."[15]

The sacrifice of human embryos, genetic engineering, surrogate motherhood, euthanasia, the demise of the "X" rating for movies, sex and violence on television, the mind-boggling lyrics of popular music, various venereal diseases, AIDS, vicious racism, and other modern phenomena testify to a cultural acceptance of radically deteriorated standards of morality.[16] The World Health Organiza-

15. Frank Kaleb Jansen, ed., *Target Earth* (Kailua-Kona, Hawaii: University of the Nations, 1989), 68.
16. There are 350,000 new venereal disease cases every day. The United States currently has more than 100,000 cases of AIDS and more than 2 million people infected with the HIV virus.

tion estimates about 2.6 million people have AIDS and at least 13 million are HIV-positive. By the year 2000, 38 to 110 million adults and 10 million children will be infected. Further, "society's knotty decisions will become even more tangled as the massive Human Genome Project lumbers towards its goal of mapping the location of every human gene, including those that govern such traits as intelligence, coordination and grace. That knowledge will expand the potential of genetic engineering far beyond the correction of disease and push it toward the realm of social engineering."[17] Medical science has added immeasurably to ethical dilemmas, especially by developing in vitro fertilization, allowing infertile women to become impregnated with other women's eggs and their own husband's sperm,[18] and by implementing the technology for prolonging the dying experience indefinitely.

Immorality and amorality have always existed, but it is difficult to pinpoint a time when they carried the aura of respectability that they do now. Indeed, "the lack of any personal accountability to a moral code has made immorality respectable in our nation. There is at times little in the press, in the entertainment industry, or in our institutions of higher (lower?) learning that can lift us up or cause us to realize that we have fallen. All of the voices are coming from below, rather than from above."[19] In 1958, 80 percent of the American people condemned premarital sex, but in only twenty years surveys showed the exact reverse: 80 percent of the populace accepted sex before marriage without condemnation. According to a national study of the reasons women have abortions, 98 percent were for convenience rather than for health.[20] Lichter and Rothman studied the beliefs of the Hollywood and media elite, those in position to influence morality on a grand scale, and found that 44 percent have no religious convictions, 93 percent attend no church, 97 percent are pro-abortion, 80 percent see no wrong in homosexuality, 70 percent see television as a social reform tool, 88 percent suggest that television is not too critical of traditional values, and 70 percent do

---

17. "The Age of Genes," *U.S. News & World Report*, 4 Nov. 1991, 76.
18. In 1991 a woman birthed her daughter's baby through in vitro fertilization with her daughter's egg and her son-in-law's sperm.
19. Cal Thomas, *The Death of Ethics in America* (Waco: Word, 1988), 22.
20. Reported by the Guttmacher Institute, the research arm for Planned Parenthood.

not think there is too much sex or violence on television.[21] Can such views fail to permeate the American culture? Have they already done so?

Addiction to an imposing variety of substances has now reached epidemic proportions in many countries, contributing to the global breakdown of social systems, including the family, health care, employment, and law. Alcohol abuse accounts for over half the motor vehicle deaths, drownings, and suicides in the United States. No one can calculate the culpability of substance abusers on divorce, physical mistreatment of spouses and children, crime, and other societal problems. Most murders committed in our largest cities—more than a score every day—are attributed to the drug traffic. Tobacco daily claims thousands of victims worldwide. The World Health Organization reports an increase in cigarette production of 40 percent in Africa, 38 percent in Asia, and 32 percent in Latin America within six years, and, as inevitably follows, an increase in cancer, heart disease, and premature deaths.

The implications of these facts upon the moral fiber of society, increased sexual violence, soaring divorce rates, and the disintegration of the family have been documented by Dr. James Dobson and dozens of other reflective Christians. Books such as Randy Alcorn's *Christians in the Wake of the Sexual Revolution* (Multnomah Press) suggest how the new morality has invaded and corrupted the church. It is particularly disconcerting to see church leaders propose new moral standards for sexual behavior that are a radical departure from a traditional Christian position on the authority of Scripture. Indeed, the 1991 report of the Presbyterian study committee on human sexuality "equates the authority of Scripture with the authority of human experience."[22] The report advocated full church acceptance of practicing homosexuals, including ordination, and pension benefits for same-sex couples; it dismissed marriage as the sole criterion for allowable heterosexual intercourse.[23]

21. Jansen, *Target Earth,* 72.
22. *Christianity Today,* "Sexuality Report Draws Fire," 29 April 1991.
23. The document, entitled *Keeping Body and Soul Together: Sexuality, Spirituality and Social Justice,* was not accepted at the General Assembly of the PCUSA. Many, however, suggest irreparable damage was done. The PCUSA continues to study the issue.

Secularization

American society is being freed from the influence of religious ideas and institutions. What happened to Christianity in Europe may be unfolding in America before our eyes. "It has often been predicted that Europe will become completely secular and that the rest of the world will end up like it. And Nietzsche, who in 1882 famously celebrated the 'death of God', was surely right to call it the most remarkable of all events or expected events. For secularisation on the European scale is without precedent or parallel."[24] The Church of England used to be the central institution of society, with spiritual values permeating social behavior, cultural activities, politics, families, and morals. But, "more recently these values have been undermined by the encroachment of secularism. . . . Its Christian community has all but disappeared. Once representing the vast majority of that great nation's population, true believers are estimated now to be only about 2 percent of the population."[25] Is American Christianity destined for such radical decline? Even a casual look at American culture reveals the deterioration of our spiritual foundations.

If, indeed, the secularization that eviscerated Christianity in Europe now threatens us, pastoral leaders must raise the alarm and take positive steps to revitalize the church. Failure to take note of trends can quickly degenerate into a dereliction of duty. The spectacle of a hemorrhaging church in an increasingly secularized society, indifferent or hostile to spiritual values, haunts us. The secular goals of neopagans are obvious and "many believe that the time for the liquidation of Christianity and the rescue of civilization from its grasp has come. New ideologies—and neopaganism is no exception—are always impelled by the belief that the worldview they want to abolish is already on the point of self-liquidation."[26]

Despite the church growth movement and the fact that a large percentage of Americans describe themselves as "born-again" Christians, traditional organized religion and mainline denomina-

24. David L. Edwards, *The Futures of Christianity* (Suffolk, England: Richard Clay Ltd., 1987), 285.
25. Barna, *The Frog in the Kettle*, 22.
26. Thomas Molnar, *The Pagan Temptation* (Grand Rapids: Eerdmans, 1987), 116.

tional churches continue to decline. Now, the church exists in a society that rejects scriptural values and a culture that is not merely neutral, but hostile to revelational truth. Broad segments of American culture view the church as the enemy. Many other people, though not antagonistic, see the church, its message, and its work as irrelevant and they give no attention to it. Pastoral leaders who continue to minister in the present context as their fathers did a generation ago cannot possibly hope to succeed in anything other than maintenance. Contemporary American pastors work not in a churched culture, but on a mission field.[27]

No longer do we live in a youthful society. Instead, the last half of the twentieth century in America has been dominated by the postwar baby boomers: "As they began coming of age, they challenged virtually all the social mores and political values that had come before. With them emerged a radical new musical form, new roles for women, a sexual revolution, unprecedented drug use and extraordinary social and personal upheaval. The old rules were thrown out, but that didn't matter. Affluence and a sense of unlimited opportunity filled this generation with confidence, even self-righteousness, as it headed into uncharted territory."[28] The legacy of this generation may not be known for some decades, but much that sustained American culture since the Puritans has disappeared, perhaps forever.

Beyond contributing to the demise of traditional religious values in the areas of sexual ethics, divorce, and abortion, the "now" generation has influenced culture in its insistence on instant gratification, its desire for constant stimulation and entertainment, and its devaluation of the nuclear family. Music and art reveal these dramatically changing standards, revelling "not in the best and the most beautiful, but in the trashiest . . . far from producing work that would elevate or transcend, Pop artists were quite content to leave their viewers where they found them."[29] Federal tax dollars have paid for so-called art that portrays Christ as a heroin-shooting drug addict and depicts the cross of Jesus in a jar of urine—and major art

27. The thesis of Kennon Callahan in *Effective Church Leadership* (San Francisco: Harper and Row, 1990).

28. David Sheff, "Portrait of a Generation," *Rolling Stone,* 5 May 1988, 46.

29. Kenneth A. Myers, *All God's Children and Blue Suede Shoes* (Westchester, Ill.: Crossway, 1989), 130.

museums display such work.[30] Many officials say that giving thanks to God on public property is a crime against the Constitution, but attacking God on public property is legal and worthy of support by taxpayer dollars. Meanwhile, in Manassas, Virginia, school officials told ten-year-old Audrey Pearson that she couldn't read the Bible on the school bus and a North Carolina judge was sued for praying for justice in the courtroom.[31]

America does less than any other industrialized society for children, according to the ninth National Conference on Child Abuse and Neglect (September 1991).[32] Our society has the dubious honor of having the highest rates of divorce, child abuse, and alcoholism. Statistics show 2.5 million children were abused or neglected in 1990—a 273 percent increase from 1976. Violent crime continues to increase dramatically across America, 8 percent or more in most states in 1991. CBS's "Sixty Minutes" recently showed how violence has escalated among children in our major cities. Many children carry guns to school.

What all this means for pastoral ministry remains to be seen, but Kenneth Myers suggests the obvious: "The aesthetic of immediate and constant entertainment does not prepare the human consciousness well for recognition of a holy, transcendent, omnipotent, and eternal God, or to responding to His demands of repentance and obedience. It could well be that modern times will prove to be the darkest age of all."[33] Our generation's moral ambiguity and malaise unravels the fabric of our society. The passing of a churched culture and the uprooting of traditional values that guided America for three hundred years multiplies the awesome responsibility of our clergy. Will the church succumb to a secularized culture as it has in Europe? Or will a renewed commitment to Scripture and a reinvigorated proclamation of revelational truth reverse the contemporary trend?

30. The National Endowment for the Arts, which supports such exhibits, is a federally funded agency.

31. Reported by The Rutherford Institute, PO Box 7482, Charlottesville, Virginia.

32. The National Conference on Child Abuse and Neglect is sponsored by the American Humane Association, the C. Henry Kempe National Center for the Prevention and Treatment of Child Abuse and Neglect, and the American Association for Protecting Children.

33. Myers, *All God's Children and Blue Suede Shoes*, 132.

Individualism, Privatization

The worldview of most Americans baffles social scientists. Fifty-one percent report no philosophy of life and another 24 percent describe a philosophy not based on Christian values.[34] Perhaps the basic absence or inadequacy of a life philosophy contributes to the myriad signs of reduced commitments in marriage, friendships, organizational memberships, jobs, and churches. A survey revealed that in 1967, 83 percent of college freshmen believed that it was very important to develop a meaningful philosophy of life; in 1982, only 47 percent thought so.

If a dominant philosophy of life exists at all in America, it may be individualism, the gospel of privatization, personal autonomy, and self-worship, summarized by Robert Bellah and his researchers: "Individualism lies at the very core of American culture."[35] What *Habits of the Heart* "reflects is simply the inevitable consequences of four decades of the steady erosion of absolute values. As a result we live with a massive case of schizophrenia. Outwardly, we are a religious people, but inwardly our religious beliefs make no difference in how we live. We are obsessed with self; we live, raise families, govern, and die as though God does not exist, just as Nietzsche predicted a century ago."[36] Indeed, "the great unifying theme at the conclusion of the twentieth century is the triumph of the individual."[37]

Individual pursuit of happiness, the American dream, material possessions, excitement, and self-fulfillment dominate the thinking of millions of Americans. Accompanying America's vast pluralism, the quest for individual attainment, privatization, and suburbanization break down our sense of community and identification in a common struggle and create alienation.[38] This opens a Pandora's box of personal greed, compromise of truth, and gratification of

34. Reported by the Barna Research Group, Glendale, Calif.

35. Robert N. Bellah et al., *Habits of the Heart: Individualism and Commitment in American Life* (New York: Harper and Row, 1985), 142.

36. Charles Colson, *Kingdoms in Conflict* (Grand Rapids: Zondervan, 1987), 214.

37. John Naisbitt and Patricia Aburdene, *Megatrends 2000* (New York: William Morrow and Co., 1990), 298.

38. See William Schneider, "The Suburban Century Begins," *The Atlantic Monthly,* July 1992.

desire at the expense of others. The "right" is determined by what one wants and is able to get; objective categories of the false, ignoble, wrong, impure, or unlovely no longer exist. "There is no true nature of things: all significance is defined by the self. Therefore, any action in any setting is justified, as long as it is 'authentic.'"[39]

Individualism has enormous ramifications for pastoral ministry, for it directly opposes the New Testament values of community, communion, fellowship, mutual interdependency and responsibility, as well as other significant biblical lifestyle teachings. Individualists cannot grasp commonality, solidarity with those who differ, accountability to a body, obligation to the poor, or commitment to a group. A few dollars to missions or charity may quiet an unruly conscience, but personal involvement in the inner city, a pregnancy clinic, prison ministry, short-term missions, or a food distribution center represent unrealistic expectations for most modern church members. Individualists interpret the purposes of God in terms of private success: a BMW, a healthy bank account, and personal leisure to enjoy life. "We will become even more self-centered, more materialistic, more driven to play. While we will value relationships, most of us will be too selfish to make the hard commitments and sacrifices that facilitate any meaningful relationships."[40]

Informational Cacophony

Our age has been dubbed the Information Age. Peter Drucker suggests that in our "knowledge-based society" information is the key resource and building block for every type of organization.

The sheer number of information-generating devices boggles the mind. By the year 2000 there will be eighty million computers in America, printing more than five million tons of computer paper yearly. About ninety-six hundred different periodicals are published in America every year, while newsstands offer a choice of more than twenty-five hundred magazines. One thousand new books are printed daily. The world's great libraries double in size every fourteen years; some already contain over eight million volumes. More information has been produced in the last thirty years

39. Myers, *All God's Children and Blue Suede Shoes,* 99.
40. Barna, *The Frog in the Kettle,* 25.

than in the previous five thousand years. The English language contains about one-half million words, with thousands of new words added yearly. Each year the average American reads 3,000 notices and forms, reads 100 newspapers and 36 magazines, watches 2,463 hours of television, listens to 730 hours of radio, buys 20 records, talks on the telephone 61 hours, and reads (only) 3 books, all of which suggests that "informational cacophony" dulls the senses and increases the difficulty of truly hearing anything, including sermons.

Much of the information reported and received is inaccurate. People hear inaccurate information, hear more than they understand, forget much of it, and resist learning more. Statistics are not apt to impress anybody, because our saturated minds cannot digest all the facts thrown at us. Information multiplies so fast nobody can vouch for its accuracy, and moreover, data are often outdated before appearing in print. Only the trends may be truly significant, and the trends are scary.

Rural, Town America

The rural and town context for pastoral ministry may vary significantly depending upon many factors. Location makes a huge difference. A church in a western ranching community may differ radically from a similar-size community and church in Illinois.

Rural and small-town churches tend to be more established, traditional, content with the status quo, and more resistant to change than urban or suburban churches. With a declining or a stable population base, new congregations form infrequently. Most existing rural and town churches celebrated their centennials years ago; those in the East have passed their bicentennials. Their long history contributes to the formation of traditions and loyalties not found in many urban or suburban churches. In addition, many of these communities have deep ethnic roots, for homesteading laws in the latter half of the nineteenth century encouraged many Europeans to settle in localized enclaves. Lyle Schaller suggests that "the small town owes its unique character to a complex web of interpersonal relationships. . . . That network of relationships sustains people, offers meaning to life, and tends to exclude newcomers until they are awarded a place in that web of relationships."[41] Church buildings tend to be modest and functional, but many have outlived their usefulness.

Traditional values change slowly in rural and small-town America, which may be both good and bad depending on which values are considered. Family solidarity and mutual dependency characterize rural and small-town culture, but pastors frequently hear the dreaded words: "We've always done it this way!" While stability generally promotes a sense of serenity, a basic conservatism makes innovation difficult, sometimes impossible.

People tend to be identified with a church whether or not they attend, making "sheep stealing" an offense that sometimes deters sincere evangelistic efforts. Many churches resist growth and a maintenance ministry often prevails, along with a status quo mentality. With a shrinking population, many find even maintenance an arduous task. The "good old days" energize more than a "bright new tomorrow." The past—often idealized in the memory—attracts interest and concern more than the future.

In some areas improved transportation has generated bedroom communities (people living in rural areas or small towns, but working in cities thirty to fifty miles away). In most respects these towns are more suburban in character than rural, and this phenomenon is called "the urbanization of rural society."[42]

Baptist and Methodist denominations predominate. Many churches are small and people tend to be older. In most small-town and rural congregations, attendance includes fewer than one hundred people, many of whom were born before World War II. Most churches occasionally participate in community affairs, but their attention and resources are devoted primarily to serving their own members. Mainline denominational churches participate in community activities more than nonmainline churches, but in general interdenominational cooperation is more common in small towns and rural communities.

Effective ministry takes place in all kinds of communities. The skills and temperaments of some pastors make them particularly

---

41. Peter J. Surrey, *The Small Town Church* (Nashville: Abingdon, 1981), 7.

42. Edward Hassinger, John S. Holik, and J. Kenneth Benson, *The Rural Church* (Nashville: Abingdon, 1988), 40.

suited to serve well in rural areas or small towns. Those who minister in rural communities or small towns must study carefully the
local culture, exercise patience in earning respect and trust, expect
difficulty in initiating new ideas or methodologies, emphasize shepherding skills, and work constructively with deeply ingrained traditions and an extensive network of relationships.

Those interested in rural or small-town church ministry might
profit from reading Anthony G. Pappas, *Entering the World of the
Small Church* (Washington, D.C.: The Alban Institute, 1988),
Harold L. Longnecker, *Building Town and Country Churches* (Chi-
cago: Moody, 1973), Peter J. Surrey, *The Small Town Church*
(Nashville: Abingdon, 1981), Lyle E. Schaller, ed., *The Rural
Church* (Nashville: Abingdon, 1988), and Gary Exman, *Get Ready
. . . Get Set . . . Grow!: Church Growth for Town and Country Con-
gregations* (C.S.S. Publishing, 1987).

Urban, Suburban America

Pastoral ministry in metropolitan areas unfolds in a context of
increasing difficulty and challenge. Many have observed the growing crisis in American cities. Great riots shook Harlem, Brooklyn,
Chicago, and Philadelphia in 1964, the worst being in the Watts
district of Los Angeles in which thirty-four people were killed and
hundreds were injured. More severe civil disturbances occurred in
1966—forty-three were reported across America. In the summer of
1967, the most devastating civil riots in American history took place
in numerous cities, especially Newark and Detroit. Urbanization,
poverty, racial hatred, and the social revolution that grew out of the
civil rights movement provided the sparks that directly or indirectly
ignited the riots. The 1992 verdict that exonerated Los Angeles
policemen in the beating of Rodney King brought still greater property destruction and the loss of sixty lives.

Obviously, the deep-seated problems of our cities continually
worsen, making great urban areas seething masses of restless discontent with overwhelming pressures caused by poor living conditions. The infrastructures of large cities continue to decay, without
sufficient funds available for their repair. The well-educated and
those in middle- to upper-income brackets tend to move to suburbs,
seeking the good life in cleaner, safer environments and in better

homes, schools, and cultural surroundings. Those in most suburbs find themselves remarkably insulated from the great tensions and stresses of the inner city, which may be only a few miles away. As the middle class leaves the city, the population left behind is increasingly dependent, unable to finance the incredible needs exacerbated by decay and inferior education. Suburban "people resent it when politicians take their money and use it to solve other people's problems, especially when they don't believe that government can actually solve those problems."[43]

Many churches also have fled to the relative comfort of suburbia, deserting vast areas of the inner cities with their minority groups, poor, blue-collar workers, transients, single-parent families, latch-key children, and ethnic enclaves. "Today many who name the name of Christ have removed themselves from human hurt and suffering to places of relative comfort and safety. Many have sought to protect themselves and their families from the poor and the wretched masses for whom Christ showed such primary concern. . . . The church's compassionless inactivity stems from being removed and out of touch with the suffering of the poor and the exploited."[44] Most churches were obviously ill-prepared for the tremendous changes of urbanization and now the church is a stranger in a culture where the majority of people live without it.

In contrast to rural and small-town environments, most people in metropolitan areas do not live in communities, but in virtual isolation and anonymity. Many people, whether in the inner city or the suburbs, live in a house or an apartment for years without ever learning the names or needs of their neighbors. "The anonymity of the city dweller results from his living among strangers. . . . Anonymity and superficial human relations may be necessary in the city but they do create problems: anonymity removes inhibitions to antisocial conduct; superficial relations can lead to calloused unconcern for persons in trouble, to deep loneliness, and general apathy."[45]

Megachurches—those with more than two thousand attendees—with state-of-the-art facilities and top-of-the-line programs

43. Schneider, "The Suburban Century Begins."

44. Harv Oostdyk, *Step One: The Gospel and the Ghetto* (Basking Ridge, N.J.: SonLife International Inc., 1983), 61.

45. George A. Torney, ed., *Toward Creative Urban Strategy* (Waco: Word, 1970), 46.

attract many parishioners from smaller churches. "They [mega-churches] offer as much in the way of activities and entertainment as they do religion. . . . As churchgoers, they are pragmatic and pressed for time, and they care passionately about amenities and services—spotless nurseries, convenient parking, dazzling enter-tainment . . . some say they are hastening the demise of traditional churches. They just suck up members from suburban churches right and left."[46] Like it or not, megachurches are transforming the religious landscape of urbanized America.[47]

The cruel depersonalization and moral megashifts that character-ize city life make the ministry of the local church even more vital. The church offers community, dignity, and purpose not readily found elsewhere in urban centers. However, traditional forms of ministry that concentrate on getting congregants and prospective members into state-of-the-art edifices will not work in the coming century. The urban environment demands greater emphasis on the church scattered, with effort diversified to minister effectively to those anguished by dehumanization in many forms. Urbanized Christians can no longer form cocoon-like churches in comfortable suburbia and devote themselves to narcissistic concerns. The crucial responsibility of city pastors, whether inner-city or suburban, cen-ters on inspiring new passions: ministry in a pregnancy home, a food distribution center, a homeless shelter, a prison, a coffee house, or a thousand other places where society experiences the rawness of life without the hope of the gospel. Churches—whether inner-city or suburban—uninvolved in meeting the city's desperate needs cannot possibly maintain credibility; they deserve to shrivel and die.

More than a hundred years ago Charles Spurgeon understood the ramifications of the gospel for a needy city and, as a result, he estab-lished orphanages, schools, shelters for the poor, meals for the hun-gry, homes for the aged, literacy programs for the disadvantaged. While doing all this and more, he preached powerfully against rac-ism, economic exploitation, and many other injustices found in the urban environment. With all of these concerns and efforts, Spur-

46. "Mighty Fortresses," *The Wall Street Journal,* 13 May 1991.
47. For "an irreverent look at church growth, megachurches, and ecclesiastical 'show-biz'" see *The Ultimate Church,* by Tom Raabe (Grand Rapids: Zondervan, 1991). The satir-ical humor carries a serious message.

geon never compromised or neglected the gospel of personal salvation through faith in Jesus Christ. Similarly, William Booth, founder of the Salvation Army, established soup kitchens, homeless shelters, employment offices, clothing centers, job-training schools, rescue centers for alcoholics and prostitutes, and many other programs to meet the needs of city dwellers. The metropolitan context for pastoral ministry demands such holistic ministry.

The popular urban culture presents great opportunity for the church, but great danger as well. Myers offers a startling observation: "It might seem an extreme assertion at first, but I believe that *the challenge of living with popular culture* may well be as serious for modern Christians as persecution and plagues were for the saints of earlier centuries . . . the erosion of character, the spoiling of innocent pleasures, and the cheapening of life itself that often accompany modern popular culture can occur so subtly that we believe nothing has happened."[48] The volatile context in which pastoral ministry takes place often defies description. For the church to be salt and light, it must resist conformity to the world while raising biblical standards of faith and lifestyle. Pastoral leaders must be spiritually authentic and innovators of new paradigms for ministry.

Those interested in urban ministry may profit from the following books: Larry L. Rose and C. Kirk Hadaway (eds.), *The Urban Challenge* (Nashville: Broadman, 1982), Harv Oostdyk, *Step One: The Gospel and the Ghetto* (Basking Ridge, N.J.: Sonlife International, 1983), Larry L. Rose and C. Kirk Hadaway (eds.), *An Urban World: Churches Face the Future* (Nashville: Broadman, 1984), and Jack O. Balswick and J. Kenneth Morland, *Social Problems* (Grand Rapids: Baker, 1990).

Steps to Contextual Appreciation

Pastors must understand and appreciate the cultural context of their ministries. Effectiveness in ministry depends upon the ability to apply ancient scriptural truths to a contemporary reality.

Become a student of culture. Discipline yourself to read the best newsmagazines that not only report but also analyze the incredible transmutations of our world.

48. Myers, *All God's Children and Blue Suede Shoes*, xii.

Seize every opportunity to travel and participate in ministry cross-culturally, whether around the world or across town. Become a pastor with a broad vision for the world; avoid a nearsighted and provincialized ministry.

Adapt methods and message to the context of your ministry, without compromising the truth of Scripture. Grapple seriously with the "so what?" question.

Lift the consciousness of the congregation to an appreciation of cultural pluralism, the opportunities available to them, and their solemn responsibility to make a difference in our world.

3

SYNCRETISM, PLURALISM, ECLECTICISM: WHAT A RIDE!

Spiritual life is fostered,
and spiritual maturity engendered,
not by techniques, but by truth.

J. I. Packer

Each generation of Christian leaders faces a distinctive challenge, a challenge similar in some ways to that of previous generations, yet remarkably different in other ways. Pastors struggle to maintain traditional values, biblical integrity, and cultural relevance. Many fail. Some pastors close their eyes to the world around them, while others close their ears to the authoritative voice of Scripture and the gentle whispering of the Holy Spirit; some lose touch with both the culture and the gospel.

At the end of the century, the church faces an identity crisis unparalleled in American history. Gone—probably forever—are the days when pastors spoke for the conscience of the nation and churches influenced the outcome of moral decisions. Perhaps the single most important question facing American Christianity is "Will the church continue to slide toward irrelevance?"

Powerful and interrelated threats to American Christianity confront our clergy. The advance of secularization and neopaganism into the church will cripple it as has happened in Europe.

A Changed Culture

The Renaissance and later the Enlightenment critically examined previously accepted doctrines and institutions from a rationalistic viewpoint. Scholars discarded traditional religious values and replaced them with the supremacy of human reason. Philosophers asked "What do you think?" "What do you want?" and "How does it feel?" Questions like "What does the Bible say?" or "What is right or wrong?" faded into obscurity. New cultural norms began to emerge, norms no longer related to any objective standard, but dependent upon the vagaries of feelings and wants. "What is 'good' is corrupted into whatever gratifies one's personal desires, whatever promotes self-interest even at the expense of the dignity and worth of others."[1] Absolutes became trivialized or mocked out of existence.

The bitter fruit of replacing revelation with rationalism, relativism, and individualism has been experienced in Europe for some generations, but only recently has American culture shed most of the constraints of religious ideas, objectives, and institutions. Secularization has labored and brought forth a society that not only rejects a Christian worldview, but also shows hostility to many biblical values. Many regard Christian ideals, moral standards, and paradigms as not only obsolete but injurious to healthful living (see chap. 2). Our culture not only is open to pagan values and goals but enthrones them.

Some interesting anomalies result. For example, officials in one of the republics that formerly made up the Soviet Union recently requested that the "JESUS" movie be shown in all public schools. Meanwhile, an American court prohibited a fifth-grade school teacher from keeping a Bible on his desk, and another court prohibi-

1. Carl F. H. Henry, *Twilight of a Great Civilization* (Westchester, Ill.: Crossway, 1988), 40.

ted a young student from reading the Bible on the school bus. Our daily newspapers carried the story that "Teen Chastity" efforts are being called unconstitutional. The ACLU has gone to court to dissolve the 1981 Adolescent Family Life Act and to prohibit funding for organizations that distribute advice to youth about avoiding premarital sex.

Today's American churches suffer significant losses to the amorphous, rival religion of secularism. Mainline denominations are losing one thousand members a week by most estimates.[2] Many now believe that evangelicalism peaked a decade ago and has been eroding in membership and strength ever since. Further, some suggest that the surge of evangelicalism during the 1970s and 1980s indicates not its understanding and penetration of culture but the church's accommodation to culture and society's manipulation of the church. "Churches that lend support to the technological mainstream are generally rewarded by the society at large. What this may indicate is not that the secular society is becoming more receptive to the message of the church but that it is taking advantage of the opportunity to use the church for its own ends."[3] The statistical success of some evangelical churches during the 1970s and 1980s may even delude many into believing no serious problem exists.

An Enfeebled Church

A culture indifferent or hostile to Christian values has dramatically penetrated and devitalized American churches. A new, rival in-church religion dominates current American Christianity, a religion that clings to many orthodox doctrines and the blessings and assurances of salvation while it rejects the disciplines of discipleship and obedience to even the most basic scriptural commands. Orthodoxy and orthopraxy have parted company, resulting in enfeebled churches.

That non-Christian society should adopt non-Christian values surprises no one. Christian ideals and institutions have always had

2. The situation in Europe is far more dismal. In England about 6 percent of the population attend church services, 4 percent or less in Germany and Scandinavia. The Church of Scotland lost twenty thousand members in one recent year. The vitality of Christianity has now shifted to Africa and isolated places in Asia, such as Korea.

3. Donald Bloesch, *Crumbling Foundations* (Grand Rapids: Zondervan, 1984), 52.

limited influence on society's norms, and there have always been vociferous critics of biblical teaching. The great problem relates to the compromise of historic Christian values within the church, the contamination and enfeeblement of the church by the surrounding culture. The enemy within our ranks is more to be feared than the enemy "out there." The antagonist has joined the church and become respectable, and in many cases associated with the norm and the blessing of God. Søren Kierkegaard's words seem more urgent than ever before: "Christianity in our times is close to becoming paganism; it has long ago yielded at least its main points."[4]

It may be that a passionate desire to make the gospel attractive and nonoffensive and the church user-friendly and influential has corrupted our fidelity to both biblical truth and ethical methodology. "Current evangelical popularity presents powerful pressures to compromise biblical values for the sake of social acceptance. . . . Our degree of compromise has reached epidemic proportions."[5]

The epidemic proportions of compromise in the church is revealed by the following factors that confront American clergy and that form a powerful challenge to meaningful ministry.

Theological Flaccidity

Historically, theologians wrestled with texts such as "No one who lives in him keeps on sinning. No one who continues to sin has either seen him or known him" and "No one who is born of God will continue to sin, because God's seed remains in him; he cannot go on sinning, because he has been born of God" (1 John 3:6, 9) and "As the body without the spirit is dead, so faith without deeds is dead" (James 2:26). Both Calvinists and Arminians concluded that no one could be saved while continuing to love that which God hates, no one could serve two masters (Matt. 6:24).[6] To the Calvinist, a lifestyle of sin meant that the individual had never been regenerated; to the Arminian, continuing in sin meant the loss of salvation, assuming the individual was once saved. For both of these

---

4. Cited in Bloesch, *Crumbling Foundations,* 39.

5. Jon Johnston, *Will Evangelicalism Survive Its Own Popularity?* (Grand Rapids: Zondervan, 1980), 2, 13.

6. Charles Spurgeon: "Let not a man suppose that he can be saved while he continues to love what God hates."

major theological systems, assurance of salvation was inextricably linked to growth in grace and obedience to the demands of discipleship, the major theme of 1 John.

The theology so popular in many of today's churches differs significantly from historic Christian teaching. The new theological wrinkle offers quick and permanent assurance of salvation in response to an easy professed belief, while at the same time allowing the convert to live indefinitely with contempt for Christ's teaching. Today's theological flaccidity separates historically unified concepts: justification from sanctification, faith from repentance, the saviorhood from the lordship of Christ, and the new birth from discipleship. Such flaccidity thereby permits the professing Christian to remain in a lifestyle indistinguishable from that of the unregenerate individual, but with confidence in eternal salvation. Many choose this new option without realizing the danger. No one is so surely in the grip of Satan as the person who falsely believes he is saved.

A New Evangelism

Evangelism differs substantially not just in style, but in fundamental content, from the days when Jonathan Edwards preached "Sinners in the Hands of an Angry God." Evangelism used to confront and condemn sin, declare death and hell as the true wages of sin, uphold the holiness of God, proclaim the person and work of God's Son, and offer forgiveness and eternal life by God's grace through faith in the Lord Jesus Christ. Those who responded to such a message became disciples as well as church members. Today's evangelism encourages easy decisions and "many people never seem to be taught just what conversion means. They register a decision for Christ, but there is no content to it."[7]

Today's evangelism aims for decisions, not disciples, opening it to the charge that easy-believism marks American Christianity: "Most mass and local church evangelism approaches today have a significant shortcoming. Attention is centered, and success judged around the goal of getting a 'decision.' That brief verbal commitment is seen

7. Klaus Bockmuhl, "Christianity Has a Moral Backbone," *Christianity Today,* 6 Oct. 1978, 54.

as the ultimate response to the Great Commission."[8] Perhaps cheap decisions explain the results of one follow-up program of two thousand evangelistic conversions. Four hundred of those people were baptized and only seven were found to be in any church one year later. Only God knows how many of these converts really understood the authentic gospel and responded with genuine faith in Christ, but there is obvious cause for concern.

Neopaganism

Neopaganism distinguishes itself from the old kind by its baptism into the church. The lifestyle of innumerable professing Christians differs but little from that of the practical atheists of our culture; indeed, in most cases their lifestyle is indistinguishable from that of the unregenerate. More than forty million Americans claim a born-again experience.[9] Yet, it is difficult to imagine a time when so many professions of faith have produced so little evidence of transformation and spiritual vitality in daily lives.

A 1984 Gallup Poll uncovered this paradox: "Religion is growing in importance among Americans, but morality is losing ground." That same poll found "very little difference in the behavior of the churched and the unchurched on a wide range of items including lying, cheating, and pilferage." In 1990, a survey by the Roper Organization showed little difference in the moral behavior of "born-again" Christians before and after their conversion experiences.[10] The Barna Research Group surveys demonstrate: "There is virtually no difference in the lifestyles of the average American and the born-again Christian. . . . More born-again Christians read *Penthouse* than watch the top-rated Christian TV shows. . . . Outside the realm of overtly religious matters, this (Christian) segment can hardly be differentiated from the unsaved masses. They have not altered their lifestyle one bit since accepting Christ. Their acceptance of Christianity has cost them nothing. In their minds,

---

8. Win and Charles Arn, *The Master Plan for Making Disciples* (Pasadena, Calif.: Church Growth Press, 1982), 9.

9. Estimates are as high as 84.7 million; e.g., Forest J. Boyd, *Decision*, December 1980, 12. A 1990 Gallup poll reported that 74 percent of Americans, eighteen years of age and older, say they have made a commitment to Jesus Christ.

10. *National and International Religion Report,* 8 Oct. 1990.

they can have their cake and eat it too."[11] Harold J. Foos, a professor at Moody Bible Institute, correctly asserts: "Today in America it's all too clear that the church corporately and Christians individually are barely distinguishable from the surrounding culture. A cursory look at lifestyle or a detailed review of statistics (for example, divorce, abuse, or business ethics) leaves little doubt that the clearly identifiable Christian is hard to find."[12]

Innumerable professing Christians nonchalantly dismiss biblical commands as hopelessly antediluvian. Intrachurch paganism repudiates even the most fundamental elements of morality. "Conversion is a change of mood, of friends, of opinions, but not of daily life. It does not reach the level of behavior. It does not include moral change."[13] "In a recent major study of sexual attitudes and practice, no major difference was seen between the *practice* of Christian kids and non-Christian kids. Christian kids are just as involved sexually as their non-Christian friends."[14] Many rationalize continuing immorality: "My personal faith affirms God's laws for the whole of man, not unreal antiquated rules" and "Christ wants us to live abundant lives; to me that includes sex."[15] "The sexual norms and codes upheld by the church through the ages are dismissed as archaic."[16]

One cannot tell which disturbs most: the paganism within the church or the casual attitude of many clergy to such facts. Can the Holy Spirit, whose responsibility includes the conviction of sin, be a failure in these professed believers?

An Oxymoron

The term *pagan Christians* characterizes many of today's church members. Every honest pastor must wrestle with the question: Are such professors of the faith truly Christians? Is it conceivable that

---

11. *Christian Marketing Perspective,* Fall 1987. The quoted statistic becomes more meaningful when compared to the fact that 13,500,000 Americans watch Christian television programs every week.

12. "When Pop Culture Loses Its Fizz," *Moody Monthly,* July/August 1990.

13. Bockmuhl, "Christianity Has a Moral Backbone," 54.

14. Rich Van Pelt, *Intensive Care: Helping Teenagers in Crisis* (Grand Rapids: Zondervan, 1988), 178.

15. Richard Quebedeaux, *The Worldly Evangelicals* (San Francisco: Harper and Row, 1978), 127. Note also *Christians in the Wake of the Sexual Revolution* by Randy Alcorn (Portland, Ore.: Multnomah, 1987).

16. Bloesch, *Crumbling Foundations,* 23.

genuine believers may evidence few or none of those characteristics that have historically distinguished the saints? Can justification be received without progressive sanctification? Can the working of the Holy Spirit be so minuscule in true Christians as to be unobservable by others even after many years? Can a person use Christ as a celestial insurance policy against condemnation, while openly and indefinitely rejecting the demands of discipleship and Christ's teaching about how to live on earth while awaiting the heavenly call? Should the old doctrine that claims that true Christians grow in grace and persevere in the way of holiness—though with imperfection—until death be surrendered?

A. W. Tozer challenged today's popular opinion: "Plain horse sense ought to tell us that anything that makes no change in the man who professes it makes no difference to God either, and it is an easily observable fact that for countless numbers of persons the change from no-faith to faith makes no actual difference in the life."[17] Similarly, Charles Spurgeon taught, "Yet, in all true conversions there are points of essential agreement: there must be in all a penitent confession of sin, and a looking to Jesus for the forgiveness of it, and there must also be a real change of heart such as shall affect the entire afterlife, and where these essential points are not to be found, there is no genuine conversion."[18] Sadly, many modern teachers only pay lip service to such truth or reject it altogether.

A Substitute Gospel

Our preaching needs reevaluation in the light of the product it has generated, for it is no longer the norm for professing Christians to take seriously their own confession: "Jesus is Lord!" Many preach a gospel gutted of substance, a gospel that suggests that true justification is possible without any consequent evidence of a changed lifestyle. The "saved" person may remain a "slave of sin," "a friend of the world," and live "according to the sinful nature." J. C. Ryle preached that a religion such as this will never save the soul; indeed, a religion that costs nothing and changes nothing is worth nothing.

17. A. W. Tozer, *Man the Dwelling Place of God* (Harrisburg, Penn.: Christian Publications, 1966), 31.
18. Charles Spurgeon, *Metropolitan Tabernacle Pulpit*, vol. 20 (Pasadena, Tex.: Pilgrim Publications), 398.

Spurgeon condemned "pigpen Christianity" and was sure that people are not saved for the sake of their works, yet he was equally sure that no person will be saved without them; and that one who leads an unholy life, who neglects the great salvation, can never inherit the crown of life.

Few churches are shaped by the demands of the gospel or witness a stirring of the Spirit of God in their services, victory over temptation, answers to prayer, fervency in devotion, or effectiveness in witness, all evidences of spiritual vitality. Such reality raises a question about the gospel being preached: Is it the historic, authentic gospel? J. I. Packer concludes that it is not: "Without realising it, we have during the past century bartered [the] gospel for a substitute product which, though it looks similar enough in points of detail, is as a whole a decidedly different thing. Hence our troubles; for the substitute product does not answer the ends for which the authentic gospel has in past days proved itself so mighty. Why? We would suggest the reason lies in its own character and content . . . it needs to be said with emphasis that this set of twisted half-truths is something other than the biblical gospel."[19]

If the gospel is gutted of substance, all pastoral efforts will amount to little except the rattling of ecclesiastical machinery.

An Antinomian Gospel

Popular antinomianism may account for the absence of serious discipleship among so many professing Christians. This type of preaching "assumes that God loves us without judgment, that grace opposes obligation, that 'oughts' are dehumanizing if not sick, and that the gospel always makes the law questionable. . . . Nothing is required by this merciful God. Don't worry about any response to God in order to feel completely OK with yourself and God. Feelings of guilt are considered neurotic. . . . How strangely different from the Holy One of Amos, Isaiah, and Jesus."[20]

Such an antinomian gospel suggests that the responsibilities and obligations of discipleship are merely options for believers, and that to reject biblical commands, growth in grace, and holiness (without

19. J. I. Packer, *A Quest for Godliness* (Wheaton: Crossway, 1990), 126, 127.
20. Thomas Oden, *Pastoral Theology* (San Francisco: Harper and Row, 1983), 8, 9.

which no one will see the Lord, Heb. 12:14) incurs no serious consequences. An antinomian gospel thus reflects the "cheap grace" so
roundly denounced by Dietrich Bonhoeffer.

A Comfortable Gospel

Preaching today emphasizes peace, comfort, happiness, and personal satisfaction. Preaching does not focus on the glory of God, the
lordship of Christ, the constraints of discipleship, the reality of
judgment, or the devastating effects of sin. "Whereas the chief aim
of the old [gospel] was to teach people to worship God, the concern
of the new seems limited to making them feel better. The subject of
the old gospel was God and his ways with men; the subject of the
new is man and the help God gives him. There is a world of difference. The whole perspective and emphasis of gospel preaching has
changed."[21]

Sunday services in many churches may serve more to entertain
than to evangelize, strengthen faith, prepare saints for spiritual warfare, or facilitate corporate worship. Indeed, the kind of church
meeting that yields personal comfort is what sells in today's narcissistic world. Our music, sermons, and prayers seem obsessed with
health, wealth, and personal happiness. Few preachers summon
parishioners to count the cost, pick up the cross, die to the old sinful nature, and "put on the new self, created to be like God in true
righteousness and holiness" (Eph. 4:24). Today's message helps
people feel better, but it does not help them know, worship, and
serve God.

Ecclesiastical Narcissism

Due to real or perceived pressures, many leaders channel effort
and funds toward recruiting ready-made members, running traditional programs, oiling bureaucratic machinery, increasing in-
house expenditures, and building expensive structures that serve
extraordinarily limited purposes. Many local congregations have
become excessively concerned with the maintenance of their own
structures and tragically unconcerned about the power of the living
God, the fields of the world ripe for harvest, or the community at its

---

21. Packer, *A Quest for Godliness*, 126.

doorsteps. In most American churches activities have become inwardly focused and exist primarily for the preservation of the organization, the running of its machinery, and the comfort of its members. This fortress mindset focuses on the church gathered. Equipping and commissioning ministries have a low priority in today's churches. Several components indicate this ecclesiastical narcissism.

Materialistic Goals

Despite the perceived advances of the church growth movement, Protestant church membership and attendance have actually declined throughout the 1980s. Peter Wagner admits: "I don't think there's anything intrinsically wrong with the church-growth principles we've developed, or the evangelistic techniques we're using. Yet somehow they don't seem to work."[22] Something may be amiss with the church's real goals, which may differ significantly from the church's stated goals.

Organizational prosperity forms the criterion for success with many and, when achieved, it deceives people into thinking that they have secured the blessing of God. Genuine leaders know that their churches desperately need revival, a fresh touch from God, and a restoration of biblical values. Many rejoice over the attainment of impressive statistics, but in reality they may be witnessing the judgment of God and the withdrawal of his Spirit from the whole affair.

Apathy for Evangelism

An incredible incongruity perplexes spiritual leaders: many express enthusiasm for church growth and few exhibit passion for evangelism or discipleship. Considerable obsession exists for creating large and powerful churches, but in many cases institutional affluence seems more important than additions to the kingdom. Are we building churches or crowds? Do our growing churches emerge from effective ministry?

With some notable exceptions, most of the growing churches in America have no aggressive evangelistic witness or disciple-making emphasis; their growth has little, if anything, to do with penetrating

22. "Church Growth Fine Tunes Its Formulas," *Christianity Today*, 24 June 1991, 46.

society with the gospel. Sociologists Reginald Bibby and Merlin Brinkerhoff researched evangelical church growth and concluded that "claims of the penetration of secularized society . . . represent an illusion."[23] *Christianity Today* reports that "church growth's greatest challenge in North America comes from research that shows that more than 80 percent of all the growth taking place in growing churches comes through transfer, not conversion."[24]

Few Christians, including many pastors, have much enthusiasm for evangelizing or discipling, the primary mandate of the gospel. "Reaching non-Christians is a low priority for most congregations. What was once the heartbeat of the entire church, particularly the early church, has diminished enormously as a priority in the minds of its members. What was once an important criteria for success has diminished to merely one item (and not a particularly important one) on the church's busy agenda."[25] In most churches numerical increase results from choice location in expanding suburbia, charismatic pulpiteers, clever promotional efforts, top-of-the-line entertainment, funding for impressive buildings, and heavy transfer growth from a highly mobile populace. Many megachurches merely suck up members from stagnant or dying churches.

Profaned Ministers

Clergy and lay leaders often lose sensitivity to the spiritual nature of their work, which inevitably leads to ministerial decay and bewilderment. In American Christianity pastoral ministry has become profane and worldly, a mere job or profession, and the church has become simply another corporate enterprise. Henri Nouwen, perhaps better than any contemporary theologian, understands and speaks to this grave danger: "The basic question is whether we ministers of Jesus Christ have not already been so deeply molded by the seductive powers of our dark world that we have become blind to our own and other people's fatal state and have lost the power and motivation to swim for our lives. . . . Thus we are busy people just like all other busy people, rewarded with the rewards which are

---

23. *Christian Education Trends* (Wheaton: David C. Cook, 1983), a private circulation to ministers and Christian educators.

24. "Church Growth Fine Tunes Its Formulas," 47.

25. Arn, *The Master Plan for Making Disciples*, 7.

rewarded to busy people! All this is simply to suggest how horrendously secular our ministerial lives tend to be."[26]

Regrettably, most people today do not view clergy as saints in touch with God, noted for their piety and skill in handling the Word of God and giving spiritual direction. Many pastors merely run an organization, which happens to be the church. One promotional piece for a church management seminar suggested that pastors spend about 70 percent of their work time in administration, which leaves only 30 percent of their time for what they claim to be their real priorities. Thus, the church is overmanaged and underled by those with upside-down priorities. Wrong priorities are often well-managed and well-promoted, producing conspicuous but nonspiritual results, while right priorities are shelved, perhaps because of the pressures of our success-oriented culture.

Helmut Thielicke warned the church against "clerical promoters" who major in fanfare rather than substance: "They are operators who are bent only upon attractive novelties and will not put an end to the unproductive rattling of the ecclesiastical machinery but will only make it run faster."[27] Such a secularized, profaned ministry jeopardizes the spiritual lives of people, threatens the vitality and existence of churches, and contributes to the paganizing of our culture.

Directional Ambiguity

In our nation's government, politicians advocate balanced budgets but increase spending and, from fear of voter reprisal, reject increased taxes, thereby adding to the deficit they condemn. Similarly, many church leaders profess deep commitment to evangelism, discipleship, social justice, and a plethora of efforts to feed the hungry, house the homeless, heal the hurting, and comfort the afflicted, but actually spend their energies and funds elsewhere, mostly in making the institution prosperous. Most pastors readily confess that their professed major priorities are not the things that occupy the bulk of their time.

26. Henri Nouwen, *The Way of the Heart* (New York: Ballantine, 1981), 10–11.
27. Helmut Thielicke, *The Trouble with the Church* (Grand Rapids: Baker, 1965), 49.

Ecclesiastical narcissism makes a coherent sense of direction and genuine ministry impossible for pastors and congregations. Many—probably most—churches and pastors rarely evaluate what has happened, never accurately determine where they are, seldom dream of things to come, and have no time to strategize for the next decade or century. Instead, they busily maintain unproductive conventional programs, oil ecclesiastical machinery, and handle myriad urgencies. Few think strategically about the purposes of God and the opportunities of the hour.

Technological Dependency

Many of today's churches and clergy depend heavily on technology, entertainment, and promotion to accomplish the agenda of the church. Os Guinness is correct: "Marketing now is overpowering ministry."[28] This brings a corresponding deemphasis upon biblical mandates like prayer, preaching, teaching, evangelism, meditation, spiritual direction, and discipleship. Many contemporary Christian leaders are indifferent to historic Christian practices, perhaps in a desperate effort to appear relevant and user-friendly, to attract the unchurched, and to become successful. "Secular methodologies have overrun too many church leaders' thinking. Evangelicals are too easily duped by the latest ways to reach people, whether it be telemarketing, nifty brochures, or musical extravaganzas. The entire approach puts more responsibility on the leadership to be creative and raise funds than it does on the members of the church to effectively penetrate their worlds for Christ."[29]

Never have churches possessed such technological proficiency, yet with so little personal morality, social justice, spiritual fervor, meaningful worship, or evangelistic compassion among its members. Many churches devote resources to telemarketing, computerized mailing lists, hi-tech media, slick promotional blurbs, state-of-the-art facilities, programming novelties, financial manipulations, power structures, staff management, organizational charts, and motivational gimmicks. Such churches depreciate spiritual war-

---

28. Os Guinness, "Guidelines for Plundering," lecture given at "The Church in the 21st Century," seminar, 21 August 1991, Denver, Colo. This lecture has been revised, updated, and included in *No God But God*, ed. Os Guinness and John Seel (Chicago: Moody, 1992).

29. Bill Hull, *The Disciple Making Pastor* (Old Tappan, N.J.: Revell, 1988), 40.

fare, prayer retreats, and hours of solitude and quiet before God. Most parishioners suffer from biblical illiteracy, while an endless number of seminars focus on technological imperatives and management techniques, especially in marketing and fund-raising strategies.

Modern methodologies and technologies can be helpful when used with spiritual discernment. We would be extraordinarily foolish to reject useful managerial insights, excellent accounting procedures, computers, modern media, and the like. Yet, anything becomes an enemy when it replaces biblical directives for the church, as has happened today in a large segment of American Christianity. Further, not all methodologies are compatible with Scripture, and we must carefully guard against the temptation to value and accept anything purely on the basis of pragmatism.

The church is the body of Christ, and the struggle for church growth is spiritual in nature. When evangelicalism takes its marketing and promotional cues from Madison Avenue and not from Scripture, it errs tragically. We wage spiritual battles with spiritual weapons "against the rulers, against the authorities, against the powers of this dark world and against the spiritual forces of evil in the heavenly realms" (Eph. 6:12). The powers of hell cannot prevail against the true church that puts on the whole armor of God.

The Challenge

Today's world and church require a new breed of committed Christian leaders—or possibly the revival of an old genre. What kind of pastors do we need, and what must they do to reverse a trend toward ecclesiastical compromise and narcissism? In the light of the imposing threats to serious Christianity, where do we go from here? In addition to suggestions found elsewhere in this book, we set out the following elementary principles.

Commit to Spiritual Weapons

Only the full armor of God will enable Christian leaders to stand against the wiles of Satan, the secularization of our values, and the contamination of the American church. Truth, righteousness, the authentic gospel, genuine faith, and persevering prayer will reverse the church's slide toward irrelevancy.

There was a day in the history of the church when "Cromwell and his army made long, strong prayers before each battle, and preachers made long, strong prayers privately before ever venturing into the pulpit, and laymen made long, strong prayers before tackling any matter of importance (marriage, business deals, major purchases, or whatever). Today, however, Christians in the West are found to be on the whole passionless, passive, and, one fears, prayerless."[30] Pastors must labor to recover the norm of long, strong prayers. In Chicago twenty-four hundred Muslim men gather at one mosque twice a day for prayer, nine hundred of them at the 4:00 A.M. service. No comparable Christian prayer meeting exists anywhere in America. "It is all too easy for churches to give lip service to prayer while, in fact, trusting in technique."[31]

Yet, some extremely encouraging signs offer hope to serious Christians. David Barrett, a mission statistician, has researched a surging prayer movement and claims there are approximately 170 million Christians worldwide who are committed to praying every day for spiritual awakening and world evangelization. About 10 million prayer groups focus on these priorities, according to the National and International Religion Report (May 1992). Some entire denominations are currently mobilizing their constituents to pray for revival. No significant revival has ever occurred except in response to such persevering prayer.

Recover an Authentic Gospel

We must renounce the kind of preaching and teaching that is producing converts who merely give lip service to Christianity and fail to become true disciples. Pastors must say clearly that there is "a different gospel—which is really no gospel at all" (Gal. 1:6–7) and that there exists a kind of faith that damns as surely as the most blatant and blasphemous forms of atheism (James 2:14–19). Prevailing or failing at such a task will largely determine the effectiveness of our Christian leaders and the health of our churches.

Evangelicals generally agree that justification followed by progressive sanctification and eventual glorification depends on God's

30. Packer, *The Quest for Godliness*, 25.
31. "Church Growth's Two Faces," *Christianity Today*, 24 June 1991, 19.

bestowal of grace and personal faith in Jesus Christ, but what does that mean? What proper doctrinal content is assigned to the word *believe*? When Paul and Silas preached "Believe in the Lord Jesus, and you will be saved" (Acts 16:31), what really was expected of the Philippian jailor? Out of the variety of current opinions, pastors must recover and preach historic and biblical truth.

What constitutes biblical, saving faith in Christ? A careful study of Scripture and a synthesis of the best teaching of history's greatest theologians suggest that genuine, saving faith means acknowledging sinfulness, renouncing self-righteousness, trusting gratefully in the finished, substitutionary work of Christ upon the cross, and thereby exchanging rebellion against God for submission to the authority of Christ. Genuine Christians "have been set free from sin and have become slaves to righteousness" (Rom. 6:18). Too much modern theology characterizes a different, more shallow gospel, allowing regeneration without reformation, birth without life, assurance without discipleship.

Pastors who will make a difference in a new century must return to an authentic gospel, one that preserves the doctrine of grace and thoroughly rejects works for salvation, but insists that genuine faith brings a person into a relationship with Christ and the Holy Spirit, producing evidence of a changed life. Indeed, "any professed faith in Christ as personal Saviour that does not bring the life under plenary obedience to Christ as Lord is inadequate and must betray its victim at the last."[32] As Martin Luther wrote, "Christ has earned for us not only God's mercy, but also the gift of the Holy Spirit, that we should have not only forgiveness, but also an end of sins. Whoever remains in his earlier evil ways must have another kind of Christ. Consequence demands that a Christian should have the Holy Spirit and lead a new life, or know that he has not received Christ at all."[33]

The historic gospel produces Christians who count the cost of discipleship, deny self, struggle against sin, and manifest the fruit of the Spirit. "Whoever claims to live in him must walk as Jesus did" (1 John 2:6) and "If you love me, you will obey what I command" (John 14:15). We are called to be saints and act saintly; God has

32. Tozer, *Man the Dwelling Place of God*, 33.
33. Cited in Bockmuhl, "Christianity Has a Moral Backbone."

saved us and "called us to a holy life" (2 Tim. 1:9). Assurance of sal-vation increases with godliness, for "we know that we have come to know him if we obey his commands" (1 John 2:3). Pastors dare not offer assurance to those whose lifestyle denies their profession, for "the man who says, 'I know him,' but does not do what he com-mands is a liar, and the truth is not in him" (1 John 2:4). Good trees bear good fruit, and bad trees bear bad fruit (Matt. 7:18). Pastors must preach such authentic truth unequivocally.

Strive for Vitality

Pastors who make an impact concentrate efforts and muster resources not for organizational prosperity but for spiritual vitality, which may or may not result in statistically measurable results. Modern paraphernalia, methods, and marketing strategies fail to penetrate our society with the gospel and fail to create vitality in our churches. We need pastors who will pray and work for a gracious visitation of God's Spirit, a revival and renewal of our churches, and who will wholeheartedly submit to the authority of Scripture.

True spiritual vitality includes "an awesome sense of the pres-ence of God and the truth of the gospel; a profound awareness of sin, leading to deep repentance and heartfelt embrace of the glori-fied, loving, pardoning Christ; an uninhibited witness to the power and glory of Christ, with a mighty freedom of speech expressing a mighty freedom of spirit; joy in the Lord, love for his people, and fear of sinning; and from God's side an intensifying and speeding-up of the work of grace so that men are struck down by the word and transformed by the Spirit in short order . . . ."[34]

Few of these traits mark today's American churches. The accepted structures of modern ecclesiology fail to quicken the con-science, soften the heart, promote humility, defeat the flesh, or pre-vail in spiritual warfare in the lives of most parishioners. Few con-gregations observe consistent demonstration of supernatural power and the joy of transformed lives. Worthy pastors bring their efforts and the church's resources to bear upon the spiritual delinquency of our generation, the authority of the Word, the grace of God, and the power of the Holy Spirit in setting believers free from the shack-

34. Packer, *A Quest for Godliness*, 36.

les of sin, "in order that you may live a life worthy of the Lord, and may please him in every way: bearing fruit in every good work, growing in the knowledge of God, being strengthened with all power according to his glorious might . . ." (Col. 1:10–11).

Techniques and secular ideologies never nourish the true life of the church. Passionate declaration of divine truth, spiritual discipline, and long, strong, fervent prayers move mountains and claim territory for God. "We cannot allow ourselves to set our sights on anything lower than revival for our churches—a new visitation by God, a new searching of hearts, a new humility, a new joy, a new quality of godliness, a new closeness of fellowship with our holy God through Jesus Christ by the Spirit, a new power for witness."[35]

Think Strategically

A shattering of the status quo and a reversal of the church's slide may be imminent. A movement in church leadership is just beginning to emerge, a movement that suggests promise. Here and there we see those who have committed themselves to making things happen, dreaming new dreams, energizing constituents, and transforming organizations into new entities devoted to excellence in genuine ministry. Some dramatic revolution in thinking about leadership and parishioner responsibility has begun to bring significant fruit and revitalization to a number of churches.

There is growing hope that Christians everywhere are taking personal responsibility for ministry. We see a few scattered churches streamlining their bureaucracies, equipping ministries, and freeing people to become involved in ministries not managed by the church's hierarchy and within the church's walls. Many are experiencing joint ventures between a variety of churches, particularly in core areas of cities. For example, in Denver, Colorado, "Mile High Ministries" carries a major impact; within one block five buildings shelter a coffeehouse, Mercy Ministries (for mothers), Where Grace Abounds (for homosexuals), Denver Street School (for public-school dropouts), a discipleship ministry, and the Church of the Open Door. More is being planned. Ten city and suburban churches have formed a coalition supporting this multi-

---

35. J. I. Packer, *The Bulletin of Westminster Theological Seminary* (Winter 1983): 5.

faceted and far-reaching ministry, with many Christian laity involved weekly.

The church cannot move effectively into the next century without leaders like these, leaders attuned to the realities of a frenetic age, determined to rise to the challenges before us and do something significant for God and for a desperately needy world.

Steps to Meeting the Challenge

The challenges—indeed, the threats—to pastoral ministry are formidable. The obstacles will not easily go away and will undoubtedly menace the church more as we enter the new century. Failure to grapple intellectually with and prevail spiritually over in-church secularization and neopaganism will guarantee pastoral failure and church irrelevance. Pastors must consider the following:

Examine whether theological flaccidity and a corrupted gospel have fostered an in-church secularization and neopaganism in the lives of parishioners. Recover an authentic gospel.

Reject ecclesiastical narcissism that compromises church goals, profanes ministerial work, fosters technological dependency, deemphasizes spiritual weapons, and engenders directional ambiguity in the church.

Give much study and prayerful thought about the use of spiritual weapons, including a faithful preaching of the demands of the gospel, discipleship, and persevering prayer. Commit to recover a faith that shapes individual lives and the corporate life of the church.

Lead church leaders to think strategically about personal responsibility for ministry. Streamline bureaucracy and free people to do ministry not necessarily managed by church leaders. Enter into joint ventures with other churches to begin ministries that exceed the capacity of any one church.

4

MINISTRY MUTANTS OR MINISTRY MODELS

We must honestly unmask
and courageously confront
our many self-deceptive games.

Henri J. M. Nouwen

Societal upheaval and church pressures present many serious problems of role definition for pastors in every generation. Today's changes, however, differ from those of previous eras in both speed and scope. How can pastors hold to biblical teaching about their ministry, maintain integrity, and respond adequately to a radically different world, a world that differs not merely from the century of the church's inception, but one that bears little resemblance to that of their fathers?

Our younger generation of pastors, and especially those preparing for ministry, struggle with role definition in a way that their forefathers did not. At the end of the twentieth century, dedicated young people look at the world and ministerial service through different lenses and they do not like what they see in traditional churches. Many of today's ministerial students who have not been reared in a church environment intelligently question the typical, established routines of many local churches and balk at devoting their lives to an institution mired in conventional, outdated practices. Parachurch, overseas, counseling, or educational ministries attract increasing numbers of our youth, because they apparently present viable alternatives of service. The traditional church often seems irrelevant and unattractive. Part of the problem may be attributed to theological seminaries and Bible schools that have been agonizingly slow to revamp methods and curricula in order to prepare students for a fundamentally different world than the professors of these institutions have encountered in their own ministries.

Of course, traditionalists remain firmly entrenched in some bastions of ecclesiastical conservatism, but decreasing numbers of parishioners take their ministries seriously. Unable to think in terms of new standards of ministry, these pastors—with honorable intentions—think in unpretentious terms of survival and maintenance, and seldom imagine penetrating their communities with the gospel of Jesus Christ. Consequently, they struggle to maintain a status quo, a struggle many pastors are losing. Eighty percent of American churches have not grown or have declined in attendance during the 1980s. Business as usual may (or may not) ensure survival, but only a change in the pastoral role will create effectiveness in the coming years of pastoral ministry.

A Historical Perspective

Of course, no single or simple historical pastoral role exists. An enormous variety of ecclesiastical traditions exist, and Scripture gives only a broad outline of pastoral work, leaving ample room for the great diversity of roles throughout history and in our contemporary world.

Denominational authorities, local church leaders, or ministerial educators have never agreed on the constitution of pastoral work, except in generalities. "Entering the ministry is more like entering the army, where one never knows where he will land or live or what specific work he will be called upon to perform."[1] Moreover, comparatively few people have a clear conception of what pastors are supposed to know, be, and do.

The pastoral role has tended to shift depending upon varying circumstances and differing biblical emphases. As Christ, the great Shepherd, is seen as Prophet, Priest, and King, so his undershepherds similarly carry out those roles to varying degrees at different times in church history. Sometimes the preaching role (prophet) became dominant, sometimes the sacramental role (priest) became central, and at other times the governmental role (king) emerged as primary. Most theologians recognize all of these roles as inherent in pastoral ministry, though many believe that the priesthood of all believers diminishes the priestly role of clergy.

The priestly role dominated clergy's priorities from the earliest times in the Roman Catholic Church. The writings of Chrysostom (*On the Priesthood*) and Pius XI (*On the Catholic Priesthood*) heavily influenced the emerging importance of administering the sacraments. Pastors or priests mediated between God and humankind in offering Christ in the Eucharist. Through that ministry "the grace of the Savior flows for the good of mankind." Other pastoral roles were adjuncts to this central ministry.

In medieval times the "government of souls" became the preeminent pastoral role. Sometimes this function became excessive and corrupted: "Preachers told kings when they could go to war and which wars were holy. Preachers told scholars what they might study and what could not be examined. Preachers told lenders what was reasonable interest on a loan and what was exorbitant. Preachers told powerful men whom they might marry and if they might get a divorce."[2] Yet, there was always the underlying purpose of directing souls so that they might escape hell and achieve eternal life. Some clergy, however, shunned worldly duties entirely and gave themselves to prayer and contemplation in a variety of monastic orders.

1. H. Richard Niebuhr, *The Purpose of the Church and Its Ministry* (New York: Harper and Brothers, 1956), 51.
2. Claude A. Frazier, *Should Preachers Play God?* (Independence, Mo.: Independence Press, 1973), 13.

During Reformation times ministers preached, taught, prayed, administered the sacraments, presided over the church, and cared for the needy. Still, it was recognized that the primary task was preaching the message of salvation by declaring God's forgiveness of sin, God's grace and love for mankind, and the sole basis of man's receiving God's forgiveness and grace, faith in Jesus Christ. Preaching, however, included not only public discourse but also "every action through which the gospel was brought home and men were moved to repent before God and to trust in him. Public discourse was never enough; private admonition, catechetical instruction, personal pastoral care, the administration of the sacraments, the leadership of public worship—all these needed to be faithfully attended to; but in everything he did the preacher had one thing to do, namely, to bring home to men the gospel of divine love."[3] Pastors often preached seven or more times a week, once each on an epistle, a Gospel, the Old Testament, the creed, the sacraments, the Lord's Prayer, and so forth.[4]

For several generations the pastoral role was shaped through the powerful influence of the great Puritan, Richard Baxter, who proclaimed to his fellow clergymen: "The *first* and main point I submit to you is that it is the unquestionable duty of all ministers of the Church to catechize and to teach personally all who are submitted to their care."[5] Such ministry included teaching the principles of religion and matters essential to salvation, and giving personal tutorials and examinations on biblical content. In Baxter's view, this primary responsibility should take up the bulk of the pastor's time and would effect reform and revival by the grace of God. Baxter describes how he procrastinated in fulfilling this duty, was convicted by God about his negligence, and how he then, with two assistants, worked with fifteen or sixteen families each week, catechizing the eight hundred families in his parish. Baxter decried those ministers who preached well, but who were unsuited to the private nurture of their members. In modern terms, such work would be called disci-

---

3. Niebuhr, *The Purpose of the Church and Its Ministry*, 61.
4. H. Richard Niebuhr and Daniel D. Williams, *The Ministry in Historical Perspectives* (New York: Harper and Brothers, 1956), 131-32.
5. Richard Baxter, *The Reformed Pastor* (Portland, Ore.: Multnomah, 1982), 5.

pling, but with a heavy emphasis upon biblical teaching, though Baxter also stressed the importance of evangelism.

Generally, it can be said that since the early days of the church Christian pastors have functioned in the roles of believer-saint, biblical scholar, preacher-teacher, priest, liturgist, evangelist, father-shepherd, and discipler. They preached, taught, led worship, administered sacraments or ordinances, exercised oversight, and gave care to individuals in need.

A stereotype of pastoral clergy in the middle of the twentieth century might be described as follows:

- He—there were few women clergy—was somber, serious-minded, perceived as introverted and bookish, and often wore a symbolic black suit and tie.

- The pastor was known more by what he did not do and by what he preached against. He was viewed as otherworldly and held to be above the temptations and passions of mere mortals.

- The pastor was an authority figure, generally unquestioned on matters of faith, doctrine, standards of conduct, and church policy and polity. He was educated, influential, politically powerful, respected, and a prominent citizen of the community. He was the *parson* (OFr. *persone*; Med. Lat. *persona*) and enjoyed the pedestal his position afforded him.

- The pastor was marked by conspicuous religiosity—even if he was not genuinely pious—a preacher and teacher of Christian values and a custodian of community morals. He was a functionary who presided at worship services, public gatherings, weddings, funerals, and baptisms. He often called in homes and hospitals. There was a transcendent quality about him that derived from his role as God's representative in the affairs of humankind.

Current Corruptions of the Pastoral Role

For all their vacillation, previous generations probably had clearer conceptions of the pastoral role than exists in America today. As we near the end of this century, widespread confusion and ambiguity about pastoral priorities handicap our clergy. What is a pastor's primary role? Is it preaching? administering? enabling? giving spiritual direction? engaging in social service? providing leadership?

H. Richard Niebuhr suggested that "if a new conception of the ministry is emerging it will be marked by the appearance of a sense of the relative importance of the activities and a definite idea of the proximate end sought by the minister in all of them."[6]

While no definitive new conception of pastoral ministry has emerged, uncertainty about pastoral authority, vagueness about priorities, and a confusion of subroles with a pastor's primary role continue to weaken churches.

A direct relationship exists between time management and the pastoral role. Those who claim their real priority is one thing, but who spend most of their time doing something else, merely deceive themselves and cannot control their lives. During the last half of the twentieth century, contemporary pastoral roles fall into a few broad categories, each excessively emphasizing certain appropriate subroles, while neglecting more primary functions.

The Fragmented Generalist

Never in history have pastors been expected to accomplish so many tasks skillfully. By almost any standard, performance pressures put upon contemporary American pastors exceed the limits of reason. Exorbitant expectations and consequent stress have caused the erosion of spiritual vitality and authenticity in many pastors, the abandonment of pastoral positions for other types of ministries or secular jobs, the emotional breakdown and burnout of ministers, a rapid turnover of pastoral positions every three years or less, and increased dissatisfaction, causing pastors to build walls around themselves, wear masks, and hang on desperately until retirement.

Sometimes, of course, pastors put excessive pressure upon themselves. More frequently, our success-oriented society and internal church politics have pushed pastors to produce substantial statistical achievement or be labeled failures in ministry. Pastors frantically attempt to do everything in order to produce visible results, fractionalizing their role and minimizing their calling. Congregational dissatisfaction with pastors who produce poor statistics manifests itself with appalling frequency. Pastoral firings and

6. Niebuhr, *The Purpose of the Church and Its Ministry*, 63.

forced resignations have dramatically increased in the last ten years, approaching 10 percent annually in some denominations. The number of battered pastors is a scandal of the American church.[7] In other times, pastors could expect persecution from the world; now mistreatment is more likely to come from within the church.

"[V]aried role pressures pile, one upon the other, in rapid fire. . . . [A]n apt analogy may be that of machine guns, grenades, and booby traps going off . . . all at once."[8] Historically, ministerial roles were defined in terms of specialties. Richard Baxter was a catechist; Charles Spurgeon was a preacher; George Whitefield was an evangelist; and so forth. Of course, they all did other things, but their reputations were gained by their excellence in their areas of concentration. They knew in what they wanted to excel and they concentrated their energies on these areas. Today such specialization only occurs in large, multiple-staff ministries, and even there pastors sometimes are fractionalized and marginalized by attempting to be all things to all people. Sometimes pastoral educators write on the chalkboard a list of all things that senior or solo pastors customarily do—a truly impressive list—and then pose questions to their students: Who could do it all? Who would *want* to?

There is a simple truth here: too many pastors try to do too many things and, consequently, do nothing well. Some wag has defined specialists as those who learn more and more about less and less until eventually they know everything about nothing. Equally ludicrous are pastors who attempt more and more and succeed at less and less, until eventually they tackle everything and succeed at nothing. In attempting to be triumphalists, they become reductionists.

Of course, pastors, especially solo pastors, must do a number of things, but when they become fractionalized so that they do not recognize or excel at a few primary tasks, their ministries are ineffectual. One cannot escape the conclusion that many of today's weak and stagnant churches are pastored by those who have attempted

7. See "The Problem of Battered Pastors," by Marshall Shelley, *Leadership,* 17 May 1985. A number of current books and articles address this subject.
8. Donald Smith, *Clergy in the Cross-Fire* (Philadelphia: Westminster, 1973), 27.

too much and majored in nothing. A corollary truth is that today's truly effective pastors define their roles carefully, decide to achieve competence in limited areas of ministry, discipline themselves accordingly, and delegate responsibilities to others.

The Therapist

In the middle decades of the twentieth century, the concept of ministry took a subtle but important shift in direction. Psychology took a quantum leap in popularity; parishioners began to have more personal problems and also seemed more ready to talk about them. Pastoral counseling suddenly became a primary activity in many ministers' schedules.

Previously, one-on-one ministry focused on the spiritual needs of people as they related to God, but that emphasis tended to fade as pastors became enamored and overwhelmed with the personal and social problems of people and society. This quickly reflected itself in theological seminaries that rushed to fill a perceived vacuum. At times, it became difficult to determine the boundaries of theology and psychology.

Pastoral ministry took this dramatic twist: whereas pastors previously thought almost exclusively in terms of applying scriptural answers to people's spiritual problems, with a view to bettering their relationship with God, now pastors dealt with a range of personal and interpersonal difficulties that were *not* seen as essentially spiritual problems. Some veteran pastors still tended to reduce all problems to a spiritual dimension, but the new generation of clergy seek solutions to an extraordinary range of crises from extrabiblical sources. Some, of course, try to integrate biblical teaching with psychology and other fields of learning.

Pastors became community and personal problem-solvers, which opened them to the charge of being little more than social workers or amateur psychologists, particularly in mainline denominations. Indeed, "in their efforts to accommodate, many clergy have simply airbrushed sin out of their language. Like politicians, they can only recognize mistakes which congregants are urged to 'put behind them.' Having substituted therapy for spiritual discernment, they appeal to a nurturing God who helps His (or Her) people cope. Heaven, by this creed, is never having to say no to yourself, and God is never having to say you're sorry."[9] Pastors were reduced to therapists, a function at which few excelled. Such a pastoral role contributed further to the secularization of the church.[10]

The impact of a therapeutic culture upon the preaching ministry cannot be overestimated. Many books emphasizing preaching as counseling appeared on pastors' shelves and exposition of Scripture became subordinated to helping people cope with their circumstances and to helping them feel better about themselves. Harry Emerson Fosdick was a pacesetter in this "life-situation preaching." The very nature of the gospel was corrupted (see chap. 3).

That counseling is an important activity is not open to question. People need help with their problems. The proliferation of professional counselors and their apparent busyness testifies to the obvious demand. Surely, however, for pastors to conceptualize their ministry primarily in terms of counseling and to devote the bulk of their time to it doesn't do justice to either biblical truth or the needs of our society. Scripture does not summon pastors to be personal therapists, nor are many clergy trained sufficiently to be good at it. Few clergy excel as personal problem-solvers or sounding boards, and many get into trouble trying to do so.

The Chief Executive Officer

In 1956 Niebuhr advanced the suggestion that the emerging pastoral role was that of *spiritual director,* which had its roots in the bishop or overseer of the ancient church, Augustine being a prototype. Of course, the pastoral director must do traditional things: preach, teach, lead in worship, administer sacraments, care for souls, and preside over the church. But the master or integrative role of the minister is to build or "edify" the church. According to Niebuhr, the pastor's first function is to "bring into being a people of God who as a Church will serve the purpose of the Church in the local community and the world."[11] Niebuhr believed the pastor should be the teacher of teachers, the primary

9. *Newsweek,* 17 Dec. 1990, 56.
10. See *Power Religion,* ed. Michael Horton (Chicago: Moody, 1992). Part 4, "Power Within," deals with the problems of psychology theory and practice as it has emerged into the evangelical mainstream.
11. Niebuhr, *The Purpose of the Church and Its Ministry,* 82.

enabler, the manager of the educational objectives of the church, the chief facilitator, and the administrator of a community of faith. Preaching and teaching, in this conception of ministry, retain a place of great importance, but with a different aim: the instruction and motivation of persons who carry out the mission of the church.

Though proposed almost forty years ago, Niebuhr's model for the pastoral role, which has considerable merit, did not achieve much recognition or actualization. Oddly, however, an aberration of the pastoral director has evolved with an impressive array of devotees.

In its decidedly perverted form, the pastoral director becomes the CEO (chief executive officer), who efficiently runs the church as one would run a successful business enterprise or Chamber of Commerce. Ministry defers to executive decision-making, corporate management, public relations, and marketing considerations. Nothing declares the contamination of the CEO role more succinctly than the following statement: "In one church growth research project it was discovered that in many churches 85 percent of available time is given to management, while only 15 percent of time is given for ministry."[12] Niebuhr foresaw this potential danger of the pastoral director concept of ministry and warned against it, but his warning was unheeded.

Few American pastors admit to adopting the mentality and modus operandi of the CEO. Yet, the evidences of this secularized, corrupted form of pastoral work proliferate. Much of current literature on pastoral ministry implicitly or explicitly suggests that the current deterioration of the church would be solved by effective CEO pastors, and that the success of the megachurches may be attributed to superior CEOs. A fair question is, Does the church need a CEO because the perception of the church as an institution has changed, or has the CEO molded the institution in his own image?

The movement to a CEO model of pastoral ministry received a major impetus through the writings of those who attempted to synthesize insights from the world of professional management with pastoral work, perhaps in a desperate effort to regain a credibility

12. Bruce W. Jones, *Ministerial Leadership in a Managerial World* (Wheaton: Tyndale, 1988), 88.

that eroded rapidly during the first half of the century.[13] This emphasis, coupled with a desperate craving for growth success and secular respect, brought about the creation of the "big operator" (Niebuhr's term) whose ministerial calling has been profaned, sometimes beyond recognition. A CEO orientation inevitably minimizes the importance of spiritual direction and preaching-teaching competence in favor of a wide range of business, marketing, and programming skills. Sometimes even the personal spiritual disciplines are not viewed as of paramount importance.

Entrepreneurship and production count in secularized religion and many benefits accrue to pastors who excel in these skills. Laity often pressure their pastors to adopt a managerial style of ministry, particularly laity accustomed to the pressures of achieving success in the corporate world. "Underlying this trend is the notion that the church must sell the gospel to unbelievers. Churches thus compete for the consumer on the same level as Frosted Flakes or Miller Lite. More and more churches are relying on marketing strategy to sell the church."[14]

Without intending to do so, church growth literature has popularized the CEO mentality among pastors. John Wimber identified seven levels of industrial management that correspond to managerial skills of pastors in various size churches, the largest requiring "chairman of the board" ability. Eddie Gibbs stressed that churches from 150–450 in size need middle management pastors who "must avoid getting over-involved in the detailed execution and allowing all the decision making to float up the organizational structure."[15] Gibbs says that churches over 1,000 must have pastors who function like the chairman of the board. Lyle Schaller made distinctions between pastors who are shepherds (the small church), those who are ranchers (the middle-sized church), and those who must be presidents or CEOs (the large church).[16] Peter Wagner advocated

13. Typical examples include Jones, *Ministerial Leadership in a Managerial World*; Ted W. Engstrom and Howard R. Dayton, *The Art of Management for Christian Leaders* (Waco: Word, 1982); and David S. Luecke and Samuel Southard, *Pastoral Administration: Integrating Ministry and Management in the Church* (Waco: Word, 1986).

14. John MacArthur, "Gimme That Showtime Religion," *Masterpiece*, Sept.-Oct. 1990, 2.

15. Eddie Gibbs, *I Believe in Church Growth* (Grand Rapids: Eerdmans, 1981), 383.

16. Lyle Schaller, *The Multiple Staff and the Larger Church* (Nashville: Abingdon, 1980).

more management for the pastor and more ministry for the people.[17] All of these authors emphasize an obvious truth: church growth necessitates adaptations of the pastoral role, changes requiring less one-on-one involvement and more administrative skill. However, the church suffers serious damage when prayer, study, preaching-teaching, and discipling ministries diminish in deference to executive skills, as is currently happening in many churches.

Obviously, the serious objection to the advice to "act like a CEO" is that to do so is to corrupt and reduce the ministerial office and defer to pressures to make the church successful according to a range of materialistic and corporate standards. A CEO model of pastoring—focusing on efficiency, PERT charts, problem-solving, public relations, budget control, delegation, promotion, programming, marketing, organizing, recruiting, and planning—eclipses more important pastoral functions. Desire for material growth, the emergence of megachurches, management seminars, and the American success-oriented culture have doubtlessly fueled this perverted view of pastoral ministry, and have certainly contributed to an impressive array of ministerial temptations, including authoritarianism, bureaucratic mentality, personal kingdom building, pretentiousness, self-deception, love of the pedestal, ladder-climbing, and thirst for materialistic success.

Some question the legitimacy of dichotomizing managerial and ministerial functions. Isn't effective management also effective ministry? Some pastors defend excessive managerial orientation by defining ministry in administrative terms, thus unfairly neutralizing objections. "Management is ministering to people. In fact, it's difficult to think of any administrative duty that is not people centered."[18] It is certainly difficult or impossible to neatly categorize all pastoral activities as either management or ministry. Yet, when pastors study for their preaching and teaching opportunities, they are not managing or ministering. Rather, they are preparing to minister, and that preparation should consume a sizable proportion of their time. Similarly, when pastors preach, teach, or disciple, they are not

17. C. Peter Wagner, *Leading Your Church to Growth* (Ventura, Calif.: Regal, 1984).
18. Don Cousins, Leith Anderson, and Arthur DeKruyter, *Mastering Church Management* (Portland, Ore.: Multnomah, 1990), 42.

managing, but ministering—unless "management" is stripped of its primary meanings and becomes an elastic and empty expression.

A few have vigorously opposed the CEO or managerial orientation of a pastoral role: "Our church is Christ's body and not an organization requiring management. . . . As an elder who is gifted in pastoring, I am learning *not* to be a manager."[19] Another writes: "Body leadership and body functions are distinctly different from leadership and functions in an organization. To confuse body and enterprise, organism and organization, is to do violence to the very nature of the church."[20] Their voices, however, seem muted and out of step with the success-minded majority.

None of this, however, is to disparage the importance of administrative skill, but organizational and managerial excellence in a church without spiritual power provides nothing but a shell. Pastors should be expert enough at doing or delegating administrative work so they can limit the time given to it, thus reserving sufficient time for prayer, study, preaching-teaching, discipleship, and spiritual leadership.

The following points summarize our discussion:

pastors must do some managerial work whether they like it or not,

the subrole of manager is biblically sanctioned (e.g., 1 Tim. 3:4–5),

managerial functions control an excessive proportion of many pastors' time (40–85 percent in surveys),

most pastors feel they have been inadequately trained in managerial responsibilities,

most pastors do not enjoy managerial tasks, consider them a low priority, and do not feel that they are efficient in performing them,

most pastors would prefer to spend the bulk of their time doing things more ministerial in nature.

19. Lawrence O. Richards and Clyde Hoeldtke, *A Theology of Church Leadership* (Grand Rapids: Zondervan, 1980), 26.

20. Norman Shawchuck, *What It Means to Be a Church Leader* (Indianapolis: Spiritual Growth Resources, 1984), 26.

The Competitor

As never before in church history, pastors are expected to be competitors. Lyle Schaller observes: "Who is the scapegoat when the numerically growing congregation of 1970 finds itself to be shrinking as the population climbs more rapidly? For many, the obvious answer is the pastor. The care-giving shepherd is in many cases being asked to assume the role of a skillful competitor."[21] In other words, the pastoral role that formerly centered on preaching-teaching, care giving, and equipping has become one focused on rivalry with other pastors and churches, with thriving organizations as the prize for competing successfully. Success or failure in pastoral ministry reveals itself in superior physical facilities, bigger budgets, more attractive programming, and fuller pews than other churches in town. In order to compete successfully, churches become reflectors of community culture, not the molders of it.

The roles of generalist, therapist, CEO, and competitor often merge into one ugly mass of confusion. In a desperate desire to compete successfully, pastors become media specialists, programming experts, stage directors, choreographers and, even more sadly, performers. The idea is to mold the church according to the desires of the consumer. "Tailor the church service to whatever will draw a crowd. As a result pastors are more like politicians than shepherds, looking to appeal to the public rather than leading and building the flock God gave them."[22] When pastors become competitors, the emphasis shifts from worship or edification to entertainment, technique supplants the offense of the cross, and easy decisions replace radical changes of heart.

Pastoral Role Definition

Undoubtedly, the New Age philosophy, including its humanistic foundations, evolutionary thesis, and cultic identity, has impacted the church negatively. Current trends suggest the church is attempting to synthesize, rather than oppose, this pernicious danger: "The '90s promise to bring a move toward syncretism—the

21. "Trends in Pastoral Care," *Leadership* (Winter 1990): 28.
22. MacArthur, "Gimme That Showtime Religion," 2.

blending of the most popular aspects of Christianity with similarly pleasing elements from other religious traditions."[23] The hazards of gradualism and indifference may render the church more impotent than we have yet experienced in American Christianity.

Francis Schaeffer pinpointed the fundamental deterrent to effective pastoral ministry: "The real problem is this: the church of the Lord Jesus Christ, individually and corporately, tending to do the Lord's work in the power of the flesh rather than of the Spirit. The central problem is always in the midst of the people of God, not in the circumstances surrounding them."[24] The most urgent need of Christianity is for pastoral leaders who resolve to do the Lord's work in the power of the Spirit. Much has changed in the world and in churches since apostolic days, but Paul's word remains the bottom line of ministry: "For though we live in the world, we do not wage war as the world does. The weapons we fight with are not the weapons of the world. On the contrary, they have divine power to demolish strongholds" (2 Cor. 10:3–4). Pastoral work is not merely a matter of human technology; rather, it is spiritual warfare utilizing spiritual weapons.

James Glasse emphasized the pastor's role: "This requires that he identify those points at which his profession is to be practiced. He must make clear what he professes to know, to be able to do, through what institution, under what standards, and to what end. Having limited his concerns to a given area of society's needs and functions, he holds himself responsible for effective efforts in that area. To be a professional in one area means precisely to be a layman in another area."[25] Tasks that do not fall under a pastor's carefully delineated role must be delegated to partners in ministry.

What are those areas for which pastors should hold themselves responsible? What priorities transcend everything else in pastoral ministry? While circumstances may vary and necessitate some flexibility in the role of a pastor, certain constants remain. The nonnegotiables are relatively few, but exceedingly important and consistent with Scripture.

23. George Barna, *The Frog in the Kettle* (Ventura, Calif.: Regal, 1990), 111.
24. Francis Schaeffer, *No Little People* (Downers Grove, Ill.: InterVarsity, 1974), 64.
25. James D. Glasse, *Profession: Minister* (Nashville: Abingdon, 1968), 44.

The Model Disciple

Pastors cannot be perfect, but, nevertheless, they must be model disciples. Pastors must reflect the working of the Holy Spirit in their lives, visible manifestations of God's grace: "You are witnesses, and so is God, of how holy, righteous, and blameless we were among you who believed" (1 Thess. 2:10). Pastors "have this treasure in jars of clay to show that this all-surpassing power is from God and not from us . . . so that the life of Jesus may also be revealed in our body" (2 Cor. 4:7, 10). Paul's most fundamental counsel to Timothy was to be a man of God and "set an example for the believers in speech, in life, in love, in faith and in purity" (1 Tim. 4:12) and "to pursue righteousness, godliness, faith, love, endurance and gentleness" (1 Tim. 6:11). Since pastors are "entrusted with God's work, [they] must be blameless" (Titus 1:7) and "the overseer must be above reproach" (1 Tim. 3:2).

This crucial role means that pastors say by their lifestyle: "Follow my example, as I follow the example of Christ" (1 Cor. 11:1). Indeed, the pastor's "true test of usefulness is whether he is whole-heartedly devoted to God" and "delights in holiness, hates iniquity, loves the unity and purity of the Church, and abhors discord and division."[26]

The Overseer

Pastors are overseers, which probably relates to the "watchman" role of the Old Testament prophet (Isa. 21:11). In its historical and biblical connotation, "overseer" does not mean "administrator"— much less Niebuhr's "big operator"—but, rather, "to see the sanctification and holy obedience of the people under our charge. To nurture our people's unity, order, beauty, strength, preservation, and increase must be our task. It is the right worshiping of God."[27] Pastors' ultimate responsibility, after modeling true discipleship, is to oversee the spiritual welfare of those entrusted to their care (1 Pet. 5:3; Titus 1:7), making certain that the unsaved are evangelized, the newly born are discipled, the weak are strengthened, the tempted are fortified, the fallen are restored, the disconsolate are

26. Baxter, *The Reformed Pastor*, 69.
27. Ibid., 68.

encouraged, and all are spiritually nourished. Through this critical shepherding ministry, church members discover their spiritual gifts and are prepared and freed to do ministry in their communities (Eph. 4:12).

Of course pastors cannot do all of this personally for everyone. Nevertheless, to "oversee" is to take responsibility for this ministry. The work itself must often be done through trained staff and laity, but that does not absolve pastors from their sacred obligation. The buck stops with them. Pastors should be sobered by the words of Scripture: "They keep watch over you as men who must give an account" (Heb. 13:17).

The Guardian and Communicator of Truth

Pastors are guardians and communicators of the revelation of God. Pastors are "entrusted with the gospel" (1 Thess. 2:4) and "entrusted with the secret things of God" (1 Cor. 4:1). Paul exhorted Timothy: "Guard the good deposit that was entrusted to you—guard it with the help of the Holy Spirit who lives in us" (2 Tim. 1:14). This sacred responsibility means that pastors must be primary guardians of sound doctrine and exponents of scriptural truth. Pastors must "preach the Word" and "correct, rebuke and encourage—with great patience and careful instruction" (2 Tim. 4:2). Oversight, referred to in the preceding paragraphs, is primarily but not exclusively carried out through pastoral guardianship and application of scriptural truth.

Obviously, to guard and communicate scriptural truth means that pastors must be diligent students of Scripture. Many pastors never fulfill God's intention because they lack the personal discipline to study. Samuel Blizzard's research on pastoral time management showed that "urban ministers spend 27 minutes a day in general intellectual activities and 38 minutes a day in sermon preparation," a disgraceful statistic by anybody's standard.[28] Floyd Shafer's words sound a wake-up call: "Fling him into his office, tear the OFFICE sign from the door and nail on the sign, STUDY. Take him off the mailing list, lock him up with his books—and get him all kinds of books—and his typewriter [computer?] and his Bible. . . . Force him

---

28. Reported by Smith, *Clergy in the Cross-Fire*, 48.

to be the one man in our surfeited communities who knows about God. . . . Set a time clock on him that would imprison him with thought and writing about God for forty hours a week. . . . Rip out his telephone, burn his ecclesiastical success sheets, refuse his glad hand, put water in the gas tank of his community buggy and compel him to be a minister of the Word."[29] Obviously, Shafer exaggerates, but probably in the right direction. William Barclay calls us to account: "The more a man allows his mind to grow slack and lazy and flabby, the less the Holy Spirit can say to him."[30]

The Visionary Guide

Effective pastors are visionary guides. Today's churches need visionary pastors, those who dream dreams, sharpen the missional understanding of the church, open themselves to new possibilities and paradigms, and articulate "a view of a realistic, credible, attractive future for the organization, a condition that is better in some important ways than what now exists."[31] Historically, the church has a record of being a reactionary organization, playing catch-up to world and local events. Current events move so swiftly and dramatically that the church can no longer be merely responsive to society's changes; it must interpret information about an anticipated future to construct a credible vision for a church that affects a radically changing world. Therefore, it is no longer optional to serve as a visionary guide; it is essential (see chap. 7).

Visionary guidance means that pastors must be philosophical strategists. Effective churches inevitably have pastors who possess a sense of identity, they know who they are, what they stand for, where they are going, and how to get there; that is, they have clarity of vision. Churches with poor pastoral leadership drift along without understanding their purpose, objectives, strategies, and place in their communities. Visionary guides become mood-setters, cheerleaders, and coaches.

A pastor, more than anyone else, must assist the church to discover answers to questions about its mission, its distinctive place in

29. Floyd Doud Shafer, "And Preach As You Go!" *Christianity Today*, 27 March 1961.

30. William Barclay, *The Promise of the Spirit* (Philadelphia: Westminster, 1960), 98.

31. Warren Bennis and Burt Nanus, *Leaders: The Strategies for Taking Charge* (New York: Harper and Row, 1985), 89.

the community, strategies for accomplishing its mission, and work-able and ethical methodologies. The entire church takes its cue from pastors who see beyond the immediate and the apparent, who generate an excitement about next week, next month, and next year. The congregation gains a sense of exhilaration as it captures a vision about what their church could be and what difference it could make in the community and world. When pastors fulfill this responsibility of visionary guidance, a congregation possesses a unique understanding of who they are and what their purpose is as God's people.

The Global Tactician

The days are past when pastors could merely support a church missionary budget and run an annual missionary conference. Jesus declared his mission: "To preach good news to the poor. He has sent me to proclaim freedom for the prisoners and recovery of sight for the blind, to release the oppressed, to proclaim the year of the Lord's favor" (Luke 4:18–19). Our mandate requires the continuing of Christ's work (John 20:21). James A. Scherer suggests this new approach to missions: "Our faithfulness to the missionary mandate cannot be measured simply in terms of multiplying converts and churches. It is urgent that we reintegrate the whole spectrum of concerns from personal salvation and church growth to social jus-tice and freedom into a single comprehensive and convincing prom-ise of 'salvation today.'"[32]

Meaningful ministry necessitates a personal awareness of world conditions, genuine concern, and sharing that burden with others. Pastoral tacticians should be guided by the following mission agenda: stay abreast of world conditions, issues, and peoples; increase awareness of global concerns throughout the congregation and community; generate ideas, strategies, and specific actions to deal with spiritual and physical needs, act locally on cultural and environmental issues and abuses of the body and soul; promote a holistic approach to missions around the world; and stimulate inter-cessory prayer for the world's peoples.

32. James A. Scherer, *Global Living Here and Now* (New York: Friendship, 1974), 115.

Pastors cannot tolerate indifference to actual conditions, whether in themselves or their churches. The personal salvation gospel that we passionately affirm sounds vacuous and hypocritical when not accompanied by genuine concern for the holistic welfare of dehumanized people and their environment. "Dear children, let us not love with words or tongue but with actions and in truth" (1 John 3:18). Furthermore, "from everyone who has been given much, much will be demanded; and from the one who has been entrusted with much, much more will be asked" (Luke 12:48). American Christians have been given much; much is required.

Today's church and culture cry for leaders, those who take responsibility to penetrate a hostile culture, rally support for needed institutional change, strategize effectively both globally and locally, and bring a refreshing vitality to the church in order to make a difference in our world.

The Team Builder

The building of firm alliances in ministry, both within the church and community, as well as across denominational barriers, form a major pastoral responsibility.

Ministry requires dealing with complexity and ambiguity. Those who excel in these difficult tasks invariably learn that they can't do it alone; they must rely on others. Delegation and cooperation in an atmosphere of collegiality and fraternity are essential skills in teambuilding. The day of the omnicompetent superstar in pastoral ministry has passed. Effective ministers study the culture in which the church exists, contextualize the gospel, and build a network of enthusiastic supporters, a community of believers committed to God and each other.

Put succinctly: pastors must be spiritual leaders who model discipleship, oversee the spiritual health of the church, guard and communicate scriptural truth, facilitate vision, strategize locally and globally, and develop congregational synergism and joint ventures to advance Christ's kingdom. Activities that fall outside of these boundaries, including many managerial functions, should be compressed into 20 percent of a pastor's workweek.

Steps to Role Definition

Pastors must clearly understand who they are and what they are to do in the local church. A carefully defined role is essential in effective ministry:

Examine the particular parameters and pressures of your ministry.

Study scriptural passages on pastoral responsibilities, especially the pastoral epistles.

Identify your special gifts, desires, and capabilities to be certain you are in a compatible calling. Some may need to change ministries.

Decide which areas of responsibility are a priority, those activities mandated by Scripture and present conditions, and delegate most other matters.

Never stop developing skills in the few major requisites of your ministry.

5

MINISTRY MINUS METHOD EQUALS MADNESS

Grant, O God, that we may never listen
to any teaching which would encourage us
to think sin less serious, vice more attractive,
or virtue less important.

William Barclay

Thousands of pastors muddle along year after year unaware that their church's lack of effectiveness and productivity is due to a missing or poorly defined philosophy of ministry. Excellence in pastoral ministry necessitates a clear and comprehensive philosophy of ministry, sometimes called a theology of ministry. Competent pastors and successful churches owe their effectiveness largely to their sense of identity: they know who they are, what they stand for, where they are going, and how to get there.

The term *philosophy of ministry* pertains to the basic principles, beliefs, and values that form the foundation of ministry for both a pastor and a church. A philosophy of ministry embodies a sense of uniqueness, purpose, and direction. A personal philosophy encompasses the system of values and fundamental beliefs by which one lives, makes decisions, and carries out responsibilities. An organizational philosophy explicates those guiding assumptions, creeds, and postulates that give distinctive character and direction to the corporation or community. Spiritual leaders use their own personal philosophy of ministry to help the church to clarify its mission and enable all members to feel that the mission is vital and worthy of their enthusiastic support.

Successful business enterprises always have a clearly defined philosophy, often relating to customer satisfaction or superior service. For example, the L. L. Bean Company in Freeport, Maine, suggests: "A customer is not an interruption of our work . . . he is the purpose of it. We are not doing a favor by serving him . . . he is doing us a favor by giving us the opportunity to do so." Marshall Field Company in Chicago built its merchandizing empire with a simple motto: "The customer is always right." IBM advertises: "When it comes to service, we treat every customer as if he or she is one in a million." Such business philosophy, faithfully implemented, leads to the attainment of a company's goals.

Obviously, none of the previous illustrations encompasses the entire business philosophy of these companies, yet each encapsulates something crucial to the function of the enterprise, particularly in marketing. The complete operational philosophy of a company like IBM is spelled out in a variety of documents, articles of incorporation, by-laws, and policy manuals. No business enterprise succeeds without these clearly articulated guidelines and principles that determine priorities, goals, and methods of operation. Similarly, pastors and churches that seek to make a difference in our world must define their philosophy of ministry and then implement it rigorously.

Successful business enterprises, effective churches, and individual pastors differ dramatically in their respective philosophies. A study of widely divergent pastoral and church philosophies leads to these conclusions:

- A variety of philosophies may contribute to success.
- The philosophy itself may not be as important as the fact that it is clearly defined.
- An effective church philosophy evolves through energetic leadership, primarily according to leaders' gifts and vision.
- Each effective philosophy is tailored to a local situation.
- A worthy philosophy proves itself valuable only as it is implemented rigorously.

Pastors need to identify their own strengths and vision, define their own personal philosophy, understand the environment in which they work, and help the church to determine its own uniqueness in ministry.

A Personal Pastoral Philosophy of Ministry

Effective long-term ministry requires pastors to accurately determine their personalities, gifts, interests, vision, and priorities. These vary for each individual and, therefore, so does a personal philosophy of ministry. Each pastor must identify and practice a personal philosophy of ministry, incorporating enough built-in flexibility to avoid rigidity. A personal philosophy guides the pastor in making decisions about every important facet of ministry: management of time, development of relationships, leadership style, preaching, family responsibility, and so forth.

The apostle Paul's theology of ministry included the following:

- preach to the Jew first, then to the Gentile (Rom. 1:16)
- preach where Christ was not known (Rom. 15:20)
- preach not with the "wise and persuasive words" of mere human wisdom (1 Cor. 2:4)
- teach publicly and from house to house (Acts 20:20)
- establish ministry on a personal foundation of holiness, righteousness, and blamelessness (1 Thess. 2:10)
- encourage, comfort, and urge people to live lives worthy of God (1 Thess. 2:11),
- model Christian discipleship (2 Thess. 3:7–9)

Philosophy translates into action. Because of Paul's philosophy, he sought a hearing first within the Jewish community, and then he turned to the Gentiles. He declined to build on another's foundation. He eschewed chicanery of every sort and endeavored to preach with a demonstration of the Spirit's power. He taught in synagogues, marketplaces, and private homes. He preached to people as a father exhorts a child. He developed many in-depth relationships. He modeled a personal lifestyle of holiness. He supported himself in order not to be a burden to others. Obviously, these are just a few examples of Paul's personal ministerial philosophy in action.

A personal philosophy of ministry evolves out of answers to such questions as:

- How does Scripture define my responsibilities?
- What is my primary calling in pastoral ministry?
- How has God gifted and equipped me in distinctive ways for the ministry? How can I serve Christ most effectively, maximizing my abilities and minimizing my liabilities?
- What opportunities has God given me to serve him?
- What family responsibilities form constraints upon my ministry?

As answers to such questions take shape, and through careful thought and prayer, a personal philosophy should emerge with respect to the following areas.

Relationships

To what degree should pastors maintain "professional distance" or promote interpersonal warmth and affection?

Those who opt for professional distance discourage the use of their first name, seldom reveal personal struggles, and discourage much familiarity. Such pastors, while not antisocial, nevertheless give credence to the saying "familiarity breeds contempt." Respect and authority, not affection, form the primary relational orientation for these pastors and, consequently, an aloofness permeates their ministry. Others conclude that interpersonal relationships characterized by affection and warmth facilitate meaningful ministry—perhaps are even required for pastoral effectiveness. Therefore, greater transparency, vulnerability, and intimacy earmark every facet of their ministry.

Obviously, the aforementioned positions represent extremes of a continuum. Wise pastors decide carefully the degree of transparency and intimacy that should characterize their ministry. Sometimes it becomes necessary to struggle vigorously against the natural inclinations of one's personality.

Change

To what degree should pastors aggressively seek change or preserve the status quo?

The preservers of the status quo maintain tradition and become the custodians of continuity for the church. Their congregations come to expect little change, and when changes do take place people seem paralyzed or blindsided. Other pastors conceive their role to be agents of change. Innovation, not preservation, represents their fundamental orientation.

Of course, change involves risk, yet not to change may be the bigger risk, and so "by talking about it, by treating change as normal (instead of as something you do only when you have to), these leaders take away much of the fear and anxiety that surround change."[1] Again, most pastors see themselves somewhere between the extremes. Excellence in pastoral ministry demands a clear understanding of one's role as an agent of change.

Preaching-Teaching

To what degree should the pastor's Sunday preaching focus on evangelism, exposition, encouragement and exhortation, verse-by-verse commentary, people's needs, contemporary topics, or entertainment?

It does not take long for visitors to identify the preaching philosophy of a pastor, and most people gravitate to a church with a pastor whose preaching philosophy is compatible with their desires. In a large metropolitan area such as Southern California a variety of large, effective churches have emerged with radically different pastoral philosophies of preaching. The congregations of each church would be dissatisfied with another church's preacher. However,

---

1. Robert H. Waterman, Jr., *The Renewal Factor* (New York: Bantam, 1988), 233.

churches that stumble along in mediocrity usually have pastors with no discernible philosophy of preaching.

Role Definition

How should the pastor balance preaching, counseling, discipling, administrating, and the dozen or so other responsibilities?

Of course, role clarification relates to the previous chapter and we will not belabor it here, except to note that many men and women in ministry experience little effectiveness or sense of exhilaration in what they do because they feel trapped in positions that do not allow them to use their gifts or practice the philosophy of ministry that characterizes their service. An individual whose major gifts and interests are preaching, teaching, and discipling will encounter great frustration with responsibility that demands twenty hours a week in administration and another fifteen hours a week in counseling. Those gifted in administration will chafe at responsibilities that demand significant preaching and counseling. To be called to one area of ministry, but to have to spend time and energy performing quite a different function is an incongruity that calls a person's integrity into question. It also breeds mediocrity, disappointment, and failure.

Time Management

How shall the pastor's workweek be divided so that time is used profitably? A worthy philosophy of ministry not only clarifies primary and long-range responsibilities, but also dictates how time is managed so that those duties are fulfilled honorably. The principle of time management according to primary role responsibilities sounds simple and obvious, but extensive surveys of pastoral time management report that clergy feel that they spend more time on activities judged least important than they spend on functions viewed as most important.[2] The most important needs in pastoral life do not usually clamor for attention. Insignificant but squeaky wheels make demands and seduce pastors to forsake their true philosophy and calling. Such mistakes often prove fatal.

Philosophical convictions involving time management should include the following commitments:

2. David S. Schuller, ed., *Ministry in America* (New York: Harper and Row, 1980).

- not to sacrifice long-range goals or primary duties to short-term expediencies
- to manage time proportionate to one's primary calling and spiritual gifts
- to not waste one's own time or someone else's time
- to reserve significant, quality time for one's family

Of course, many other time-management considerations should be clarified, such as time for relaxation, exercise, vacation, prayer, study, discipling, and so forth.

Leadership Style

Leadership style relates to the use of power, authority, or influence in the decision-making process of boards, committees, or congregations. To what degree and on what issues should pastors be autocratic, participatory, or laissez-faire? Autocratic behavior (dictatorship) is at one end of the continuum and laissez-faire behavior (hands off) is at the other. Obviously, many options exist between the extremes, and effective leaders fluctuate up and down the continuum, depending upon many factors.

Each pastoral leader must develop a flexible leadership style that grows out of scriptural interpretation, personality, ecclesiastical tradition, personal convictions, and sensitivity to one's conscience.

A philosophy of leadership style includes the following basic tenets:

- Christ is the head of the church and spiritual leaders serve as undershepherds to his authority.
- Scripture forbids authoritarian behavior (1 Pet. 5:1–3; Matt. 20:25–26). A spirit of servanthood characterizes church leaders (Matt. 20:27–28).
- Effective pastoral leaders cultivate group involvement in major decisions and work for consensus, the "one accord" of Scripture (Acts 15).
- Effective leadership demands flexibility in style according to clearly understood parameters.[3]

3. An extensive philosophy of spiritual leadership, including these parameters, is discussed fully in the author's *Leadership in Christian Ministry* (Grand Rapids: Baker, 1989).

Within such fundamental guidelines, much room exists for diversity and personalization. An individual philosophy of ministry guides many specific leadership actions. An unclear or absent philosophy of ministry causes pastoral leaders to vacillate wildly and unpredictably, creating distrust and confusion throughout the church body.

A Church Philosophy of Ministry

Just as an individual pastor must clarify a personal philosophy of ministry, so each church must identify its philosophy of ministry. A clear church philosophy normally is based on pastoral leadership, scriptural interpretation, current trends in the community and world, available resources, acceptable levels of risk, corporate values, and a church's vision, all of which are discussed extensively in this book.

Beyond these points, meaningful church philosophy of ministry should address the following issues.

Declaration of Mission

A worthy church philosophy begins with a clarification of the church's mission. The mission statement should be relatively brief, a few concise sentences that declare the church's purpose or reason for existence. An illustration from a secular organization might be helpful. The Center for Creative Leadership, with headquarters in Greensboro, North Carolina, publicizes its mission as follows: "Our mission is to encourage and develop creative leadership and effective management for the good of society overall. We accomplish our mission through research, training and publication—with emphasis on the widespread, innovative application of the behavioral sciences to the challenges facing the leaders of today and tomorrow." The first statement relates to ideology, the primary business of the corporation. The second statement concerns methodology, the primary ways the corporation expects to achieve its ideological mission.

Obviously, the ideological mission (but not the methodological mission) of the church is biblically mandated, though the differing scriptural interpretations of diverse traditions results in significant variations. Many churches understand the biblical mission of the church as fivefold:

Worship: the celebration of life in Christ, the corporate act of rendering unto God praise, tribute, adoration, and devotion, through liturgy, music, meditation, homily, and prayer.

Evangelism: the communication of the gospel of Christ to the community and to the world in obedience to the Great Commission (Matt. 28:18–20).

Edification: personal growth toward spiritual maturity through scriptural teaching, obedience, and the disciplines of the Christian life.

Fellowship: the interpersonal sharing of Christian experience, corporate prayer, mutual care, and interdependency.

Social Concern: action in the community and world to bring about a more equitable and just society.

Some churches may add or subtract from this list and most churches place a greater emphasis on one or two of these than on the others.

The Adoption of Goals

Particular goals change constantly, depending on such factors as the season of the year, changes in resources, available personnel, or new priorities. However, comprehensive goals that involve basic philosophy change rarely and only after great deliberation or radically altered circumstances. The Center for Creative Leadership lists its broad, changeless goals as follows:

- To contribute significantly to the theoretical and practical knowledge relevant to creative leadership.
- To improve the practice of leadership and the effectiveness of management across a broad range of organizations and groups both public and private.
- To build a robust professional organization capable of achieving our institutional mandate over the long term—with particular regard for the development of individual staff members.

Goals provide teeth and impetus to the mission of the church. For example, assuming evangelism is a primary mission, the following goals might be developed that will realize that mission: to train church laity in witnessing effectively, to present the gospel effectively in public services, to develop evangelistic home Bible studies, and to stimulate missionary and church planting efforts in areas removed from the immediate locality of the church. Or, assuming discipleship is a fundamental mission, these goals could be chosen: to equip mature Christians to disciple newer believers, to provide spiritual formation groups focused on Bible study and mutual encouragement, to emphasize Bible teaching and exhortation in preaching ministry, and to involve staff in one-to-one discipling ministry.

Church goals should be as specific and measurable as possible without becoming bogged down in trivialities. Spiritual leaders must exercise care that these basic goals do not become either so general as to be meaningless or so numerous as to be overwhelming and self-defeating. No church can do everything well. Effective churches carve out a special niche in the community, decide what the church proposes to do, and develop sensible goals designed to meet the mission and the needs of the community.

Individual church goals differ for many good reasons. For example, churches located near a college or a university campus may differ dramatically from those located in a retirement community. Churches in areas with a high proportion of yuppies—young, urban professionals—naturally would particularize their ministry goals to reach these people. In other words, community demographics is a consideration in the development of church goals—and in the staffing to meet those goals. Others factors also guide churches and leaders in their identification of worthy and workable goals.

Priorities Achieved by Consensus

In every church many different programs and interest groups compete for the talents, financial resources, time commitments, and support of leaders and constituents. Should a $50,000 gift be used to install a new church organ, or should the money be used to improve a missionary hospital in Zaire? Should the next staff addition be a youth pastor or a worship pastor? Should the church launch a new building program and incur heavy indebtedness or promote multiple congregations in rented facilities? What percentage of the church budget should be allocated to overseas missionary work, pastoral staffing needs, or debt reduction? Would a new recreational center contribute significantly to effective ministry in the community? Dozens of such questions perplex spiritual leaders and many churches flounder in finding answers to them.

Answers to the questions depend upon the church's philosophy of priorities. The determination of philosophical priorities flows from decisions about church goals—or ought to. Obviously, a church with strong goals to reach a university campus might well conclude that a college pastor is a high priority, far more important than the addition of a visitation pastor. A church in a retirement community might decide the reverse. A church with strong teaching and discipling goals must prioritize resources to meet those objectives. An inner-city church in a community with many poor and homeless people might correctly consider a homeless shelter and a food distribution center high priorities.

Helping the church decide its priorities is one of the most important tasks of spiritual leadership. In order to fulfill this task well three pivotal considerations must be kept in mind: many people with vested interests clamor loudly for pet projects that often do not help the church fulfill its mission or reach its primary goals, some people—large donors, for example—always have more clout than others, and they often tend to control the process of deciding priorities, and priorities must be determined by consensus, not power plays, to be functionally efficient. Frequently, people try to inflict their personal philosophy upon the whole church, often with catastrophic results. A church sets itself up for disaster when squeaky wheels decide priorities contrary to established church goals.

Clear Government Structures

Who makes what decisions, how, and why? Does the church have elders, deacons, trustees, a general board, an executive board, or committees? Assuming that the church has at least some of these, what decision-making authority does each have? What remains under the jurisdiction of congregations acting with a quorum of church members? What functional relationship exists between the professional staff, lay leaders, and the constituency? What authority does the pastoral staff hold?

With denominational churches and most independent churches, plenty of room usually exists for governmental self-determination. Most churches write their own by-laws, thereby regulating decision-making and the boundaries of congregational and leadership authority.

The importance of clear governmental questions and answers cannot be overestimated. Churches that languish in mediocrity, stagnation, and slow death almost invariably have church governance structures marked by some or all of the following shortcomings:

- poorly conceived and written by-laws
- too many layers of bureaucracy
- a cumbersome and confusing decision-making process
- unclear lines of authority
- lack of trust in leadership
- inadequate consensus-building mechanisms

The particular governmental structure does not seem to matter as much as does its clarity and functional efficiency. Certainly, effective churches differ widely in their forms of government, some with strong congregational authority, some with heavy authority vested in a few highly trusted leaders, and many with structures between these extremes.

Many diverse configurations can be efficient and compatible with the sketchy biblical guidelines. However, no structure compensates for poor leaders. No governmental design is any better than the people who implement it, and unworthy or unscrupulous leaders will sabotage the most carefully crafted structures and by-laws.

Unanimity of Values

For a number of reasons, values may be the most difficult part of a church philosophy of ministry. Most churches in our day, particularly urban and suburban churches, are extremely pluralistic: races, nationalities, ages, educational achievements, economic status, professions, marital status, levels of spiritual maturity, denominational backgrounds, and so forth. Married couples know how difficult it is for two people from differing backgrounds to agree on a set of values. How much greater the task of getting a church to agree!

What are values? The philosopher Allan Bloom considers the term a piece of barbarous jargon, yet everyone uses it. Politicians desire to identify with the mainstream values of the American people, and therefore desperately try to find out what they are, usually settling for family, neighborhood, community, country, justice, peace, and prosperity. Hunter Lewis suggests the following: "Although the term values is often used loosely, it should be synonymous with personal beliefs, especially personal beliefs about the 'good,' the 'just,' and the 'beautiful,' personal beliefs that propel us to action, to a particular kind of behavior and life."[4]

Church values are shared beliefs about what is important, good, useful, and rewarding. Can "beliefs that propel us to action" be agreed upon by an entire church? Yes, they can, and they must be for the church to make a significant impact in its community. Effectively ministering congregations unite around a set of values that propels them to action.

The Center for Creative Leadership lists its four essential values: our work should serve society; our mission and our clients deserve our best; our organization should be a good place to work; we should do our work with regard for one another. Several attached paragraphs explain each stated value. The L. L. Bean Company was started with a twofold value statement now called "L. L.'s Golden Rule": "Sell good merchandise at a reasonable profit and treat your customers like human beings." Dozens of such examples can be given from successful businesses because their leaders have learned that clearly stated values catapult the organization to success. Fuzzy values lead to stagnation and death. Individuals, churches, and large business enterprises become successful largely because of dynamic values tenaciously held.

Churches disagree significantly in their values, but in every effective church, values make a huge difference. For example, a newly installed pastor was dismayed to discover that the church had few young couples and those who visited did not stay. Then, through the pastor's leadership, the congregation made the nursery a primary value: cribs and toys spotlessly clean, a separate sleeping room for infants, a registered nurse on duty, and so forth. Soon the church

4. Hunter Lewis, *A Question of Values* (New York: Harper and Row, 1990), 7.

had a number of young couples with small children. The new, shared, and publicized value made a profound difference.

Excellent leaders inevitably play a major role in fashioning the organization's values, surely one of their most crucial tasks. The values of the apostle Paul shaped much of the early church. The convictions of Martin Luther launched the Reformation. The unshakable values of John Knox, Richard Baxter, and other Puritan preachers and writers impacted all of Britain—and early American history. In a similar way, the fixed values of an exemplary pastor, working closely with other spiritual leaders, influences and propels an entire church. However, clergy must exercise caution not to force everyone to adopt all of their personal values. Paul supported himself with his own hands, but he did not insist on all ministers doing the same thing (1 Cor. 9:12–14). Similarly, Paul valued his unmarried status and believed that his ministry was more effective thereby, but he recognized the right and wisdom of others who differed (1 Cor. 7:8–9).

Great patience and care must be taken to arrive at stated values not only endorsed but also enthusiastically supported by the congregation. "There is a tendency when formulating basic beliefs to settle, at least initially, for what 'looks good' or 'sounds right' rather than to achieve what reflects the true and deep-seated values of the organization. Those beliefs are few in number and are hard to articulate."[5] No individual or small group can be allowed to dictate values; consensus is of paramount importance.

Because of the supreme importance of a clear philosophy of church values, chapter 6 is devoted to the values of effective churches.

Efficient Methodology

Church philosophies of ministry diverge widely in methodology. Some leaders maintain that Scripture offers only descriptive methodology and nothing prescriptive. Anything pragmatically effective in accomplishing the church's mission and goals—assuming ethical propriety—may be used.

---

5. Benjamin Tregoe, John Zimmerman, Ronald Smith, and Peter Tobia, *Vision in Action: Putting a Winning Strategy to Work* (New York: Simon and Schuster, 1989), 170–71.

The temptation to use an "end justifies the means" ethics must be recognized and avoided. Some church leaders use highly questionable tactics to attract a crowd and build the church. Paul "renounced secret and shameful ways" (2 Cor. 4:2). He refused to use deception and distortion in his methodology, even if he suspected such tactics might prove effective at achieving a worthwhile goal. Indisputable methodological integrity ultimately pays handsome dividends; dubious methods and shadowy maneuvers eventually and inevitably lead to embarrassment, whatever their short-term benefits.

In terms of methodology, five realities characterize leadership thinking in many effectively ministering churches. These are the foci of successful church methods.

Effective methods concentrate on Sunday morning activities. Productive methodology begins with passionate, even fanatic, concern for Sunday morning, or whenever primary meetings take place. What happens on Sunday morning truly matters, and many other things do not.

Excellent church leaders scrutinize everything that takes place during the crucial hours of major services: ushering, nursery operations, selection of music, classroom equipment and teaching, parking arrangements, preaching, temperature, greeting visitors, and cleanliness of restrooms. Meticulous care for detail marks ministering churches. Count on this: in superior churches a visitor is greeted by someone with a smile and clean fingernails—and without bad breath. No excellent churches in America tolerate shoddiness on Sunday morning. Any effective church methodology treats Sunday morning as pivotal.

Effective methods stimulate constant church renewal. In the business world "maximum results come from *anticipating what will be needed and getting it in place before it becomes necessary.*"[6] In the same way, healthy churches have leaders who habitually anticipate and innovate, thereby continually transforming and renewing the church. Long-range and continued effectiveness requires creativity to meet the needs of a rapidly changing community and world.

6. Frederick G. Harmon, *The Executive Odyssey* (New York: John Wiley and Sons, 1989), 193.

Effective pastors stress the basics, but always with an awareness that what worked yesterday may not be appropriate today or tomorrow and, if so, must be replaced. Today's most successful churches are on the cutting edge of change. They don't hesitate to have a "Sunday morning" service on Friday night, disperse the Wednesday evening prayer meeting to cell groups meeting in homes, move into a warehouse or a shopping center, and so forth. A few exciting churches have instituted innovative ways of doing things far more radically than these examples. Dozens of methodological changes mark every truly effective American church. An entire chapter (8) of this book considers church transformation.

Effective methods design and promote evangelistic growth. Competent leaders think strategically to present the gospel to the community. The methods of leaders differ significantly, but outreach fuels their thinking. They may utilize Evangelism Explosion, Campus Crusade, Navigators, lifestyle evangelism, evangelistic Bible studies, literature distribution, public evangelistic meetings, or whatever, but they always think in terms of reaching the unchurched. The church that concludes "the job is done" has ceased to become a vital force in the community. A maintenance mentality means inevitable stagnation.

Effective methods train and equip laity. A healthy church's leaders always focus on methods that "prepare God's people for works of service, so that the body of Christ may be built up" (Eph. 4:12). Any worthy work must encompass the training of laity, perhaps the weakest ministry in traditional churches. Genuine spiritual leaders identify the guidelines, resources, and accountability that enable laity to develop expertise in accomplishing specific objectives in ministry. Churches that fulfill their reason for existence produce a large body of congregants who serve effectively in a great variety of ministries.

Effective methods stress motivation. Equipping laity inevitably involves motivation, and a church's philosophy of motivation reveals a great deal about both church and leaders. The success of any church greatly depends on effective motivation and mobilizing of laity resources of time, talent, and money. Whatever else real leaders do, they motivate. Failure to motivate guarantees mediocrity, if not disintegration. Unfortunately, many churches have leaders who motivate with highly questionable tactics: coercion in a variety of forms, appeal to direct revelation, guilt, cajolery, and manipulative tactics of all sorts. An exemplary philosophy of motivation respects human dignity, gives responsibility, clarifies possibilities and choices, and encourages spiritual growth.

Four Church Philosophies

Jim Abrahamson, a pastor in North Carolina, took a three-month sabbatical to visit a wide variety of effective churches across America.[7] He discovered great diversity: authentic, excellent churches can be relatively large or small, denominational or independent, charismatic, culturally mixed, traditional, or atypical. However, four broad philosophies of ministry emerged in the effective churches included in his study.

An Evangelistic Philosophy

A "reaching-out," market-driven church philosophy focuses on creative and sensitive evangelism of the unchurched. Contemporary style music (as opposed to traditional hymns), need-oriented sermons, and upbeat, user-friendly, nonthreatening services mark this philosophy of ministry. The Willow Creek Community Church in South Barrington, Illinois, exemplifies such a philosophy. The church has geared itself to speak the language of a yuppie culture and reach many people that a more traditional church would probably never touch.

Many pastors have attended seminars sponsored by the Willow Creek Church and numerous churches across America have embraced its market-driven, pro-growth philosophy. The strengths of this philosophy are easily recognized: efficiency, excellence, and stewardship of resources appeal to professional people accustomed to such values in the business world; the centrality of evangelism in Sunday services produces new converts and generates an atmosphere of excitement conducive to personal witnessing; upbeat, contemporary worship style relates well to younger generations; clarity of goals and shared values motivate—perhaps drive—the entire leadership team. Other strengths could also be recognized.

7. See "In Search of the Effective Church," *Leadership* (Fall 1990).

Every clearly delineated philosophy engenders concern about balance, as does this philosophy. Is there a comparable emphasis upon discipleship as there is upon evangelism? Does devotion to program and performance excellence (e.g., first-class music, top-notch drama, relevant and entertaining sermons) create a spectator mentality in the congregation? Do a significant number of people feel herded rather than shepherded? Are people used to fulfill the leader's vision, or are parishioners cared for, listened to, and appreciated for who they are? Each pastor and church must grapple with these and similar questions.

A Nurturing, Fellowship Philosophy

As indicated by the nomenclature, a "reaching-in" philosophy emphasizes the importance of community, interpersonal warmth, and strong support groups. The focus of such a philosophy is not upon performance in public services, but upon significant, encouraging, and cooperative interaction among parishioners during weekday activities. Evangelism tends not to be emphasized in public services, but personal lifestyle evangelism among members is preferred and encouraged. Some pastors and churches that embrace this philosophy accentuate intrachurch affirmation, particularly among those who struggle and hurt—generally a large percentage of any congregation. Others seem to stress personal commitment to meaningful ministry within the community, particularly to the down-and-outers. Always in these churches, personal involvement in the community life looms large.

The strongly relational philosophy has a number of strengths. Members feel involved and cared for as individuals. The church body represents a safe environment, a place where failure, hurt, struggle, and honesty are understood and accepted. Teaching may not be formal and structured, but the lives of caring people provide valuable examples of discipleship. Spectator Christians may well feel uncomfortable in this kind of church.

Most relationally-based churches grapple with a few sticky problems. Church growth, especially new convert growth, tends to be slow. The fellowship may become ingrown and newcomers may find difficulty breaking into the family. Also, a strong emphasis on love and acceptance may foster a dangerous inclusivism, reducing the cost of discipleship and making church discipline difficult or impossible. Some people do not want deep involvement and lots of personal attention; it may be that their own extended families provide all their fellowship needs, and they may have a meaningful ministry altogether separate from the church. Such people may merely want solid preaching and teaching, and to be left alone. Could such people find a niche in a strongly relational church?

A Worship Philosophy

A "reaching-up" philosophy focuses on worship and prayer. Many churches that embody this philosophy are charismatic or liturgical, but always they emphasize the spiritual power of corporate worship and intercessory prayer. Some of these congregations and denominations are among the fastest growing Christian groups in America.

Spiritual leaders in these churches strongly believe in deliverance from spiritual bondage—and, often, physical bondage as well. Public services tend to be emotionally and spiritually satisfying, with their robust accentuation of burden bearing, unity of the Spirit, power in prayer, celebration of fulfillment, and expectation of spiritual liberation.

Evangelism seems to thrive in an environment of praise and anticipation of spiritual deliverance. Social and racial barriers dissipate more readily and a healthy heterogeneity marks churches that stress a "reaching-up" philosophy. Generally, considerable deference to spiritual leaders, emphasis on personal experience, and respect for direct revelation typify congregational norms. A trust in God to display authentic power generates excitement and enthusiasm, qualities often lacking in traditional churches.

Sometimes churches with this basic philosophy struggle with internal confusion about "special revelations" in the absence of consensus. Many people also tend to follow—even idolize—powerful and charismatic leaders without exercising sufficient spiritual discernment. Dramatic crisis intervention often receives more attention than the slow, routine process of spiritual growth through application of the disciplines of discipleship. Disillusionment sometimes sets in when expectations of deliverance are not realized.

A Teaching Philosophy

A church that prioritizes the teaching of Scripture concludes that a clear understanding of God's Word accomplishes more than anything else in transforming individual lives and society. This philosophy theorizes that knowing the Bible produces healthy Christians and a vigorous, dynamic church body. Expository Bible teaching, therefore, represents the heart of church ministry.

Obviously, truly gifted preachers and lay teachers are essential for a teaching philosophy to work effectively. Not surprisingly, a number of people won to Christ through "reaching-out" churches gravitate to Bible-teaching churches because of the superior opportunity for learning Scripture and continued spiritual growth. Such churches appeal to the large number of Christians that desire to understand the Bible and have often been unfed in churches that make serious Bible study a low priority.

As with all philosophies, problems perplex leaders who endorse a Bible-teaching philosophy. For example, the assumption that greater biblical understanding necessarily equates with more spiritual maturity can be challenged. Many people know a lot of Scripture, but show little evidence of changed lifestyle, mature discipleship, or resistance of temptation. Further, frequently the sermon dominates all services; worship and fellowship fade in deference to learning. Sometimes gifted expositors gain celebrity status and become gurus to their fanatically loyal parishioners who do not exercise sufficient personal discernment about what they hear.

Balance in Church Philosophy

Each of these four church philosophies emphasizes one of the missions of the church: evangelism, fellowship, worship, and discipleship—perhaps at the expense of the others. Other church philosophies may stress social service in their communities. Obviously, some balance in a philosophy of ministry is desirable since all of the church's missions are important, but a study of effective churches suggests that few of them achieve much real balance, and they may not even try. An exact balance probably is impossible and perhaps undesirable.

C. Peter Wagner reminds us that no church can do everything or meet everyone's needs, and therefore, choices must be made. He cites examples of four differing philosophies: the *classroom church,* the *life-situation church,* the *rock generation church,* and the *spiritual high church,* and gives examples of each.[8] Obviously, in focusing on their specialties, each church surrenders the opportunity for excelling in something else.

There may be valid reasons for emphasizing one mission more than others; no one church can minister well to all people. A church with many new Christians may properly decide to give discipleship ministry temporary preference over other facets of ministry. Another church with many hurting and troubled people may need a philosophy that focuses on fellowship and caring ministries. A community in transition may require a church to change its basic philosophy to meet changing needs.

Further, balance does not seem nearly as important as clarity in philosophy. When a congregation unites behind a clearly defined philosophy, though the philosophy may be somewhat skewed, remarkable results can be expected.

Steps to an Effective Philosophy of Ministry

Both pastors and churches must develop a clear and concise philosophy of ministry that articulates the most fundamental principles by which they operate. After clarifying their own philosophies, effective pastors lead their churches to the following convictions about ministry:

Identify your spiritual gifts and calling to ministry.

Be sure that your present ministry enables you to use effectively your spiritual gifts. If not, negotiate a different role definition with your congregation. It may be necessary to seek a new place of service.

Give prayerful and reflective thought to the primary ingredients of a personal philosophy of ministry: relationships, change agency, preaching-teaching, role definition, time

8. C. Peter Wagner, *Leading Your Church to Growth* (Ventura, Calif.: Regal, 1984), 176–79.

management, leadership, and others. Don't hesitate to seek wise counsel and then make intelligent decisions in each major category.

Rigorously discipline yourself to practice your philosophy.

Begin to work with the spiritual leaders of the church to fashion its philosophy of ministry. Give particular attention to the mission, goals, priorities, government, values, and methodology of the church.

6

VALUES—THE MEASURE OF A MINISTRY

So then I have observed that God seldom blesses
any man's work if his heart is not set on success.

Richard Baxter

Despite many resources and prodigious effort, much of
American Christianity is characterized by feeble ministry and lack
of growth. The church exists for worship, instruction, and fellowship so that disciples might be strengthened and prepared for
"works of service" (Eph. 4:12) in the neighborhood, factory, school,
and marketplace. When a church no longer focuses on ministry, it
ceases to be the church and becomes a religious artifact, an anach-
ronism in a desperately needy world. A dynamic church that enthusiastically embraces and shares the revelation of God is gradually
replaced by a church that embraces vague theological abstractions
and clergy who "throw [themselves] into the hectic business of 'run-

ning' a congregation, the busyness that sucks up all one's energy and creates the illusion that one is consuming oneself in the service of the kingdom of God."[1]

We must distinguish both the stagnation and the relative success of many churches from those with a true missional orientation. Some thriving churches may be as unfocused and indifferent to ministry as stagnant churches. Busyness, full pews, attractive buildings, and impressive balance sheets do not necessarily indicate spiritual health or the blessing of God. Material and numerical strength may easily hide functional and ministerial impotency, deluding those involved into believing all is well. The church at Laodicea typifies exactly this type of church: "You say, 'I am rich; I have acquired wealth and do not need a thing.' But you do not realize that you are wretched, pitiful, poor, blind and naked" (Rev. 3:17). Success, as typically judged, may or may not indicate God's blessing or an effective ministry.

Similarly, material and statistical shortcomings do not necessarily indicate delinquency by God's standards. Sometimes churches and pastors minister effectively, but for a variety of reasons, they do not enjoy big budgets or booming crowds. The leaders of these churches are the unsung heroes of Christian ministry. God measures achievement in terms of integrity, faithfulness, devotion, and righteousness, qualities that do not always produce statistical impressiveness.

The Missional Church

Most churches and pastors think of themselves as unconditionally and unalterably committed to ministry—the obvious reason for their existence. Yet, many congregations run programs, conduct services, operate facilities, manage budgets, and involve scores of people in frenzied activity without much genuine or intentional ministry ever taking place—a tragedy of monumental significance.

On the other hand, missional churches that nourish and cherish ministry emphasize worship, evangelization, discipleship, development of spiritual gifts, correction of the wayward, preparation of people for service, and a wide range of caring services such as aid

1. Helmut Thielicke, *The Trouble with the Church* (Grand Rapids: Baker, 1965), 81.

and comfort to the sick or bereaved, shelter for the homeless, food for the hungry, recovery for the divorced, encouragement for the depressed, and so forth.

Two kinds of pastors are found in American churches. The first kind identifies a new family visiting the church and thinks instinctively, "This is a family we can use around here!" The other kind observes a new family and prays instinctively: "Thank you, God, for the privilege of ministering to this family!" Missional churches have the latter kind of leaders, leaders who see people not as building blocks to be used, but as recipients of the church's ministry.

Obviously, there are many differences in the declared values of ministry-oriented churches, depending upon traditions, affiliations, doctrinal positions, location, and so forth. However, certain characteristics mark those missional churches that are supremely passionate about ministry. These qualities may be found in large, average, or small churches, and in rural, town, suburban, or urban churches. Leaders who desire a church distinguished by robust ministry might weigh themselves and their church according to the following values consistently held by missional churches.

A Passion for Ministry

Missional churches invariably have leaders—especially pastors—possessed with a deep, personal intensity and fervor to win people to Christ, to nurture them to maturity, and, through personal sacrifice, to meet real needs. That all-encompassing agenda fuels a driving enthusiasm that pervades the entire church. It takes a great deal of uncompromising self-scrutiny to honestly appraise one's real values and to determine whether one truly esteems such ministry over numerous other attractive and rewarding alternatives. Many in pastoral offices become disoriented and compromise their values. The human mind is capable of infinite self-deception.

Undeniably, the apostle Paul epitomized this passion for ministry, particularly in his desperate desire to see the people of Israel come to Christ: "I speak the truth in Christ—I am not lying, my conscience confirms it in the Holy Spirit—I have great sorrow and unceasing anguish in my heart. For I could wish that I myself were cursed and cut off from Christ for the sake of my brothers, those of my own race, the people of Israel" (Rom. 9:1–3). Indeed, the record of Paul's struggle to save the lost staggers most of us. Nevertheless, missional leaders and churches demonstrate, in numerous ways, this very passion and desire to meet the salvific and nurturing needs of people.

A Priority on Ministry

In missional churches, the thinking and action of every staff and board meeting is centered around the primary concern of meeting needs, not on secondary concerns, as most nonmissional churches do.

One church board spent an entire evening discussing the problem of bat manure in the belfry; another group haggled for hours over the color of paint and carpet for the new sanctuary; another church had numerous members spend untold hours trying to decide how to spend money donated for a carillon. Ministry-focused leaders do not let such things happen.

In the missional church, the creation of an atmosphere in which people worship God, mature in the faith, and meet the needs of others is the primary concern of every staff member, group leader, and minister. Programs, property, money, and structures are never valued as indicators of success, but only as a means to accomplish evangelism, disciple-making, and serving others. Trustees do not merely talk about buildings, insurance, and budgets, but about how property and funds can be used more effectively to meet needs of people.

Pastors who truly desire to evaluate the missional status of their churches could spend some time wisely by studying the agendas and time usage of their meetings. Does an attitude of nurturing concern govern every meeting, dominate every agenda, and generate enthusiasm and excitement for new converts and their spiritual growth?

Attention to the Needy

Leaders in missional churches care intensely about people, all kinds of people, and because they care, they orient everything to helping people in realistic ways, focusing particularly upon the needy rather than on the healthy.

One of the cruelest inconsistencies of the nonmissional church is that ministry tends to focus on less needy people, while the most needy are often excluded from pastoral care. Most churches have a core of "beautiful" people: socially desirable, financially secure,

maritally stable, biblically literate Christians with children to popu-
late the Sunday school. They hold key positions, attend church
regularly, and give generously. Every pastor rejoices over their success and presence; we think the church couldn't exist or function
well without them. However, the temptation to savor and cater to
such people, and in the process neglect other more needy people,
overwhelms the judgment of many in ministry.

Singles, the divorced, the elderly, the poor, the widowed, the
AIDS patient, the unemployed, the alcohol abuser, the homosexual,
the non-Christian, the depressed, and other troubled people generally do not receive pastoral care commensurate to their desperate
needs, often because time spent with the "beautiful" people seems
more pleasant and productive. The most needy often fall through
the cracks. Indeed, in nonmissional churches, the most needy
people are often shunned and treated with disdain, much as the lepers of the New Testament. This is not true in missional churches.
Missional churches keep James 2:1–4 clearly in focus, and the compassion these pastors have for needy people, kindles a compassion
that pervades the entire church.

The Urge to Equip

Many properly argue for spending time with healthy people who
in turn can minister effectively to others, much as Jesus spent time
with the Twelve. This may seem contradictory to the previous sec-
tion, but the example of Jesus guides us. He trained the Twelve, but
did not neglect the desperately needy. He did not hobnob with the
beautiful; he devoted himself to healing lepers, the blind, and the
lame; he had time for Nicodemus, Mary Magdalene, and Zacchaeus,
but he equipped the Twelve. Missional pastors have a consuming
desire both to minister and to facilitate the ministries of others.

In missional churches, training for ministry occupies a place
near the top of every leader's agenda because it is both biblically
sanctioned and effective time management. "Many church leaders
bear incredible loads because they haven't mastered the art of raising up fellow leaders and releasing responsibility to them."[2] Leaders

2. Don Cousins, Leith Anderson, and Arthur DeKruyter, *Mastering Church Management*
(Portland, Ore.: Multnomah, 1990), 115.

observe what goes on and involve themselves in helping people improve their efforts to serve. Challenging, equipping, enabling, and delegating are primary tasks of every pastor.

In one church, a mature man was asked to teach a Sunday school class, but responded: "I always thought I might like to do that, but I don't know how." In his thirty years of church attendance and Christian experience, no one had bothered to help him find out whether he had a gift for teaching, or to help him learn how to teach.

In churches where ministry is a priority, pastors preach and teach the "Good Samaritan" and such texts that emphasize caring, the human touch, personal warmth, hospitality, visitation, sacrificial giving, helping others, and so forth. People are motivated and trained to engage in ministry through an understanding of the scriptural mandate, through the inner working of the Holy Spirit in their lives, through leaders who, by example and training, patiently equip them to serve. An atmosphere of caring pervades such churches, a caring that begins with leaders who commit themselves to sacrificial service and who train persistently. One couple who operated an inner-city mission had the motto: "Everlastingly At It!"

The Celebration of Ministry

Missional congregations constantly recognize and celebrate those involved in ministry. Newsletters, bulletins, and reports (written and oral) feature stories about those who minister in the church or in the community. One lady served her church as the "flower woman" for decades; she came to the church several times a week to water, clean, and sometimes replace the numerous plants that beautified the building. She never received recognition or a thank you for her sacrificial service. The fact that she did not seek crowd approval is irrelevant. Such oversight is rare in ministry-oriented churches.

Churches that truly value ministry think of creative ways to show respect and celebrate people in ministry, much as a business enterprise gives recognition to its best salespeople. Sunday school teachers, nursery staff, custodians, youth workers, musicians, leaders of home Bible studies, volunteers at the local hospital or pregnancy center, and others involved in a great variety of ministries know their efforts are noticed and appreciated.

One pastor bought boxes of thank-you notes and committed himself to write one note of appreciation to some parishioner each day for six months. He was astounded at the significant difference in the entire atmosphere of the church. Ministry thrives in a church where people know their efforts are appreciated. Few people can persist in effective ministry without ever receiving a "well done" by those who notice. We live in a world where people need the encouragement of those who care deeply about ministry.

Responsiveness to Feedback

Missional churches value, solicit, and respond to feedback. In the best corporate enterprises, senior management personnel never spend less than 30 percent of their time in direct contact with customers, soliciting feedback, and checking up on themselves. Spiritual leaders in a missional church should spend no less time in direct contact with these recipients of their ministries.

Genuine leaders—those determined to excel—seek feedback constantly, and they take it seriously. Such leaders have an ear to the ground; they put a premium on listening. In their visitation, telephoning, group encounters, board meetings, and one-to-one counseling, leaders hear what people say, and then they do something about it.

Three ingredients constitute the value of responding to feedback.

Every Parishioner Matters

Missional churches and leaders never sweep dissatisfaction under the carpet, no matter how minor or from whom it comes. Response to parishioners' needs, impressions, and dissatisfactions tends to be minimized in nonministering churches, who often have leaders who brush off disapproval, label displeased people as dissidents, and dismiss dropouts with a "good-riddance" attitude. Ministering churches have leaders who seek feedback and who take action on parishioner response to their ministries.

Sometimes pastors rationalize a cavalier attitude about disapproval by suggesting that we must please God, not people—which is true up to a point. But pastors who hear "the nursery is dirty" or "the sermons are too long" or "the church is unfriendly," and do nothing, condemn themselves to obscurity and insignificance. Some pastors never make an effort to hear the legitimate concerns and discern the discontentment of their parishioners, much less act upon them.

Listening Is Empathetic

The strategic advantage of every effective church begins with compassionate leaders who listen empathetically to congregants. "When I say empathetic listening, I mean listening with intent to *understand*. I mean *seeking first* to understand, to really understand. It's an entirely different paradigm. Empathetic listening gets inside another person's frame of reference. You look out through it, you see the world the way they see the world, you understand their paradigm, you understand how they feel."[3]

The business world occasionally discovers dramatic, "new," productive techniques that effective ministers have known for generations. One of the latest such techniques in the corporate environment is MBWA (Management by Wandering Around). Whatever the business pros and cons of this technique, a simple, incontrovertible thesis has proven itself valuable: supervisory personnel get out of their executive suites and "wander around," empathetically listening to factory workers and customers, and then institute changes in response to what they hear.

In a similar way, leaders of missional churches "wander around" attentively throughout the congregation. They get the message, spoken or unspoken, blatant or implied, positive or negative. Then they act. Robert Greenleaf suggests "that only a true natural servant automatically responds to any problem by listening *first*. . . . This suggests that a non-servant who wants to be a servant might become a *natural* servant through a long arduous discipline of learning to listen, a discipline sufficiently sustained that the automatic response to any problem is to listen first. . . . Remember that great line from the prayer of St. Francis, 'Lord, grant that I may not seek so much to be understood as to understand.'"[4]

The objective in constructively soliciting feedback is threefold: to let parishioners know they are important, to uncover church problems that need to be addressed, and to give leaders a constant

---

3. Stephen R. Covey, *The Seven Habits of Highly Effective People* (New York: Simon and Schuster, 1989), 240.

4. Robert Greenleaf, *Servant Leadership* (New York: Paulist, 1977), 17.

reminder of the real world full of hurting people desperately in need of ministry.

One businessman testified that he forced himself "to adopt the simple habit of calling, religiously, three or four customers a week to ask, 'How are we doing for you?'"[5] The result was nearly revolutionary; he was told exactly how his business was doing, and he did something about the feedback received. Pastoral leaders might do well to adopt the same simple strategy of empathetic listening.

Responding to Feedback Promotes Church Growth

In many churches, particularly large churches, pastors spend virtually no time in direct contact with parishioners, except perhaps with a few lay leaders. All leaders favor church growth, but one constant problem of increasing size is the formidable difficulty of keeping pace with the needs of more and more people. Not all leaders possess the capability of adjusting to their own success. However, that which separates the missional church from the generic variety is superior ability to discover real needs, muster ministry to meet those needs, measure church effectiveness in terms of meeting needs, and make adjustments to meet needs better—all regardless of how much the church grows.

Some churches and leaders do an effective job of ministry with a small constituency, but, unable to cope with their achievements or God's blessing, they give up little by little on the enormous task of keeping current with a larger group of people. Such churches settle back into the routine of running programs and conducting services for a church full of spectators; their days of effective ministry have passed. Their numbers then frequently decrease, giving rise to the "yo-yo" church syndrome: when the church becomes small enough, it begins to grow; when it becomes larger it begins to shrink. Some churches, of course, continue to thrive statistically, but not because of effective ministry. Rather, dynamic personalities, public relations efforts, superior location, or spectacular Sunday programming keep the crowds coming.

Ministry-focused churches utilize the meeting of needs to fuel further growth, and they structure themselves in a way that does not

5. Tom Peters and Nancy Austin, *A Passion for Excellence* (New York: Warner), 104.

merely facilitate spectators. This necessitates the ongoing development of ways to generate feedback from an expanding base of parishioners. Missional churches are creative in discovering real needs of people, regardless of church size. Nonmissional churches give up on this ongoing struggle.

Dedication to Detail

Missional church leaders pay attention to details. Little things matter in ministry. Those who make good movies, or manage politicians, or build quality automobiles, or skydive always attend rigorously to details. Missional leaders must do the same.

Missional churches contain people who constantly give meticulous supervision to particulars, to those matters often considered insignificant by nonministering churches. They care for details and do so rigorously, even while attending to the responsibilities of the "big picture" and strategizing for future ministry. While senior pastors in thriving churches cannot personally handle a limitless number of details, they can and must delegate responsibilities and hold others accountable.

In his visit to the Willow Creek Community Church, Jim Abrahamson noticed a smudge near a cleaning closet, and his guide assured him that it would be scrubbed off or painted over before the next service: "Young executives go to work every day in a world that does not tolerate smudges. When they come here, we want them to say, 'Hey, these people care as much about their ministry as my company does about my business.'"[6] To some that may seem excessive, or even paranoid, but it illustrates the painstaking care of excellent leaders for little things which eventually add up to distinguish those passionate about ministry.

Every church that aspires to ministerial excellence must give exacting attention not merely to smudges, but to little things that communicate concern for people. One family transferred from their church because nobody seemed to care when an elderly parent, who attended a different church, died. A little thing to many, but it communicated the wrong message to those who grieved. Conversely, a sizable pastoral staff spent some time each week praying

6. Jim Abrahamson, "In Search of the Effective Church," *Leadership* (Fall 1990): 54.

on a rotation basis for individual families in their constituency, then sent personalized letters to those families, assuring them that the church's pastors had prayed for them that week. Each family got at least four reminders during the year that they were prayed for by their pastors during the previous week. A little thing—maybe—but extraordinarily effective in communicating the right message.

Church leaders should remember these simple but profound words from the business world: "Excellence is a game of inches, or millimeters. No one act is, per se, clinching. But a thousand things, a thousand thousand things, each done a tiny bit better, do add up to memorable responsiveness and distinction—and loyalty (repeat business) and slightly higher margins."[7] Ministerial excellence is not a game, but it is a matter of a thousand little things that add up to impact people's lives for Christ. "SAS's Group President Jan Carlzon led the remarkable turnaround at SAS [Scandinavian Air System] with this premise: 'We don't seek to be one thousand percent better at any one thing. We seek to be one percent better at one thousand things.'"[8]

Some years ago Jack Nicklaus was the leading money winner on the PGA tour. At the end of the year, the difference between Nicklaus and the forty-eighth man on the money-winning list was less than one stroke per round of golf. A small superiority made hundreds of thousands of dollars difference in paychecks. So in churches a little bit of extra attention to improvement in many areas can make a vast difference in ministerial terms. A little more care in sermon preparation, or attention to the nursery, or warmth in greeting visitors, or commitment to the elderly, and to dozens of other matters add up to significantly greater ministry. In the business world "the situation is so bad (or, conversely, the opportunity so good!) that a tiny step in the direction of responsiveness sets you way ahead of the pack."[9] The same is true in churches. Churches that desire to be way ahead of the run-of-the-mill churches should give rigorous attention to a thousand little things that the other churches ignore.

7. Peters and Austin, *A Passion for Excellence*, 53.
8. Ibid., 68.
9. Ibid., 106.

Commitment to Small Groups

An increasing number of missional churches realize that the personal care offered in small groups forms the heart of their long-range effectiveness. Nonmissional churches depend excessively on impressive facilities and the meetings that take place there. Missional leaders know that meaningful interpersonal relationships and spiritual growth are developed and sustained most readily in effective small groups. Enduring and meaningful ministry necessitates the kind of discipleship and individualized attention established only in small groups.

The structure and agenda of such groups allow the development of laity interaction, interdependence, and mutual ministry. Nonmissional churches generally depend too heavily on pastoral superstars, public meetings, and formal structures.

The following principles constitute missional churches' approach to small group ministry.

Scripture Requires Community

The fierce individualism of American culture contrasts with the close communal relationships modeled in the New Testament. "We extol the virtues of friendship, yet our own loyalties to other people are more fluid and unreliable than ever. Our friends are most likely to be the people who can be most useful to us at our stage in life. Because our lives are changing faster than ever, we find that our relationships are less enduring, too."[10] Our culture resists intimacy, interdependency, and commitment, but these qualities are extolled in Scripture. Missional churches and their leaders resist cultural isolationism, commit themselves to meaningful relationships, and structure small groups that facilitate friendships, caring, and mutual edification.

Group Ministry Requires Relationships

Effective ministry necessitates healthy relationships. Inability to build and sustain relationships undermines any attempt at ministry. Substantial alliances with laity and between laity facilitate every level of pastoral care.

10. George Barna, *The Frog in the Kettle* (Ventura, Calif.: Regal, 1990), 159.

Pastoral staff members in missional churches know that effective and congregational ministry depends on interpersonal care among laity, especially as the church grows. Pastors bear responsibility to see that the spiritual needs of everyone in a growing church are satisfied to the extent possible, for this is the core meaning of what "oversight" means. Yet, wise pastors know that this enormous task cannot be accomplished without wide participation of laity in mutual ministry.

The service of such people as Phoebe of Cenchrea,[11] Priscilla and Aquila,[12] Onesiphorus[13] and many others seem dwarfed by the more spectacular achievements of the major missionary leaders, yet their lay ministry was crucial and commended repeatedly by the apostle Paul. Similarly, pastors of missional churches understand that caring relationships within the congregation must be established, maintained, and nurtured under competent leadership in order to accomplish the real work of the ministry. Most pastors have concluded that this task can best be done through the establishment of small care groups where people learn to know, love, and minister to one another.

Group Attendance Requires Encouragement

Some of the best churches put teeth into their small-group ministry. Both the New Song Church of Walnut, California, and the Community Baptist Church of Alta Loma, California, require a weekly small group involvement for membership in the church. The true size of the church is not how many attend public services, but how many are involved in the discipleship of small groups.

Some people will naturally desire a small-group experience; many others will not. Pastoral leaders err if they think that the creation of groups and announcements of their locations will suffice. Rather, efforts must be made to encourage people to join a small group, along with constant monitoring of attendance. Some people require continual encouragement until they see for themselves the

11. ". . . she has been a great help to many people, including me [Paul]" (Rom. 16:1).

12. "They risked their lives for me. Not only I but all the churches of the Gentiles are grateful to them" (Rom. 16:4).

13. "You know very well in how many ways he helped me [Paul] in Ephesus" (2 Tim. 1:18).

intrinsic value of regular meetings with other Christians to share needs, intercede, and provide care.

Groups Require Variety

Successful small-group ministry demands the choice of a variety of groups according to time of meeting, special interests, topic of study, maturity of members, and so forth. The New Song Church has groups entitled "The 30–40 Something Care Group," "T.G.I.F. Group" (Thank God It's Friday), "R.A.W." (Reading the Word, Accountability, and Worship), and "Diverse Disciples." It also has groups meeting in certain geographical areas, special interest groups for men, groups for those in junior and senior high school, groups for those interested in modern missions. Other churches have groups for senior citizens, alcoholics, drug addicts, those who have eating disorders, parents of teenagers, mothers of preschoolers, and so forth.

Group Ministry Requires Competent Leadership

Church leaders err, sometimes tragically, when they assume that establishing small groups automatically achieves worthy goals. Bad things happen in small church groups about as frequently as good things, especially in groups composed of spiritually immature people. Sometimes disastrous consequences can devastate the lives of individuals and whole congregations.

What, then, is the indispensable ingredient for small church groups to be truly helpful? Leadership! Establishing any small group without competent leaders invites catastrophe. Good leaders keep discussions on the right track, encourage participation by all, create an atmosphere of caring, model Christian discipleship, and lovingly discipline the wayward. No church care groups should function without designated, trained leaders. Some kinds of leaderless groups seem to work in certain settings, but not in churches with immature Christians. Competent leaders ensure that a small group does not function merely on a social level, but with genuine spiritual care for one another. Training lay leaders for the church's small group ministry must be at the core of pastoral ministry.

Groups Require an Evangelistic Emphasis

Groups that concentrate on developing church evangelism are important because people need help and encouragement in developing friendships with unbelievers. Leaders of evangelistic Bible study groups need some specialized training, useful materials, and competent examples. Fortunately, an abundance of good training books and manuals is available for this purpose, but pastoral leaders must model the behavior they expect of others. Not all are capable of leading neighborhood evangelistic studies, but leaders for these groups should be identified, trained, and encouraged.

Allegiance to Institutional Integrity

In secularized churches, truth often becomes confused with popular approval. The pressures to compromise institutional integrity in exchange for high marks on the congregant report card can crush genuine ministry in many churches.

A church's institutional integrity is characterized by the following values.

Commitment to Scriptural Authority

Few things so clearly reveal the difference between a missional church and a nonmissional church as their views of Scripture and the place it occupies in the church. Secularized churches simply do not take the Bible seriously. They explain Scripture according to cultural norms. Missional churches interpret culture in the light of Scripture.

Today's secularized churches make no diligent, disciplined attempt to allow Scripture to govern and order their lives. Many such churches have conventionally approved doctrinal statements about Scripture, but nevertheless in practice they dismiss its truths, often substituting self-help and utilitarian principles in their place. In many churches humanism wins out over biblical theology and scriptural precepts are often flippantly dismissed as obsolete. "Positive image building" tends to dominate over divine truth, prayer, the sovereignty of God, and obedience to scriptural commands.

In contrast, missional churches view Scripture as a living Word through which God seeks to order his church and govern his people. Pastors in ministering churches echo Charles Spurgeon: "If your creed and Scripture do not agree, cut your creed to pieces, but make it agree with this book."[14] Bible interpretations can and do vary, but missional churches treat Scripture as the unequivocal authority on matters of doctrine and conduct; their leaders conscientiously seek to apply scriptural truths to contemporary issues. Pastors committed unalterably to ministry proclaim the whole counsel of God, including those teachings that confront and oppose the popular opinions of our culture.

Resistance to Reductionism

Missional leaders resist reductionism, an attitude that erodes commitment to ethical objectivity and treats people as consumers, customers, respondents, receptors, or targets, thus denying their dignity and value as individuals created in the image of God.

Much evidence suggests that too many leaders treat people with a "herd" mentality: count them rather than love them, and use them rather than serve them. Such tactics sometimes produce crowds, but they will be uncommitted crowds, people with lifestyles void of grace and Christ-likeness and without loyalties to the church. Such people "inspect congregations as if they were restaurants and leave if they find nothing to their taste . . . they don't convert—they choose."[15]

In the ministry-focused church, leaders fiercely resist the popular demands and subtle temptations that lead to reductionism and loss of institutional integrity. They see people as individuals of incalculable worth. They proclaim the whole gospel with its demands of repentance and commitment, its summons to discipleship, and its warnings and judgments intact. They desire church growth, but only the kind of growth that produces committed disciples, not throngs of spectators. The leaders of missional churches do not dilute truth in exchange for crowd patronage.

14. Charles Spurgeon, *Metropolitan Tabernacle Pulpit*, vol. 20 (Pasadena, Tex.: Pilgrim Publications), 335.

15. *Newsweek*, 17 Dec. 1990, 52.

Resistance to Consumerism

Institutional integrity demands resistance to consumerism. Undeniably, a secularized, consumerized orientation characterizes many churches, and an increasing number of pastors jump on this bandwagon without carefully weighing the dangers.[16] In the minds of many, selling Jesus and marketing the church differ but little from the selling of soap.[17] One person, summarizing this slippery slope of compromise, said: "You begin by trying to find an audience to hear your message and you always end by trying to find a message to hold your audience."

Pressure for a secularized marketing strategy will increase in the coming years. Church growth and success are frequently tied to efficient marketing, not to effective ministry. Consider the following bold statements: "My contention, based on careful study of data and the activities of American churches, is that the major problem plaguing the Church is its failure to embrace a marketing orientation in what has become a marketing-driven environment. . . . Most churches' inability to grow is not due to lack of desire, or even a lack of resources. The truth is, we simply have not grasped the basic principles of marketing and applied them to the Church. . . . All we as a community of believers need to do is gain a proper perspective on the Church and how it can be marketed effectively. Then new and exciting doors of ministry will be opened to us."[18]

George Barna's thesis must be challenged and debated, for marketing often operates on unbiblical assumptions and exposes the church to further secularization. It may be more valid to suggest that the major problems plaguing American Christianity include the absence of prayer, the scarcity of godly leaders, and casual views about scriptural authority. At any rate, the assertion that "all we need to do is gain a proper perspective on the Church and how it can be marketed effectively" seems uncomfortably commercial and secular in its implications. "In all this, the secular church—changing its offerings and samples in response to the appetites of con-

16. See Bruce Shelley and Marshall Shelley, *The Consumer Church* (Downers Grove, Ill.: InterVarsity, 1992).

17. See "Selling Soap and Jesus" in Kenneth A. Myers, *All God's Children and Blue Suede Shoes* (Westchester, Ill.: Crossway, 1989), 20.

18. George Barna, *Marketing the Church* (Colorado Springs: NavPress, 1988), 23, 40.

sumers—more nearly resembles a delicatessen than it resembles its historical namesake."[19]

When ministers become entrepreneurs, when people become targets, and when churches become activity centers, institutional integrity has disappeared and ministerial passion along with it. That we would allow our religious institutions to degenerate into merchandizing agencies and our traditional Christian values to be reduced to consumer commodities is cause for alarm—and repentance.

Missional leaders utilize the best ethical techniques available. Yet, they never sacrifice truth on the altar of pragmatism. Missional leaders subject all methods to the severest scrutiny to determine their compatibility with Scripture and the highest standards of ethical propriety, thereby maintaining institutional integrity. The blessing of God accompanies such thinking, whether or not the crowd approves or statistical success accompanies their efforts.

Steps to Clarifying Missional Values

Organizations that identify and unite behind a clear set of values tend to be successful. The following steps may help pastors to fulfill their responsibility to help their churches identify the values that propel them toward effective ministry.

Identify the historical, denominational, and doctrinal values of the church in which you minister. Identify those worth retaining and publicizing.

Identify the uniqueness of your church and its resources. Especially consider the location, traditions, gifts, and scriptural positions of the church's members and how these factors might help define worthwhile church values.

Weigh carefully the values of other missional churches: their passion for ministry, responsiveness to feedback, dedication to detail, commitment to small groups, and allegiance to institutional integrity.

Draft a list of values, solicit contributions and response from other spiritual leaders, and cooperatively decide on those

19. C. Leonard Allen, Richard T. Hughes, and Michael R. Weed, *The Worldly Church: A Call for Biblical Renewal* (Abilene, Tex.: Abilene Christian University Press, 1991), 14.

values that will characterize the church during the coming decade. Be sure the list is neither so long as to be unwieldy nor so short or vague as to be meaningless.

Keep the values constantly before the congregation, share them with newcomers, and publicize them in the community.

7

IMAGINEERING IN MINISTRY

A rock pile ceases to be a rock pile
the moment a single man contemplates it,
bearing within him the image of a cathedral.

Saint-Exupéry

The art of pastoral guidance requires the ability to interpret available signposts about the future and to influence the church to prepare for it. "Just as the historian takes piles of information about the past and constructs an interpretation of what must have happened, so must the leader select, organize, structure, and interpret information about the future in constructing a viable and credible vision."[1] Today's changing world and the stagnant state of the church demand such ability and influence.

Visionary leaders avoid two great temptations: excessive time spent on managerial trivialities and urgencies, and fascination with an unrealistic dream world. Genuine leaders delegate most internal minutia and focus on the future, yet without becoming utopian.

1. Burt Nanus, *The Leader's Edge* (Chicago: Contemporary Books, 1989), 64.

Leadership Dilemma

Americans currently live in the "Me Generation," distinguished for its self-indulgence, individualism, and indifference to global problems—which reminds us of Paul's prophecy: "There will be terrible times in the last days. People will be lovers of themselves . . ." (2 Tim. 3:1–2). Surveys indicate that 60 percent of adult Americans feel powerless and alienated and 33 percent do not lead happy lives. Insecurity and hopelessness have become appallingly common-place in our dysfunctional society and, as a result, psychological treatment of troubled people has mushroomed. As one comedian reportedly expressed our dilemma: "One path leads to despair and utter hopelessness, the other to total extinction. Let us pray we have the wisdom to choose correctly."

Confidence in American institutions has been shrinking for several decades. Frustration and disappointment have become epidemic in our churches. "Americans have become disenchanted by what they perceive to be a great void—a sort of black hole of leadership into which problems and issues are fed and out of which nothing much seems to emerge."[2] This malady includes religious institutions; most people believe that the church is irrelevant and the clergy are not to be trusted. Clergy rank below lawyers and just above politicians on the "trust factor."

The television generation evaluates sermons and worship services on style, relational significance, and high-impact entertainment, not on the basis of truth or spiritual power demonstrated in changed lives. People patronize churches that cater to their desires and shifting whims irrespective of sound theology, missional orientation, or godly leaders. "Most churches grow by transfer. The rule of the day is the rotation of the saints. The number of real conversions to Christ by some 'great churches' is meager. . . . In reality the churches with the best programs are crowded, along with the best restaurants and theaters, because they entertain."[3] These facts and their ramifications stagger serious Christians.

Theologians have focused on eschatology, while secular futurists concentrate on the next decade or two, usually for commercial rea-

2. Ibid., 6.
3. Bill Hull, *The Disciple Making Pastor* (Old Tappan, N.J.: Revell, 1988), 20.

sons. They generate images of possible futures and probable futures, but bend their efforts toward creating preferable futures. Many pastors spend their energy on managing extant structures and traditions, and thereby fail to prepare their institutions for the next decade or the next century. We need, however, leaders with a vision. "A vision is an attempt to articulate, as clearly and vividly as possible, the desired future state of the organization. The vision is the goal that provides direction, aligns key players, and energizes people to achieve a common purpose."[4] Without visionary leaders our churches will sink further into mediocrity and irrelevancy.

Many religious leaders have a fortress mentality and doggedly maintain the status quo. Visionary leaders possess an unflagging commitment to rouse their constituencies from lethargy and to rekindle aspirations. They never see the future as a mere continuation of past traditions and methodologies. Leaders think in terms of new opportunities. Visionary pastors are wise strategists, not merely clever religious entrepreneurs. The latter sometimes achieve notoriety and statistical prosperity, but they cannot produce significant change. The church desperately needs visionary leaders.

Skills of Visionary Leaders

Change threatens power structures, comfort, hallowed traditions, cultural norms, and institutional rules, but excellent leaders overcome resistance to change. Leaders reverse entropy, understand people power, communicate enthusiasm, resolve conflicts, and create an atmosphere of trust. They energize constituents to unite in achieving commonly held goals.

How can these major pastoral tasks be accomplished? Visionary leaders have unique and identifiable skills.

Collegial Diplomacy

Today's environment differs substantially from a few decades ago when laity were undervalued and pastors received deference as authority figures. Congregations now require collegial relationships, involvement with decisions, and participation in ministry.

---

4. Ralph H. Kilmann, Teresa Joyce Covin, and Associates, *Corporate Transformation: Revitalizing Organizations for a Competitive World* (San Francisco: Jossey-Bass, 1988), 135.

Autocratic pastors find themselves out of step with contemporary reality and increasingly ineffective.

Some traits, formerly recognized as praiseworthy, now are liabilities. Rugged individualism, competitiveness, isolated adequacy, and autocracy hinder progress in our complex society. Today's real leaders master cooperation, pool talent, divide power, share information, decentralize ministry, and inspire trust. In other words, a visionary leader forges a team and stimulates all members to do their best to achieve worthwhile, mutually held goals.

Contemporary culture requires leaders to work cooperatively with constituents to be creators of solutions, explorers of new ideas, and risk-takers. Empowerment of others replaces autocracy; sharing preempts individualism; networking supplants partisanship. Any leader is like the king on a chessboard, weak and vulnerable unless surrounded by others with differing abilities. Such collegiality and teamwork are biblically sanctioned and were illustrated dramatically in the early church, particularly in Paul's ministry (1 Cor. 1:11–13; 3:4–9).

The necessary collegiality crosses parochial, denominational, and community boundaries. Coalitions, joint ventures, and global concerns dominate the thinking of leaders. Those concerned about unilateral control will fail in a world intolerant of tyrants and partisanship. Collegial leaders, not overlords, have never been more needed by the church.

Foresight

Our contemporary crisis in Christianity demands great foresight. Lack of foresight has contributed heavily to the fact that about 80 percent of American churches have plateaued or are declining. Long-range thinking represents a truly fundamental need in every local church.

Many profit from experience, but only leaders learn from anticipations of the future. Leaders question present structures, and restless dissatisfaction with the status quo stimulates a foresight to discover new ways of doing things. Leaders study demographics, economics, politics, sociology, and technology to learn trends and forecasts from experts. Visionary leaders weigh relevant facts in the light of new options. They look for early warning signals, likely scenarios, available resources, and current options. Then they relate these harbingers to the church's mission. Strategy, not maintenance, dominates thinking. Yet, leaders do not lose touch with a sense of history and tradition.

Design Aptitude

The local church embodies the means through which God intends to evangelize and disciple. Leaders cooperatively frame the church to accomplish these objectives. Visionary pastors bring wisdom, godliness, and facts to the unique design process required in each local church.

Most churches recognize a few biblically necessitated, axiomatic, and transcultural design principles. However, many operational standards must be carefully tailored to individual situations. Effectiveness demands contextualization, cultural and temporal adaptations. For example, the New Song Church of Walnut, California, targets young singles and "yuppies in training" (Baby Busters) and gears music (primarily rock), programs, sermons, and cell clusters to meet the real and felt needs of this age group. As a result, about 75 percent of the more than twelve hundred attenders are in their twenties and single. At the time of this writing, Pastor Dieter Zander is preaching a five-week series on "Great Sex"—a subject of obvious interest. Acceptable contextualization—a demonstration of relevance—does not compromise the integrity of the message.

Many of the church's activities can benefit from care in design: kinds and times of public services, evangelistic and disciple-making efforts (Awana, Bible School, cell groups, camps), policies and priorities that determine the community lifestyle, structures of governance, philosophy and schedules of church staff, and methods and implementation procedures used in achieving the mission. Organizational and procedural design never guarantee God's blessing; yet, carefully designed environments normally encourages fruitfulness, and poor design promotes ineffectiveness.

Change Artistry

Contemporary leaders are not problem-solvers in the old sense of the word, but agents of change in dynamic situations. Visionary leaders focus on evolving conditions and changing circumstances to accomplish ongoing adaptation and continual transformation.

A constant stream of events takes place, both inside the church and outside in society. Visionary leaders note the fluid movements of our culture and regulate information flow, decision-making, direction, and the rhythm of the church so that internal evolution keeps pace with the dynamic changes occurring in the environment.

Both change and stability represent danger. Change can be for the worse and stability often leads to stagnation. Effective leaders calculate the risks involved in both stability and change, examine the consequences of all possible actions, and choose directions most likely to promote healthy and constant transformation.

Intentional Action

Genuine pastoral leaders possess ability to begin a plan or task and to follow through energetically. This necessitates initiative, creativity, and determination, which express themselves in nonmanipulative and nonoffensive ways. Genuine pacesetters never fear change; they thrive on it, cultivate it, and nurture it through resourcefulness, imagination, and inventiveness.

Leaders learn where to exert influence to make positive things happen, while delegating most matters of lesser importance. Managers climb ladders of success, but genuine leaders determine whether the ladder is leaning against the right wall, or put in a different metaphor, "Effectiveness—often even survival—does not depend solely on how much effort we expend, but on whether or not the effort we expend is in the right jungle."[5] Visionary leadership demands intentional action in carefully selected areas.

Elements of a Credible Vision

Answers to a series of key questions guide credible vision. These questions can be expanded as necessary, but answers are crucial to the formation of worthy visions.

- What clear scriptural guidelines assist our determination of God's will for our future?

5. Stephen R. Covey, *The Seven Habits of Highly Effective People* (New York: Simon and Schuster, 1989), 101.

- What current and future trends in our community and world are likely to affect our church? What unexpected events or conditions are possibilities?
- What available or expected resources may help or hinder our future?
- What level of risk are we willing to take? What risk might be foolhardy?
- What values aid or hinder our development? How deeply entrenched is tradition and how open are we to change?

Obviously, no generic vision can suit all churches. Each pastor and church must wrestle with the parameters of their local setting and determine the individual ingredients of a worthy vision from which strategy emerges. However, a credible vision includes the following minimal elements.

Ministerial Focus

Any worthy vision includes a missional focus (see chap. 6). Many churches make only feeble attempts at ministry and thus fail to justify their own existence. Entertainment, social agendas, edifices, traditions, statistics, and other values usurp ministry in many churches. In thousands of American churches, ministry happens serendipitously, not intentionally. A credible vision centralizes the essential purposes of evangelism and discipleship. That vision branches out to include various and extensive forms of ministry, limited only by imagination and consistent with opportunity and resources: healing the sick, comforting the grieving, feeding the hungry, housing the homeless, freeing the oppressed, encouraging the disheartened, restoring broken relationships, and so forth. The greater and more worthy the vision, the more focused it is on ministry.

Ability Threatens Community Norms

Worthwhile vision intimidates many people, because it inevitably stretches beyond the common norms or values of society. Satisfaction with the status quo means absence of vision. Vision strains the limits of imagination. It can threaten deeply entrenched precepts; occasionally it kindles ferocious anger, but it always threatens the equilibrium of comfortable constituents.

Many examples testify to the inevitable struggle of vision. Branch Rickey, president and general manager of the Brooklyn Dodgers, envisioned integrating major league baseball, which had excluded various minority groups prior to 1946. When Rickey announced that Jackie Robinson had been signed to a Dodger contract, some of the Dodgers refused to play and other teams threatened to strike. Hate mail poured into New York, vicious editorials were written, and some of Rickey's colleagues refused to speak with him. In the great storm of controversy, Branch Rickey's dream and conviction remained intact. The norms of the baseball world were threatened and eventually shattered.[6]

Similarly, Martin Luther King's dream of a racist-free America and Gandhi's image of a new India stirred deep emotions and jeopardized and shattered the status quo. "Leaders know the environment and members of the system itself will exert incredible energy to maintain the status quo. They know this; they expect it; and they don't waver from their plan when it occurs. They recognize that a necessary part of their task is to influence others to examine their assumptions and values. Such determination and unwillingness to knuckle under to the system often earn them the label *radical*."[7] Vision requires the courage to threaten norms and value systems, much as Paul and Barnabas did with the Jewish community in Antioch.

Plausible Imagination

Vision walks the thin line between fantasy and practicality. It depicts a functional possibility. As Tom Peters and Nancy Austin put it: "Excellence happens when high purpose and intense pragmatism meet."[8] Dreams laden with insurmountable obstacles must be quietly and privately laid to rest. Care must be taken, however, because most of us tend to label difficulties "insurmountable" far too easily!

In 1985 Apple Computer, Inc., was in trouble. Founder Steve Jobs was fired and 20 percent of the employees were laid off. Many doubted that Apple could become a major factor in the business market, but John Sculley had a vision. Within two years Apple was

6. See Jackie Robinson, *Baseball Has Done It* (Philadelphia: J. B. Lippincott, 1964).
7. David P. Hanna, *Designing Organizations for High Performance* (Reading, Mass.: Addison-Wesley, 1988), 160.
8. Tom Peters and Nancy Austin, *A Passion for Excellence* (New York: Warner, 1985), 490.

the leader in the new field of desktop publishing, Sculley's imaginative but wonderfully practical dream. Similar visions have kindled the successes of Henry Ford, Albert Einstein, Colonel Harland Sanders, and Raymond A. Kroc, the man who dreamed of the possibilities of a small hamburger chain called McDonald's. A worthy vision may emerge from a dreamer's imagination, but it must be plausible and attainable.

Intolerance of Mediocrity

A worthy vision never settles for the haphazard, the inferior, or the average; rather, vision aims for qualitative excellence. Peters and Austin mock the motto of a mythical corporation: "We Are No Worse Than Anybody Else."[9] Such a credo speaks for itself. In corporate America, the business philosophy in manufacturing firms was the 95 percent quality standard—until the Japanese insisted on 100 percent! Toyota's *Basic Management Handbook* articulates the philosophy adopted by many Japanese firms: "The only acceptable quality percentage is 100%. Every car must be manufactured *exactly* according to specifications. No Toyota should *ever* leave the factory without passing quality tests perfectly."[10] American manufacturers have played catch-up ever since.

Christopher Espinosa described Jobs' greatest strength at Apple: "In a word laden with irony, intolerance. Intolerance of inadequate quality, intolerance of compromise, intolerance of bureaucracy, intolerance for doing something because 'That's the way we always do it.' A constant, maddening, frustrating drive to do it better than you've already done it or better than you want to do it."[11] Effective pastors carry a similar passion for excellence and an intolerance of mediocrity. Today's most effective churches devote painstaking effort to achieve quality, even in seemingly inconsequential details.

Commitment and Discipline

A vision that costs nothing changes nothing and is worth nothing. Pastors who work to shape a vision for the church's future must

9. Ibid., 119.

10. *Board Room Reports*, October 15, 1986, cited by Fred A. Manske, Jr., *Secrets of Effective Leadership* (Memphis: Leadership Education and Development, Inc., 1987), 47.

11. Frederick G. Harmon, *The Executive Odyssey* (New York: Wiley, 1989), 52.

realize that anything worthwhile will exact a price—upon themselves and their constituency. All who dream great dreams pay dearly for their fulfillment. Sustained success demands systematic, and sometimes sacrificial, labor and cost. Worthy visions never come cheap. One needs only to consider the enormous sacrifices of the early disciples to realize the truth of this.

The cost principle applies to personal, corporate, and ministerial excellence. Pablo Casals aspired to be the world's greatest cellist. Like all significant achievers, he did not gain his status by talent alone. Even in his nineties Casals practiced hours every day in his home in San Juan, Puerto Rico. His lifetime discipline ended only at death. No one excels at anything—marriage, politics, preaching, athletics, or business—without extraordinary discipline. Unwillingness to pay the price negates many a lofty vision.

Sometimes leaders do not see their dreams come to fruition. Robert Goddard, the pioneer of rocket science, dreamed of space travel, but the material and technology did not yet exist for him to see his dream realized. He spent most of his life in pursuit of his goal, but few scientists took his work seriously. True visionaries recognize that, despite their own incredible dedication, lofty visions sometimes find realization only in future generations. Many worthy pastors find their visions fulfilled during the ministries of their successors.

Each of the elements of a vision mentioned are found in the life of the apostle Paul and in his teaching. Vision must be ministry-focused and Paul's evangelistic passion for both Jews and Gentiles was intense (Rom. 9:3; 10:1; 15:17–20); his discipleship ministry was obvious (2 Tim. 2:2); and his concern for the sick, the poor, and the elderly was exemplary (Rom. 15:25; 2 Cor. 8:6). Vision threatens norms, and Paul's vision of the Gentiles obtaining righteousness by faith, while the nation of Israel was set aside, provoked sharp antagonism in the Jewish society in which Paul was reared and educated (Acts 22:22; Rom. 9:30–32; 11:11). Similarly, Paul threatened the cultural norms of Ephesus (Acts 19:23–29) and many other places. A vision must be large enough to qualify as imaginative but practical, and Paul's vision for Macedonia, Rome, and Spain eminently qualifies (Acts 16:9–10). Worthy vision never tolerates mediocrity; Paul's vision demanded great personal effort and sacrifice. He was never content with what had been accomplished (Phil. 3:12–14). Such great vision necessitated discipline; Paul's personal discipline and the price he paid for enduring ministerial effectiveness shames most of us (1 Cor. 9:19–27; 2 Cor. 11:22–29). In a similar way one could examine the vision of Martin Luther, many notable missionaries, and some contemporary church leaders.

Persistence

Those aspiring to effective leadership meet obstacles. Many, like Moses' spies, will suggest abandoning the dream. The cutting edge of pastoral ministry requires great courage as we approach a new century. Pain invariably accompanies the journey. The fainthearted soon give up and settle into a comfortable maintenance ministry.

We look briefly at the impediments to visionary leadership, not to frighten or to warn, but to bring realism and challenge to those determined to make a difference in our world. Four giants inhabit the land of visionaries; they must be overcome for pastors to effectively realize their vision.

The Comfort of Well-Defined, Familiar Territory

Many pastors experience considerable fear at the prospect of getting outside the prosaic, comfortable walls of their traditions and structures. Traditional values give solace, routine services offer security, and innumerable meetings lend a degree of authenticity. Assuming reasonable pastoral competence and modest statistical increase, the established environment breeds a sense of comfort, much like a warm fireplace on a cold winter night. The known represents security; the unknown spells risk and peril. That illusory sense of comfort, however, presents a monumental obstacle to leaders.

Leaders overcome the natural but deadly desire for a sure thing. Leaders harbor a deep suspicion of cozy, untroubled circumstances, perhaps remembering that the apostle Paul—and many others— took risks and rarely experienced those amenities most Americans treasure. Visionaries do not suffer from the debilitating need to be loved by everyone. They say no to inappropriate demands placed upon them. They often take unpopular stands on important issues.

Genuine leaders do not fear possible failure. Failures represent steppingstones to a brighter future.

Insistence on Immediate, Tangible Results

Few things sap energy and kill vision more quickly than pressure for immediate, tangible success. Temptations to short-circuit long-range, strategic thinking abound everywhere. Business enterprises face pressures to cut costs and increase profits at the expense of research, strategic planning, and market analysis. In a similar way, a thousand urgencies crowd the pastor's schedule. Efforts gravitate to those things that translate into instantly visible results, and strategizing slides down the list of priorities.

Pastors with low self-esteem crave statistical results as a way of proving self-worth. Well-publicized, short-term gains give a false sense of security and success. For example, one church set a new Sunday school attendance record after the pastor spent eight hours on the telephone the previous day urging straying members to be present. Such use of time is obviously ridiculous, and such records are meaningless. In addition, pressure for immediate results can come from unwitting church boards who suffer from myopia. We can no longer afford to sacrifice purpose-driven, long-range objectives for the gratification of quick, short-term results.

Aversion to Interdependence

Many pastors fail because of their antipathy to interdependence and their thirst for power. Some falsely believe that autocratic control determines effectiveness. Love of the pedestal and hostility to interdependence demonstrate insufferable egotism, the pride that leads one to believe in personal, unilateral rightness. Such pastors never tap the rich resources of the laity and have time only for managerial tasks. Ecclesiastical power-wielders rarely, if ever, experience spiritually productive ministries. They are the antithesis of visionary leadership and are vigorously condemned by Paul in 1 Corinthians 3.

Visionary leaders master the art of interdependence. Their churches benefit from the integrated judgments of groups characterized by teamwork and mutual trust. Healthy vision demands a wide-angle as well as a telephoto lens. Such breadth and depth of perspective can be achieved only by those absolutely committed to interdependence.

Commitment to Bureaucracy

When distrust of leadership increases, decision-making bogs down in the quagmire of bureaucratic bungling. Congregations have never distrusted their clergy more than now. This threatens to paralyze definitive action and extinguish vision. The most perplexing question confronting clergy today is how to restore confidence in their leadership. All too often clergy prove themselves untrustworthy, a factor that tends to increase bureaucracy everywhere and add to the burden of many worthy pastors. The integrity of pastors must be so obvious that the congregation does not harbor suspicion. Otherwise, the bureaucratic jungle will abort many a promising vision and condemn to obscurity the most praiseworthy strategies.

Let no one think that breaking down the bureaucracy will be easy, but it is essential! Peters and Austin speak of their senior management meetings: "At each, it seems, some fair share of the time is spent railing against unnecessary bureaucracy. . . . [L]ogically, inescapably, cleaning up the bureaucratic gunk *must be* the number one strategic priority."[12] However, it takes a courageous church led by brave leaders to streamline church bylaws, which in most cases have grown hopelessly cumbersome and inefficient. In the business world "the organizational model known as *bureaucracy* [traditional management] is disappearing, while a new modus operandi called the *ad-hocracy* [participative management] is emerging."[13] The church cannot afford to lag behind.

Today's most effective churches have few standing boards and committees. Decisions do not evolve through a bureaucratic jungle; they are made by those responsible for ministries, freeing church members from the onerous task of interminable meetings. The Community Baptist Church of Alta Loma, California, with five worship services (two on Friday night), dozens of cell groups, and more than two thousand attenders, has no deacons or elders, has one

---

12. Peters and Austin, *A Passion for Excellence*, 368.

13. Philip R. Harris, *High Performance Leadership: Strategies for Maximum Career Productivity* (Glenview, Ill.: Scott, Foresman and Company, 1989), 180.

board that manages facilities and budgets, and entrusts the staff with all programmatic and ministerial decisions. Pastoral care, normally provided by professional staff, is administered through cell group leaders who are the functional shepherds of the congregation. The church operates efficiently; energy is channeled into ministry, not into hacking through bureaucracy.

The Development of Visionary Skills

Visionary skill seldom develops unintentionally. Leaders are not born; they develop and mature in the grueling climate of education and experience. No personal endowment ensures excellence without the discipline of learning and incessant diligence. Pastoral leaders evolve through the tedious, sometimes boring, always challenging task of seizing opportunity, profiting from trial and error, and learning from mentors.

How did the apostle Paul become a visionary leader? His supremacy in leadership emerged through wearisome years of education, decades of experience—including obscurity, the mentoring of Barnabas, and the exercise of personal discipline. No shortcuts lead to leadership excellence.

Cognitive Development of Visionary Leadership

Thousands of pastors simply do not know how to get their churches moving or how to penetrate their communities with the gospel message. They lack missional vision and merely conduct business as usual. Our educational system must share responsibility for such a depressing reality.

Academia has historically undervalued courses designed to produce and cultivate competent leaders. Some have justified this oversight with the erroneous belief that academics cannot contribute significantly to leadership. Similarly, Christian literature on relational ministry and leadership development has been nonexistent until recently.

Now we need a massive effort to reeducate and retrain ministers presently serving churches. School faculties must evaluate their programs and strengthen leadership training curricula. Students must carefully monitor their own education, select courses to include interpersonal relationships, motivation, administration, cross-cultural communication, missional formation, strategizing skills, and leadership development. Pastors must play a desperate game of catch-up or wither further into mediocrity. Fortunately, opportunities abound, literature is available, many large churches give seminars and training, and seminaries offer continuing education programs. Pastors who cannot stomach mediocrity or hemorrhaging churches must learn the strategizing skills of leadership, the discipline most likely ignored in their seminary career.

The cognitive development of visionary leadership skills requires extensive reading on leadership and interpersonal relations, attending leadership seminars offered by churches or professional leadership training companies such as the Center for Creative Leadership,[14] and study at theological seminaries or universities.

Experiential Development of Visionary Leadership

Visionary leaders mature through experience. Would-be leaders must seek leadership responsibilities at every stage of life. "Here is a trustworthy saying: If anyone sets his heart on being an overseer, he desires a noble task" (1 Tim. 3:1). No academic training substitutes for hands-on experience under the guidance of an excellent mentor. Successful mentors impart leadership philosophy, perspective, a behavioral paradigm, and inspiration. This counsel transcends all others: *Find worthy mentors, those noted not for what they overlook, but for what they oversee.* Seldom do pastors rise above the level of their teachers and models. Poor role models invariably produce inept leaders. Few things contribute so heavily to the development of effective leadership as identification with one who models excellence in leadership and who is willing to invest time and share experience with learners.

Trainees for ministry must surround themselves with people dedicated to teamwork and avoid power-wielders intoxicated by their own authority and importance. Leaders learn to cultivate collegial relationships, work at developing consensus, and seek responsibilities open to joint venture. Effective leadership emerges from environments in which people work together in small groups to

14. The Center for Creative Leadership is a rich resource for those studying leadership skills. It is located in Greensboro, North Carolina, with a center also in Colorado Springs, Colorado.

resolve issues and plan strategy. Visionary leadership never emerges in people who merely receive and execute directives from superiors.

Cross-cultural experience adds a priceless dimension to leadership training. Gordon Aeschliman reminds us: "The major cities of the United States are beginning to look as if the world has moved to our very doorstep. Theologies of church growth and strategies of evangelism that are dreamed up in the boardrooms of suburban churches will be irrelevant in such environments."[15] International and interracial churches in large cities will become commonplace in the next century. An inner-city Lutheran pastor in Oakland, California, ministers in a church with sixteen nationalities and languages. As our world continues to shrink and change, the church cannot tolerate pastors with parochial visions. "Foreign" cultures have become the norm in the cities of America, and pastors bear the responsibility of penetrating an unchurched, multinational, and multiracial society in their own communities. Learning how effective leaders operate in a variety of cultures contributes to learning how to lead in one's own environment.

Steps to Creating Vision

Vision must come from pastoral leaders; it seldom—perhaps never—arises from the members. The following steps may serve to facilitate the evolution of a vision for the church.

> Assemble a small group of committed and highly qualified individuals to study the purpose, nature, and structuring of the church. Biblical and denominational guidelines must be considered, along with local church history. Do not rush this vital work for an emerging vision.
>
> Assemble another small group to exegete community and intrachurch culture. Take careful note of the real and felt needs of the church constituency, value systems, prejudices, openness to change, and resources (see chap. 8).
>
> After these groups accomplish their primary purposes, bring the two groups together to form the pastor's visionary and strategic leadership team. Develop clear understandings

15. Gordon Aeschliman, *Global Trends* (Downers Grove, Ill.: InterVarsity, 1990), 114.

about the kind of changes necessary to achieve the church's theological and missional objectives. This becomes the church's vision for the future. Build in flexibility, the ability to adapt to changing circumstances.

At each point test the evolving vision against the criteria for a credible vision: Is it ministry focused? Does it threaten norms? Is it imaginative but plausible? Is it intolerant of mediocrity? Does it require commitment and discipline? Does it lessen bureaucracy, decentralize ministry, equip laity, and generate enthusiasm for the future?

8

TRANSFORM OR PERISH

Churches and Christians today are sadly Laodicean:
complacent, somnolent, shallow, stuffy.
We need reviving.

J. I. Packer

American churches need a transformation that critiques
and changes customary ways of doing business, a spiritual renewal
and reorientation to the purposes of God. Today's humanistic secular wasteland challenges the people of God to be spiritually authentic, culturally sensitive, and missionally minded. Far too often
churches resemble social institutions marked by latitudinarian
thinking, mundane concerns, and narcissistic activities.

Many churches claim orthodoxy but disavow orthopraxy, value
liturgy but depreciate devotion, and affirm the Great Commission
but confine missions to overseas endeavors. Other churches demonstrate their "relevance" by purging the church of everything religious. Honest efforts to package the gospel attractively and build
membership often result in eliminating the scandal of the cross,

deemphasizing the demands of discipleship, and monopolizing resources for narcissistic purposes. Such strategy produces attendance without participation, belonging without commitment, and membership without discipleship. Such models of "success" bear ominous implications for American Christianity.

Many American churches need transformation, and pastors must be primary architects of renewal.

The Traditional Church Model

Historically, churches have relied on a hierarchical model of organizational structure, with high dependency upon clergy for results. The primary work of the traditional church is done within its walls and under its jurisdiction. Professionals do the main work of ministry; laity serve on committees and pay bills. Effort centers on efficient operations, getting the unchurched involved, keeping youth in approved activities, teaching biblical facts and stories, sending missionaries overseas, and conducting innumerable meetings. Pastors and staff initiate various programs and recruit members to run them. Bulletins and newsletters report weekly activities and beg people to staff them, finance them, and participate in them. Ministry focuses on the Sunday school, worship services, meetings, and a variety of activities. Strategy centers on getting people "in here," not on an "out there" invasion of the community. Only rarely does a traditional church have an aggressive evangelism or discipleship emphasis.

Vast sums of money now support ministries that originate and operate outside denominational or church jurisdiction. In a traditional church, these parachurch efforts often threaten leaders who lack control over them. Many people think of their home church as a comfortable place to socialize, provide certain necessary amenities, and enjoy inspiring music and a sermon. However, they tacitly understand that "real ministry" takes place elsewhere.

The conventional church model still exists and will continue, especially in rural and small-town America, but it is passing rapidly from the urban scene. Metropolitan churches unable to think in terms of new prototypes will become increasingly survivalistic, ineffective, and irrelevant. Even in smaller cities, cultural upheaval requires transformation.

Church Transformation Defined

What kind of change constitutes transformation? It is helpful to clarify and reject a few popular misconceptions.

First, transformation must not be confused with the popular understanding of church growth or success in materialistic terms.

Much of today's church planning focuses on producing quantitative indicators of organizational prosperity as opposed to building a faithful community of Christian disciples who proclaim and manifest the life of Christ in a hostile culture. Transformation relates to effective ministry, not numerical increase, though enlarged attendance may be an expected and a natural outcome of significant transformation.

Second, transformation differs from organizational and operational excellence, and bears no relationship to incremental, operational improvements that produce necessary but minimal change.

Many leaders work hard to achieve a congregational tune-up. Churches often use consultants who specialize in making things run more smoothly. Management seminars extol the virtues of operating the church efficiently and attaining corporate orderliness—a worthwhile endeavor. A well-managed church is decidedly preferable to a poorly managed church. Nevertheless, a church may run like a fine-tuned Porsche and yet be marginally effective—or clearly ineffective—in today's world. Transformation is more closely connected to re-creation than managerial competence. Transformation strikes at the core of the church's identity and methodology, not refurbishment of its extant structures.

Third, church transformation is not the intensified effort of greater numbers of people.

Mobilization and motivation of untapped laity resources improve many aspects of church life, but industry alone will not impact our culture for Christ, nor will it bring spiritual renewal to our privatistic and self-indulgent generation. Increased activity may even be antithetical to genuine transformation.

Fourth, church transformation differs from programmatic additions or deletions.

Generally, pastors think of change only in terms of instituting new programs or removing ineffective ones. While genuine transformation inevitably necessitates some of this, renewal cuts into the church's patterns of thought, behavior, foundations, and value systems. Genuine church renewal will not happen through initiating new activities or subtracting others.

What, then, is genuine transformation? The Center for Parish Development, a research and consulting agency specializing in the area of planned church transformation, defines the ultimate goal: "Church transformation is a process of intentional planned change which involves the entire church organization in retrieving its historical grounding, becoming clear about its current situation, exploring its theological heritage and commitment, envisioning a dynamic and creative future, building plans to enable the vision to become a reality, and developing new and more faithful and effective systems that will enable the church organization to manage itself more faithfully and effectively—being informed and challenged by the Gospel at every point along the way."[1]

Stress must be placed upon the process of transformation. Change can never be a *fait accompli*. "Corporate transformation is a process by which organizations examine what they were, what they are, what they will need to be, and how to make the necessary changes."[2] When the church becomes static, it soon becomes stagnant. When leaders stop thinking of change, they inevitably think of maintenance and their churches degenerate into missional lethargy and inertia.

Transformative change is systemic and strategic, challenging the existing structures, programs, and methodology of the congregation. "The important point to remember about cultural change is that behaviors rarely change without a change in the underlying assumptions, values, and attitudes."[3] Organizational traditions form a frame of reference that bends or breaks in transformation. In all cases, real change requires new ways of perceiving, intense theologi-

1. Inagrace Diettrich, *An Evaluation of Approaches to Church Transformation: An Analytical and Comparative Study Funded by the Lilly Endowment, Inc.* (Chicago: The Center for Parish Development, 1991), 3.

2. Ralph H. Kilmann, Teresa Joyce Covin, and Associates, *Corporate Transformation: Revitalizing Organizations for a Competitive World* (San Francisco: Jossey-Bass, 1988), xiii.

3. David P. Hanna, *Designing Organizations for High Performance* (Reading, Mass.: Addison-Wesley, 1988), 159.

cal reflection, careful gathering of data, precise exegesis of culture, fresh vision, new strategy, motivational struggle, intelligent decisions, and follow-through action. Frequently, the process strains and bruises visionaries, and always tests the faith of constituents.

Outlook of the Architects of Renewal

A recurring theme of this book is that the crucial questions of today are theological questions about the message, mission, and demands of the Christian faith, not technological questions about successful marketing and management.

Today's architects of renewal need an outlook that can encompass the demands of an ailing society and inspire the church forward in the Great Commission of Jesus Christ. Some essential characteristics of that outlook are fundamental to spiritual renewal.

Theologically Centered

No hope for spiritual renewal and constructive change can exist without restoring theology to its proper place, a crucial task of ministerial leaders.

In today's ecclesiastical environment, theology has been minimized in favor of methodology, sociology, psychology, and management. For example, the publishers of a leading conservative Christian leadership journal pointed out that less than 1 percent of the hundreds of articles they had printed contained any reference to Scripture or any serious theological component for answers to church problems. Scripture and theology apparently seemed irrelevant.[4] "Theology is quickly dismissed as being divisive, a noncontributive factor to the 'life, unity and purity' of the congregation. . . . The heresy of the contemporary church and her ministry lies in an excessive preoccupation with busyness, public relations, and 'I'm okay, you're okay' sessions without theological direction. Isn't this an effective route to hastening the church's death?"[5]

4. Reported by Os Guinness in his "Guidelines for Plundering" message in Denver, Colo., 21 August 1991. See also *No God But God*, ed. Os Guinness and John Seel (Chicago: Moody, 1992), 151.
5. Carnegie Samuel Calian, *Today's Pastor in Tomorrow's World* (New York: Hawthorn, 1977), 118.

Genuine transformation begins with a recommitment to the centrality of theology in ordering the life of the church. Catalysts of change think theologically and direct others in purposeful biblical study. Most importantly, the required theological centrality is not a simple reaffirmation of orthodoxy—we have quite a bit of that—but a fresh determination to order the mission and the life of the church according to scriptural guidelines.

The absence of serious theologizing reduces churches to mere semireligious fraternities and church members to neopagans. No human action can have a more profound impact upon the church than the decision to make sound theology a prime concern. When theological focus yields to pragmatic and statistical concerns, pastors become technocrats and therapists. Clergy then remove or redefine unpopular scriptural precepts. "Under the impact of secularism, sin becomes merely a psychological concept. We begin to speak, not so much of sinful behavior as of unhealthy, neurotic, or repressive behavior. Popular preachers redefine sin as low self-esteem and insist that the Christian life is a divinely sanctioned 'ego-trip' and that pride is a virtue and humility a vice. In less blatant forms such views appear to underlie a great deal of what we are hearing in our churches today. Sin is out, self-help is in."[6] Other offensive or unpopular doctrines are similarly made palliative. However, the architects of church transformation must return to primitive apostolic positions: the ultimate problem is sin (Rom. 3:10); the definitive answer is Christ (Eph. 2:8, 9). The power and consequences of sin are eclipsed only by the power of the cross and the grace of God.

American culture downplays contemplation, study, and theological reflection in favor of activism, thus giving credence to those who suggest the ministry is a profession of "accredited mediocrity." Rabbi Hillel's words may be worth remembering: "An ignoramus cannot be a righteous person."[7] The current loss of confidence in the institutional church may well be due directly to the weakening of theology in the practice of Christian ministry.

---

6. C. Leonard Allen, Richard T. Hughes, and Michael R. Weed, *The Worldly Church: A Call for Biblical Renewal* (Abilene, Tex.: Abilene Christian University Press, 1991), 65.

7. Cited by Rabbi Joseph Telushkin in *Jewish Literacy* (New York: Morrow, 1991), 555.

Culturally Informed Exegesis

The architects of church transformation integrate painstaking cultural exegesis with theological orientation. "We need the courage to adapt to a new jungle, a new uncharted world in which the accomplishments of the past have produced a global society that desperately needs a new visitation from the people of Jesus."[8] That new jungle must be recognized, studied, and evangelized, without sacrificing theological integrity. Failing in this task, church leaders will never see a church transformation with both local and global implications.

The following factors are vital to understanding our current situation.

Community demographics. Relevant questions include: What kind of a community do we live in? What racial, economic, ethnic, gender, age, family, and moral diversity contribute to the community? What is the percentage of single-parent families, the divorced, widowed, and aged who struggle for survival and acceptance? How many latch-key children are there? How many unemployed, poor, and/or homeless people live within the immediate neighborhood of the church? How many people of the community are white-collar workers? Blue-collar workers? How has the population's pluralism affected churches, schools, and other institutions in our neighborhood? How does transiency affect this community? What demographic changes have taken place in the last ten years and what additional changes can be anticipated in the next twenty-five years? Demographic trends must be recognized early because a church that constantly plays catch-up cannot possibly hope to make much difference.

Demographic study of inner cities is of particular importance. These areas have become melting pots for many diverse groups. Few church leaders have the courage to invade these wildly heterogeneous communities and, moreover, suburban ministry often pays richer numerical dividends. Viable church ministry in the coming century must penetrate diverse ethnic, racial, and international groups, particularly in our large cities. Failing this task ensures missional catastrophe.

8. Gordon Aeschliman, *Global-Trends* (Downers Grove, Ill.: InterVarsity, 1990), 11.

The mobility of today's parishioners adds considerably to the task of community exegesis. Many people live great distances from the church they attend. Large churches typically draw people from many different types of community. Some churches attempt to minister to a population that no longer exists, while the present population receives no attention from what has become an irrelevant church. The typical answer to this dilemma has been for churches to flee to the suburbs in an attempt to recover their lost constituency, leaving the mission field destitute of witness.

Community values. Relevant questions include: How has the passing of a churched culture affected community values? What are current community statistics on the availability and use of pornography, drugs, and deadly weapons—especially among children and youth? What community or governmental services exist for unwed mothers, the poor, substance abusers, and other desperate individuals? What schools are available, and what are their educational standards? What are the available recreational facilities and programs? How much leisure or discretionary time is available for families? What values are held by the community on abortion? How many churches are there and who attends them? What are the television-viewing habits? What are the region's sports events and teams and how are they supported? Answers to such questions reveal community values and can help the church determine its strategy.

For example, if inadequate recreational facilities and programs exist, the church may find building a gymnasium feasible as both a service to the community and as a vehicle for effective ministry. The First Evangelical Free Church of Rockford, Illinois, maintains a community center with a variety of ministries some miles from its main church. If the community does little to counsel and provide for unwed mothers or substance abusers, such ministries could be extremely worthwhile, and need not be located in the church building. Far too many churches run programs according to traditional values no longer present, instead of developing ministries that address genuine community needs.

Congregational identity. Congregational exegesis is figuring out what the congregation has become, why and how it has become that way, and identifying its problems, needs, possibilities, and resources. Cultural exegesis includes the study of denominational and local history, doctrinal positions, missionary commitments, pastoral contributions, leadership adequacies and weaknesses, dynamics of power (politics), decision-making processes, program successes and failures, preferences in worship style and content, educational achievements, and the degree of homogeneity and/or heterogeneity. No credible strategy can evolve without such scrutiny and evaluation of a church's history and present reality.

Failure to understand congregational identity causes leaders to press for unrealistic goals or to misinterpret the group's capacities for achievement (note Luke 14:28–39). Congregations then become disillusioned and embittered and lose the will to press for any meaningful objectives.

In short, the message of the gospel must be contextualized, but not contaminated by the culture. Information previously discussed can be of help in understanding the church's current global status, as can many of the books listed in the bibliography.

Forward-looking

Architects of church transformation constantly think in terms of strategy for the future—next week, month, year, and decade. They direct others away from the past and from a status-quo mentality into a forward-looking mode of vision and planning.

Church regeneration never occurs in an environment where people contemplate the "good old days" or focus only on present circumstances. Pastors who are futurists experience a deep and continuing dissatisfaction with the status quo, an unrest that matures into an earnest congregational quest for alternatives. They create a church atmosphere conducive to change through a few crucial activities.

First, futurists celebrate past achievements only in terms of providing a foundation for the realization of tomorrow's goals. Many people revel in accomplishments for purposes of self-congratulation and self-satisfaction, but futuristic leaders think of the past only as a base for far greater attainments. For example, one church observed the completion of a major building program with the theme "The Past Is Prologue." The milestone was only a stepping-stone to further action.

Second, futurists and strategists generate new ideas—lots of them. Some concepts inevitably prove too idealistic and unfeasible.

Some suggestions evolve into other, better plans. Some notions die a natural and well-deserved death, but this does not matter, because good leaders never tie their egos to their ideas and so they do not take offense at rejection of their proposals. They risk failure, but in doing so they stimulate discussion, evaluation, and possibility thinking. Genuine leaders think and speak constantly of opportunities and inspire people to seize them.

Third, futurists motivate their constituencies through personal integrity, constant encouragement, confidence-building, and collegiality. No leader, regardless of his gifts or charisma, can achieve church transformation without widespread cooperation and participation. Spiritual leaders galvanize and infuse a congregation with a spirit determined to achieve great things for God.

Fourth, futurists preach with a positive and optimistic approach. In many respects, pastors resemble coaches; they cheer on and instruct. Tom Landry, former coach of the Dallas Cowboys, defines coaching as "making men do what they don't want, so they can become what they want to be." A good coach takes great pains to teach fundamentals and instill winning attitudes, much as Nehemiah approached his gigantic task with a "we-can-do-it" and "we-will-do-it" perspective. Enthusiastic preaching emphasizes God's intentions for the church and inspires people to be more cooperative and excited about the future. Optimism is a contagious disease—as is pessimism—and futurists breathe confidence and enthusiasm about the future!

Fifth, futurists are not slaves to pragmatic concerns for numerical prosperity. Earnest efforts to package Christianity in appealing terms frequently result in the domination of utilitarian concerns. God can become a useful tool for people who seek the good life, and the church can become little more than a successful business enterprise. Effective strategists reject popular pragmatism in favor of proper missional orientation.

The description of an effective church as articulated by Kennon Callahan is a conspicuous example of devotion to pragmatism.[9]

9. Kennon L. Callahan, *Twelve Keys to an Effective Church* (New York: Harper and Row, 1983). This book, along with the *Leader's Guide* and the *Planning Workbook,* and his follow-up book, *Effective Church Leadership: Building on the Twelve Keys* (New York: Harper and Row, 1990) are used widely, especially within the United Methodist Church and the Evangelical Lutheran Church in America.

Callahan's "twelve keys" are grouped into two categories: relational sources of satisfaction, emphasizing such things as objectives, visitation, dynamic worship, small groups, leadership resources, and participatory decision-making, and functional or organizational sources of dissatisfaction, emphasizing programs and activities, accessibility, visibility, parking and landscaping, space and facilities, and financial resources. Inagrace Diettrich correctly evaluates Callahan's keys: "The [recommended] long-range planning process is a quasi-consensus building and goal setting process which does not include serious educational efforts to deepen the theological awareness and commitment of church people or to expand their expectations regarding the nature and purpose of the church. . . . The process is a short-term 'tune-up' of the existing situation, which does not intend to bring about, and will not bring about a fundamental reorientation in the life and practice of the church."[10]

Callahan studiously avoids theological formulations—apparently in the belief they would be divisive—in favor of pragmatic principles. He offers no valid research data other than his own experience, and his books contain no documentation or footnotes. "When certain characteristics of growing churches become the 'holy grail,' simply because they work, not because they are biblically sound, then pragmatism has become an idol."[11] Many church critics unwittingly endorse such idolatry.

Disciple-making Concentration

The fundamental task of the church is disciple-making (Matt. 28:18–20), but American churches rarely require either commitment or discipleship from members, and many churches make only feeble efforts to teach discipleship principles. Those who desire renewal must reverse the modern trend and bend themselves to an unpopular and sometimes costly endeavor: the reproduction of true disciples and insistence upon discipleship. Worthy leaders ask and require more, not less, of their church members.

"Successful" religious entrepreneurs have become the church's celebrities and heroes, but they often appear uninterested in the

---

10. Inagrace Dietterich, *An Evaluation of Approaches to Church Transformation* (Chicago: The Center for Parish Development, 1991), 20.

11. Bill Hull, *The Disciple Making Pastor* (Old Tappan, N.J.: Revell, 1988), 40.

quality of their products. Failure to accentuate discipleship has fostered a dangerous inclusivism, and encourages a form of neo-paganism that is infecting our churches. Members refuse submission to scriptural authority, mutual accountability, or the Holy Spirit's tutelage. Genuine architects of transformation must reverse this trend and concentrate on making disciples through effective preaching, teaching, one-on-one efforts, and training co-laborers. The Calvary Community Church of Westlake Village, California, stresses a six-fold commitment to its members: worship attendance, participation in a growth group, a ministry endeavor, financial stewardship, a family night, and personal time spent with God.

The wise words of Kenneth Strachan, written before the current emphasis on church growth, tell us what pastors should be about:

> Let us begin as our Lord began, with discipleship. The time has come to give up the unscriptural and ultimately profitless driving for numbers of converts or church members and to return to the fundamental condition Christ laid down for membership in His church. . . . Here we simply reaffirm that for His church Christ sought only disciples, and that to the end of His earthly ministry He did not lay down any lesser condition. His demand is one of absolute commitment for every Christian—this is Christ's goal and God's best for every man. . . .
>
> The important thing to remember is that the call to membership in the church can be on no condition other than discipleship. And the relationship of pastor to His people must always be that of disciple to disciple in the making of disciples. . . .
>
> Any decision to settle for the discipleship of a select few and to accept second-class status for the rest is the death of mission. It merely caters to the spiritual pride and ambition of the few and relegates the majority to ineffective passivity.[12]

Leaders who fear the sifting process that invariably accompanies emphasis upon discipleship condemn themselves to a lifetime of ministerial futility and surrender any hope of being positive agents of change, though ironically they may attain statistical success.

12. R. Kenneth Strachan, *The Inescapable Calling* (Grand Rapids: Eerdmans, 1968), 88–89.

A lengthy, involved description of a disciple is not necessary here.[13] Most basically, disciples live under the authority of the Word of God. Or as Strachan has written: "Discipleship begins with an unconditional commitment to Jesus Christ and with the acceptance of a sentence of death."[14] Nothing so transforms and empowers the church as Christians who live their lives according to biblical teaching. Nothing so enfeebles the church as hordes of pewsitters who refuse submission to the plain teaching of Scripture. Spiritual leaders who truly desire to transform the church major in disciple-making.

Church-scattered Emphasis

Ministry belongs to the entire church family, those who live daily in unchurched, irreligious, and hostile environments. No one states this critical need more forthrightly than Bill Hull: "The pastor who does the ministry rather than training the people to do it, behaves in an unloving and noncaring fashion. . . . When the pastor must control the ministry and save the best parts of it for the professional staff, people will continue to be weak and parasitic."[15]

Pastoral agents of change shift the emphasis from the church gathered to disciples scattered. Genuine ministry necessitates abolishing professional elitism, affirming the believers' priesthood, and entrusting laity with both authority and responsibility to carry out the mission of the church in neighborhoods, factories, offices, schools, hospitals, coffee houses, playgrounds, marketplaces, and a thousand other places removed from church buildings.

The implications of this aspect of transformation mean that leaders enter into a collegial and supportive role with constituents, a role that does not jealously monopolize people's time, money, or talents for the institutional church. Also, it means that some conventional church activities may die for the lack of staff and participants—a paralyzing thought for traditionalists. The rapidly growing New Song Church in Walnut, California, thrives without a Sunday school, but aggressively promotes a network of cell groups that

13. Hull includes an excellent description of a disciple in *The Disciple Making Pastor.* See chapter 3, "The Product."
14. Strachan, *The Inescapable Calling,* 89.
15. Hull, *The Disciple Making Pastor,* 129.

stress teaching, fellowship, worship, prayer, power, ministry, and evangelism.

Evangelism and pastoral care, formerly the almost exclusive domain of the clergy, is shared freely with many individuals gifted in evangelizing, caring, serving, and giving. Parishioners understand that laity, not a professional staff, are primary instruments of one-to-one ministry. Such a paradigm shift is crucial as the church becomes larger.[16] The church becomes a vital worship and training center for those in various stages of spiritual discipleship.

Churches and leaders who continue to focus on the church gathered rather than on the church "scattered" develop a fortress mentality and will not make much of a difference in their communities or in our world. To be sure, a lot of good things have been done and will be done with the old mindset, but transforming the culture for Christ will never be one of them. The architects of church transformation know that their task is to equip people for a vast range of opportunities in a malevolent culture and to free them to get involved in noninstitutional ministries, including parachurch efforts, which can no longer be perceived as threats and intruders. The church must concentrate on corporate worship and maturing disciples, preparing the saints for the work of the ministry (Eph. 4:12).

Holistic Ministry

Transforming architects promote radically different ministerial structures; they focus on a holistic ministry to the community and the world. The desperate social needs of our culture mean that churches must be involved with the poor, the sick, and the homeless. The inner-city St. Barnabas Episcopal Church in Denver, Colorado, faced a real crisis a few years ago. The congregation was diminishing; the sanctuary was unsafe for occupancy. Rather than flee to suburbia, the congregation floated bonds, remodeled, and stayed where they had been for one hundred years. Now the church's ministry includes twenty alcohol and drug-abuse pro-

---

16. Carl George emphasizes this crucial concept in his book on the metachurch model. See *Prepare Your Church for the Future* (Tarrytown, N.Y.: Revell, 1991).

grams, Project Angel Heart (which provides hot meals to terminally ill people), and numerous other ministries to the community.

Our shrinking, interdependent, and rapidly changing world means that churches must redefine their concept of missionary work. Church members do things that have largely been left to governmental agencies. The pastor of Our Savior's Lutheran Church of Denver, Colorado, strikes the right note: "We're not here to be served or to protect our institutional survival, but to reach out and respond and to be concerned with the needs and hurts of our neighbors." Inner-city health clinics staffed by Christian volunteers, including physicians and nurses, are joint projects of numerous churches and Christians. Churches sponsor food banks, clothing closets, child-care centers, homeless shelters, and immigrants. Church members form hospice care groups for the terminally ill, including AIDS patients. Such efforts obviously provide evangelistic opportunities, but evangelism does not represent the solitary concern. Holistic ministry represents genuine orthopraxy.

Overseas short-term missionary opportunities abound and the new model of ministry seizes them. For example, the Faith Evangelical Free Church in Milford, Ohio, budgets about two thousand dollars per year to involve one of their pastors in an overseas missions project each year and aggressively encourages laity in short-term, cross-cultural missionary efforts. A medical team, including a dentist, podiatrist, orthopedic surgeon, and children's dentist, recently spent two weeks in Mexico. Thirty laity have gone overseas within the last few years in a variety of ministries, revamping the concept of missions and revitalizing missionary vision.

Literally hundreds of opportunities must be seized by today's Christians, for only through coupling meaningful care for human needs with a clear presentation of the gospel can our society be transformed for Christ. The Vineyard Christian Fellowship in Westchester, Ohio, has pioneered a concept known as "Servant Evangelism" in which members scatter throughout the city to serve in a great variety of tasks, free of charge, thus opening the door to effective evangelism. Pastor Steve Sjogren reports more than forty such efforts within the past year, including free gift wrapping during the Christmas season at a major shopping center, free laundry service at a nearby laundromat, free car washes, and free Polaroid photos given away in parks. Within one year more than four hundred people have had opportunity to witness to sixty thousand people in this nonconfrontational method of evangelism. The church has grown from forty people to eighteen hundred in less than five years, while planting five new churches in surrounding communities. In doing such things, the church is transformed from an isolationist, religious fraternity to a dynamic group of witnessing disciples.

A mature, noncompetitive, and collegial relationship exists with other churches and parachurch ministries. A level of cooperative struggle eclipses anything that traditional churches experience, but in this new partnership the church fulfills its God-given mission to the world. In addition, the church is transformed into a vital worship and training center for those in various stages of spiritual discipleship.

Synopsis of Church Transformation

Attribute	Traditional	Transformational
Ideological Mission	Worship, fellowship, evangelism, edification, caring	Worship, fellowship, evangelism, edification, caring
Methodological Mission, Corporate Strategy	Traditional worship, programs, conducting meetings, providing services, celebration	Innovative and contemporary worship, fellowship, disciple-making, caring, small groups, cells
Functional Strategy	Getting people into church, emphasis on church gathered, professional pastors, elitism, programs, limited social efforts	Equipping people for ministry in the world, emphasis on church scattered, every-member mission within culture, risk-taking
Missionary Strategy	Church planting, in-church evangelism, altar calls, mass evangelism, literature efforts, apologetics	Holistic, social services coupled with evangelism, servant evangelism, short-term lay missions, relational, friendship evangelism
Theological Posture	Weak, marginal, subordinate to methodology and marketing considerations, theoretical	Strong, central, preferential over methodology and marketing considerations, practical
Membership Standards	Emphasis on decisions, little commitment required, relaxed attitude toward biblical lifestyle, low expectations	Clear discipleship agenda, emphasis on commitment, obedience to scriptural teaching, high expectations

Structural Posture	Centralized hierarchy, rules, by-laws, bureaucratic control and decision-making, suspicious of leadership	Decentralized network, collegial, participative decision-making, trusting of strong leadership
Time Orientation	Emphasis on tradition, continuity, status quo, past and present structures	Emphasis on the future, opportunities, planning, vision, strategy
Cultural Awareness	Marginal, little exegesis, culturally ignorant or insensitive	Careful exegesis of culture, adaptive to culture, yet without compromising message

Barriers to Church Transformation

The architects of church transformation face formidable barriers. Awareness of obstructions to change may provide clues to overcoming the natural resistance that people experience in facing threats to their religious environment. The following hurdles must be faced and overcome by pastoral architects of change.

Denial of the Need for Change

Many people simply disavow the need for change, particularly when a church has a long and stable heritage. Ruts often become comfortable. Denial of need is probably the most pervasive of all obstructions to church renewal.

Traditional practices are often identified with theological correctness. For example, for decades a Sunday evening service and a Wednesday night prayer meeting represented evidences of conservative Christianity in many churches. Proposed changes in these criteria of orthodoxy were perceived as attacks upon the core of Christianity. However, altering such forms has nothing to do with jeopardizing fidelity to sound doctrine. Many may still disagree with this claim.

Denial of the need for change has its roots in fear: "Most people fear it [change], for they are comfortable and secure with the status quo. The real issue is whether one will permit fear of the unknown to paralyze us into inaction. . . ."[17] Patient reassurance is an exact-

---

17. Philip R. Harris, *High Performance Leadership* (Glenview, Ill.: Scott, Foresman and Co., 1989), 169.

ing and time-consuming endeavor, but essential to the process of change.

Inadequate or Incapacitated Structures of Authority

Hopes for church transformation frequently collapse because of a disregard for authority. Our culture has grown accustomed to contempt for authority, a state of affairs affecting the church as well as our governmental agencies. Few churches today have clear, scriptural teaching and congregational understanding about authority:

> recognition of God-ordained authority of the church's spiritual leadership, authority intended to "direct the affairs of the church" (1 Tim. 5:12),
>
> the biblical requirement of congregational respect and submission to leaders who conduct themselves within scriptural parameters (1 Thess. 5:12–13; Heb. 13:17),
>
> the need for church discipline and accountability to one another. The absence of accountability within the church allows individualism, moral pollution, and defiance of authority, which lead to antinomianism and makes leadership ineffectual.

For many churches the first effected change must necessarily be proper structures of authority. Malfunction here means failure in virtually all other objectives of transformation.

Lack of Vision

The lack of a compelling vision makes meaningful change impossible. Few tasks are more crucial and difficult than sharpening a vision of a desirable future—imagineering. A thousand urgent chores pressure pastors to postpone the development of a credible, imaginative image of the church's tomorrow. This topic has been covered in detail in chapter 7.

Absence of Tenacity

Weak personal resolution, the inability to persevere, makes transforming action unlikely or impossible. Many pastoral leaders fail simply because they meet resistance, get discouraged, and then divert their attention to easier tasks. Tenacity is a quality of leadership essential to change efforts. "They [change agents] may even come to feel that they are walking into a wall time after time after time. The key is to have the desire, commitment, and simple doggedness to keep walking into that wall until it finally collapses. We believe that effective change influencers exhibit a unique 'stick-to-itiveness' that, over time, makes their vision salient and begins first to create and later helps to carry out the formal change process."[18] The average American pastoral ministry lasts less than three years, an impossibly short time to effect worthwhile change. Such pastors can never hope for meaningful change. Church transformation seldom comes easily and never quickly.

Poor Relationships and Defective Communication

Jesus reminded the disciples that they were sent out as sheep among wolves and therefore must be "as shrewd [Greek *phrōnimos*, wise, thoughtful, prudent[19]] as snakes and as innocent as doves" (Matt. 10:16). The context of this verse differs substantially from our present argument, but the principle remains the same. True church reformers must be wise, thoughtful, and prudent; they must possess a searching intelligence combined with sound judgment.

Pastors with closed, one-way, authoritarian styles of communication must expect extraordinary and well-deserved resistance. Those who meet resistance with defensiveness, censoring, punishment, or arm-twisting will only engender greater hostility. On the other hand, those who open the process and participate in two-way communication will likely avoid the shock of adversarial relationships and aborted attempts at change. The decision-making process in most organizations, particularly churches, demands the cultivation of collegial relationships and careful nurturing of strategic plans to ethically influence those whose enthusiastic support is vital to transformation.

18. Ibid., 137.
19. See Gerhard Kittel and Gerhard Friedrich, *Theological Dictionary of the New Testament,* abridged (Grand Rapids: Eerdmans, 1985), 1279.

Steps to Initiating Transformation

Renewal will not happen without pastoral leadership. Passive pastors will never see church revitalization. Pastors may consider the following steps to initiate transformation in their churches.

Decide how to communicate the emerging vision (chap. 7) and enlist widespread support of the congregation. Be patient and persevering. Expect antagonism, conflicts of interest, and criticism. Sometimes it is necessary to modify the vision. A lesser vision that succeeds is better than a grandiose vision that fails.

Work hard to correctly appraise and tap resources and capabilities. In cooperation with all spiritual leadership, identify the driving forces in favor of change and analyze the resisting forces. Sometimes trial balloons must be launched and sometimes those with closed minds must be bypassed.

Think through a strategy of education and action and expect to make mid-course corrections.

Lead the church to make decisions to implement the strategies to fulfill the missional objectives.

Follow through the decisions with dogged determination.

9

GROWTH—SERENDIPITY
OR STRATEGY?

He who delights in contemplating
whereto he has attained, is not merely sliding back;
he is already in the dirt of self-satisfaction.

George MacDonald

Pastors of stagnant churches face three options: sacrifice dreams and settle for maintenance, move to a different place of ministry, or become a catalyst for renewal and growth. The first alternative is distasteful, even deadly, and the second option is a last resort, a choice that often results from frustration. Many pastors choose to move every three years or thereabouts, but usually find no greener grass or more fertile field. Fruitful pastoral ministry involves both spiritual and numerical growth. The alternatives to growth are unacceptable.

178

Most churches grow when given appropriate leadership and sound ministry. Some congregations in the inner city or in rural America may not grow much numerically. Still, the absence of growth usually indicates leadership malfeasance or inadequacy and church complacency.

Archimedes said: "Give me a place to stand, and I will move the earth." Where do pastors stand and what propels a church to grow? What primary pastoral actions serve to attract God's blessing and facilitate growth?

Rather, out of the vast range of possible pastoral activities, what few endeavors pay the richest dividends in terms of healthy growth? Certainly, actions of leaders in church renewal, summarized in the previous chapter, stimulate church growth as well. Along with those crucial functions, pastoral leaders who desire progress concentrate efforts in the following areas of ministry.

Galvanize Church Commitment

Effective pastors commit themselves to church growth and galvanize their churches to make the same resolution. Such a statement may seem obvious, but many churches and pastors aspire only to maintain the status quo—a shocking reality.

One survey of five thousand pastors revealed that fewer than half of them gave high priority to planning and implementing church growth. "Rather than growth, their priorities were centered on maintenance."[1] Some churches flatly oppose growth. People often have deep feelings of attachment to outdated buildings, traditional methods, governmental bureaucracies, forms of service, and the like. Indeed, "most small churches are not likely to grow substantially either in affluence or size. Because their members don't want them to. The desires and needs of these members set definite limits on the quantitative growth of many, if not most, small churches. Denominational units seeking to 'improve' the effectiveness of small churches by increasing their size are often frustrated by small church members who need a small scale experience."[2] Such

---

1. C. Peter Wagner, *Leading Your Church to Growth* (Ventura, Calif.: Regal, 1984), 44.
2. Douglas Alan Walrath, *Finding Options for Ministry in Small Churches* (New York: National Council of Churches, 1981), 24.

churches put pastoral leadership to an ultimate test: can a commitment to growth replace a comfortable but noxious rut?

One young pastor's experience typifies the problem. Nearing graduation from seminary, he visited a stable (stagnant?) church in the East. During his stay he was told that the church of about one hundred needed new blood and the membership wanted an evangelistic effort to reach the community and enlarge the church family. The graduate enthusiastically accepted the call, fully believing that great opportunity awaited him. All went well for the first year and a half. Evangelistic home Bible studies were beginning to bring in a harvest, and the pastor cultivated young couples who moved into the area. Suddenly, however, things went sour. Some new people accepted places of leadership and some old-timers felt bypassed and complained that young people were "taking over the church." Growth threatened the positions of those accustomed to the strings of power. People grumbled that the pastor spent too much time with new families and did not "make the rounds" as previous pastors had done. The young pastor discovered the truth: many parishioners desired the status quo. Paradoxically, many of the same people who criticize growth also castigate pastors who do not produce growth.

In traditional churches, a conducive climate and commitment to growth must be established before a church body is ready to receive and assimilate new members. Commitment to growth seldom comes easily, except in newly formed congregations. This means that in order to energize a congregation to grow, pastors must work toward the following essential objectives.

Maturity in Leaders

Prior to major outreach ventures, pastors may need to focus on the maturation of those who hold key positions of church leadership. God gives the increase; people do not. In agriculture, only God can make a seed grow and produce a harvest, but better farmers normally produce better crops. In ministry, God sees fit to bless deeply spiritual leaders. The recognition and development of spiritual gifts and graces inevitably produce enthusiasm for reaching the unchurched. Genuine evangelism according to the Great Commission means making disciples, not converts, and "the church that has established a disciple-making flow will be healthy and will grow, and

God wants this for both His church and a lost world."[3] This is the essence of Paul's counsel in 2 Timothy 2:2. Stagnation in many churches is due to insufficient spiritual maturity among members. Adding new believers to a body of spiritual dwarfs promotes unrest and hostility.

Earn Respect of Congregation

Significant change meets resistance when it takes place before leaders achieve love and approval from the constituency, but congregations who highly esteem (1 Thess. 5:12–13) their pastors will follow them anywhere. No shortcut or substitute exists for earning the respect and love of parishioners. Pastors who fail to earn the enthusiastic support of their constituency cannot hope for church growth. Respect and love cannot be demanded; they can only be earned through wise and godly leadership, which often takes time.

Consensus in Goals and Values

Many pastors err in plunging into activities that produce growth without first developing consensual goals and values. When members feel that a few power wielders set agendas and monopolize decisions, dissatisfaction may be expected. Disenfranchisement of members may be a major cause of resistance to growth, but a meaningful plan developed through cooperative effort reduces the discomfort of change. Any significant division over the mission, values, strategic plan, and specific goals creates a climate unfavorable to growth. Unless people enthusiastically come to consensus on the necessity of reaching their community, there is little chance of healthy growth.

Efficient Structures and Organization

Activities that produce growth are counterproductive if leaders neglect the structures and organization that must assimilate the growth. A dysfunctional government never produces desirable results. Ninety percent of American churches have inefficient by-laws and cumbersome bureaucracies that cripple leaders, hinder decision-making, and enfeeble congregations. Particular attention must be given to biblical standards for spiritual leadership; few things sink progress so quickly as unqualified leadership.

3. Bill Hull, *The Disciple Making Pastor* (Old Tappan, N.J.: Revell, 1988), 135.

Congregational Education

The uninformed must be patiently educated about church growth because ignorance increases anxiety and resistance. Many people simply do not understand the scriptural mandate and principles of church growth and that to resist evangelism and disciple-making is to place oneself in opposition to the fundamental purposes of God.

Some recalcitrant people refuse education and leadership and, regrettably, these people must be bypassed. A few obstinate individuals cannot be allowed to bully the entire church and frustrate plans for growth. However, if a sizable minority of people adamantly and unalterably oppose progress, growth is unlikely or impossible. Usually, patient and wise leaders can tactfully overcome resistance and galvanize a team.

Diligent effort in these five areas of ministry should lead to church commitment to growth. If a pastor provides constructive leadership in these essentials for a reasonable length of time and there emerges no commitment to growth, the pastor must decide whether to settle for a maintenance ministry or "shake off the dust" and seek another place of service. Opportunities for effective pastoral ministry abound—sixty-two thousand American churches are currently without pastors[4]—and to waste one's time indefinitely with obstructionists who refuse leadership and reject God's will is simply not good stewardship. Moving is a distasteful activity for those who enjoy roots, but it sometimes becomes necessary.

Clarify a Philosophy of Growth

Opposition to growth is at odds with the purposes of God. This is axiomatic; no extensive biblical defense of church growth is offered here.[5] Donald McGavran strikes the right note: "Any truly Christian theology in the most responsive world ever to exist must demand church growth. Any fully Christian theology in America,

4. Earl Pavin, *Missions USA* (Chicago: Moody, 1985), xi.

5. Excellent biblical defenses of church growth include "God Commands Church Growth" in Donald A. McGavran, *Effective Evangelism: A Theological Mandate* (Phillipsburg, N.J.: Presbyterian and Reformed, 1988), and "The Mandate to Make Disciples" in Donald McGavran and Win Arn, *Back to Basics in Church Growth* (Wheaton: Tyndale, 1981), and others.

where at least four-fifths of the population is either very nominally Christian or totally non-Christian, must pray for, give to, and work for substantial church growth."[6] Devoted Christians share the passion of Jesus: "when he saw the crowds, he had compassion on them, because they were harassed and helpless, like sheep without a shepherd" (Matt. 9:36). Indeed, "the harvest is plentiful" (Matt. 9:37), and true Christian disciples desire to see more workers and a greater harvest. "There is no way for a Christian to avoid open search for the lost. The real Christian candidly avows that he desires men to become fellow disciples and is bending all his efforts to that end."[7]

If church growth through making disciples is an indisputable premise of Christianity, leaders need clear convictions about its meaning and how it is to be achieved, convictions compatible with Scripture. The following principles represent an effort to assist a church struggling to make sense out of the many conflicting church growth philosophies and to formulate a philosophy consistent with Scripture and Jesus' Great Commission.

Growth the By-product of Ministry

Numerical growth should be the result of faithful service to Christ in the multifaceted work of the ministry. Our job is to minister well; Christ will build his church.

Some churches experience statistical success, but not as the result of effective ministry, and "results in themselves are not a proof that God is pleased. It is possible to win attendance contests and disseminate the Gospel and see results; all these activities can be done without pleasing God! Such results can be achieved by deceptive gimmicks or for purely personal satisfaction."[8] Bigger crowds sometimes result from advantageous location, charismatic personalities, promotion, technological expertise, marketing gimmicks, scintillating programs, and literally dozens of other methods. Many—perhaps most—of these strategies are not harmful, but they have little if anything to do with effective ministry. They have no

---

6. McGavran, *Effective Evangelism*, 109.
7. Donald A. McGavran, *Understanding Church Growth* (Grand Rapids: Eerdmans, 1970), 42. The chapter "God's Will and Church Growth" is especially recommended.
8. Erwin W. Lutzer, *Failure: The Back Door to Success* (Chicago: Moody, 1976), 25.

value at all unless they buttress ministry; they become liabilities if they substitute for ministry.

Pastors who truly desire the kind of growth that matters must stress bedrock, ministerial activities: faithful preaching-teaching, evangelism, disciple-making, worship, fellowship, and caring for and meeting needs of people. Those who slight ministry in favor of courting crowds simply do not serve well. God desires the multiplication of saints, not the convening of a crowd.

Equipping Precedes Growth

Faithful service to the few precedes responsibility for the many: "Well done, good and faithful servant! You have been faithful with a few things; I will put you in charge of many things" (Matt. 25:21). If pastors would give themselves faithfully to shepherding and edifying those whom God has already entrusted to their care, God may well bless them with more people who need nurturing. Richard Taylor strikes a somber note: "Too many young pastors have been poisoned in their thinking before they even take their first charge. They dream of the megachurch, and do not want to settle into such a lowly role as shepherding a flock. . . . They think only of leading a church that is exploding in size."[9] Contaminated ambition has sunk many a pastoral ship, and has crippled church growth as well. Scripturally, oversight takes precedence over outreach.

The vast numbers of professing Christians and church members who have never discovered their spiritual gifts reveal leadership ineffectiveness and dereliction of duty. Few things so stimulate church growth as a body of believers exercising their spiritual gifts in their communities. Pastors with growing churches help people discover, develop, and utilize their spiritual gifts in the work of the ministry.

One fair-sized church in the western United States has a paid staff of one hundred, including part-timers. Such churches demonstrate a disturbing trend, a tendency to give up on the task of equipping and mobilizing laity in favor of simply paying professionals to do the church's work. Genuine ministry disciples, equips,

9. Richard S. Taylor, *Principles of Pastoral Success* (Grand Rapids: Francis Asbury Press, 1989), 76.

mobilizes, and entrusts many people with significant responsibilities. The atmosphere of this kind of a church favors church growth.

How do pastoral leaders accomplish the important work of helping people discover, develop, and utilize their gifts? Pastors regularly preach and teach on the spiritual gifts. They challenge and counsel people individually regarding their spiritual gifts. Leaders pair people expressing interest in a spiritual gift with others who obviously have a similar gift. Many testify that discovering and development comes by observing and doing and, therefore, people must be provided opportunities to use their gift in a great variety of church ministries. Leaders encourage and free people to become involved in ministries outside the institutional church. Administrative streamlining liberates laity for ministry; if people spend excessive time on committee or board meetings, they are hindered in using their spiritual gifts. Peter Wagner suggests five steps necessary for discovering one's spiritual gifts: explore the possibilities, experiment with as many as possible, examine your feelings, evaluate your effectiveness, and expect confirmation from the church.[10]

Trust God and Work Hard

Two approaches to growth usually fail. The first error depends excessively on human effort. In some churches, massive efforts are mobilized to respond to society's wants. Such churches find themselves in a mad whirl of aerobics, volleyball nights, ski outings, camping weekends, retreats, and activities too numerous and varied to mention—all in heroic attempts to attract more people. In doing all of these good things, many churches and their leaders fail to recognize the need of and depend sufficiently on importunate prayer, spiritual warfare, study of Scripture, teaching, one-on-one discipling, expository preaching, and various spiritual disciplines.

Anything that substitutes for scriptural necessities ultimately fails. The church's battles are primarily spiritual and will not be solved by technology or mere human exertion. We have been entrusted with spiritual weapons for our spiritual battles (2 Cor. 10:4). Absolute trust in the sovereignty of God and utilization of the means of grace promote healthy growth.

10. C. Peter Wagner, *Your Church Can Grow* (Ventura, Calif.: Regal, 1984), 82.

On the other hand, some err through passivity, rationalizing their ineptitude or laziness by claiming dependency upon God. The Holy Spirit has an affinity to work through well-prepared, innovative, and diligent human vessels. Jesus said "the harvest is plentiful but the *workers* are few. Ask the Lord of the harvest, therefore, to send out *workers* into his harvest field" (Matt. 9:37–38, emphasis added). The apostle Paul "worked night and day laboring and toiling" (2 Thess. 3:8). Some people try to excuse their slovenly habits, administrative sloppiness, and inattendance to the spiritual disciplines by claiming dependency upon God.

Effective pastoral ministry fuses unflagging human labor with trust in God and reliance on the spiritual means of grace for church growth.

Lead Without Manipulation

Leaders think clearly, prioritize correctly, galvanize constituents, and direct churches to become what God wants them to be. Leaders possess a sense of what God wants done and display a steely determination to get at it. C. Peter Wagner testifies: "I have observed that pastors who tend toward being leaders, whether or not they are also administrators, will most likely be church growth pastors. Pastors who see themselves to be administrators and use that kind of management style tend to be maintenance-oriented. Making sure that the church functions smoothly and harmoniously is usually where a manager is. A leader, on the other hand, is willing to take risks and upset the status quo in order to move out toward new horizons."[11]

Spiritual leaders are governed in everything by the spiritual realities that underlie their calling: persevering prayer, wisdom, diplomacy, consistency, and evident fruit of the Spirit. Spiritual pastors refrain from authoritarian manipulation, viewing that method of governing as antithetical to genuine leadership: "If a pastor ever has to cajole or beg or threaten a congregation in order to gain leadership, it is a sure indication that he or she does not have it and will probably never get it."[12] The graces of spiritual leaders are more in

11. Wagner, *Leading Your Church to Growth*, 89.
12. Ibid., 111.

evidence than their gifts and this produces congregational willingness to follow.

Enhance "Moments of Truth"

Pastors who truly desire church growth thoroughly examine the quality of experience that parishioners and visitors experience on Sunday mornings and at other such "moments of truth." Some churches attract people, others repel people. Some pastors create a climate of beauty, warmth, enthusiasm, caring, and acceptance. Other pastors unwittingly engender an atmosphere of coolness, objectivity, and insensitive unconcern. "We define climate in the church as the combination of factors which determines how it feels to be a part of the church."[13] Frankly, the corporate personality of some churches sickens and rebuffs.

The totality of a church atmosphere is too multifaceted and complicated to examine at great length here.[14] Pastoral leaders would profit from a lengthy brainstorming session with their lay leaders to uncover components that attract or repel people. We can suggest only a few of the factors that contribute to people's evaluation of their church experience.

Cleanliness and Orderliness

Clean and orderly facilities are necessary to church growth. As the commercial reminds us, "You only get one chance to make a first impression." If a visitor's first impression is bad, seldom does the church get a second opportunity. Few things disgust people so much as nurseries with dirty sheets and slovenly or unqualified attendants; restrooms with no soap or towels and dirty toilets or sinks; ushers with grimy hands or bad breath; unmown, weed-choked lawns and parking lots littered with trash; unvacuumed floors and pews with week-old bulletins in them; Sunday school classes marked by lack of discipline.

13. Ron Jenson and Jim Stevens, *Dynamics of Church Growth* (Grand Rapids: Baker, 1981), 98.

14. Excellent literature is available on this subject, including Melvin L. Hodges, "Creating Climate For Church Growth," in Donald A. McGavran, ed., *Church Growth and Christian Mission* (New York: Harper and Row, 1965), "Climate" in Jenson and Stevens, *Dynamics of Church Growth,* and others.

Disorder, dirt, and carelessness do not communicate caring, beauty, and invitation. A pastor can find no better place to start than here in looking to improve the church's atmosphere and the quality of the people's experience who visit and attend the church.

Warm Relations

The degree of congeniality or aloofness communicated to people who are not the in-group has an instant effect on them, positive or negative.

A fundamental drive exists in all people, a desire to be accepted and thought of as important. To feel as though you are invisible is an unpleasant experience. Most people do not and cannot bash their way into acceptance. They require others to reach out to them, make them feel important, and include them as family members.

Pastors who lead their churches in growth promote a hospitable, receptive, and gracious spirit throughout the church family by such actions as mingling with people before services, talking with people, demonstrating interest in their lives, and welcoming newcomers to the fellowship. They work hard to learn names and needs, not merely to promote church growth, but because they genuinely care about people. Leaders give serious thought about how the church can recognize and receive visitors warmly—without making them feel conspicuous and being sure to avoid the cliquishness that afflicts many churches and stymies their growth. Pastors truly desirous of church growth carefully exegete James 2:1–12 and preach, teach, and model the truths of such texts.

Optimism and Enthusiasm

A healthy atmosphere conducive to growth reveals an optimism and enthusiasm in the church family, particularly among the church staff, including lay leaders and Sunday school teachers. People want to be part of something significant, where there is a sense of expectancy and excitement about what is going on and what will take place in the future. An indifferent or defeatist attitude among the church staff sounds the death knell to church growth. A sanctified discontent with the status quo, coupled with a joyful expectancy about the future, communicates to the community that to be a part of this church is to see God at work transforming human lives.

Many pastors do not realize that they convey negativism. Sermons often tend to focus on what Christians should not do. Conversations in boards and committees bog down on problems, and difficulties are perceived as obstacles that give rise to frustration and futility, not as opportunities for God to work. People do not want to board the Titanic; they look for a place that radiates confidence, positivism, and cheerfulness. The church that communicates the attitude that its greatest days lie just ahead attract people who hunger for evidence of spiritual vitality.

Authentic Preaching

No single action of pastors attracts or repels people so directly as the pulpit ministry. Visitors come to church hoping for spiritual nourishment and will not return if the sermon is boring, irrelevant, or wearisome. Established members with deep ties to the church may stick through the ministries of poor pulpiteers, but growth—both spiritual and numerical—is unlikely without good preaching. Indeed, "if a preacher will not—or cannot—think himself clear so that he says what he means, he has no business in the pulpit. He is like a singer who can't sing, an actor who can't act, and an accountant who can't add."[15] Never underestimate the cumulative effect of good preaching. Many of today's sizable churches can attribute their growth mainly to good preaching.

The late psychologist George Crane shocked many preachers by saying: "Many clergymen couldn't rate even a D in any high school public-speaking class! You are an ally of Satan if you drive parishioners away from church by your stodgy public-speaking methods."[16] The torrential outpouring of words week after week simply makes no difference in thousands of churches. Mediocrity in the pulpit stunts church growth, wastes thousands of hours, and injures the spiritual lives of millions of Americans. What kind of preaching scratches where people itch and effects both spiritual and numerical growth?

15. Haddon Robinson, *Biblical Preaching* (Grand Rapids: Baker, 1980), 39.
16. Quoted in "The Shepherd as a Preacher: A Word to Speak," *Focal Point*, vol. 6, no. 3 (July–Sept. 1986). *Focal Point* is a quarterly publication of Denver Seminary.

Thematic Preaching

Effective preaching features major biblical themes and identifies, illuminates, underscores, and applies one of God's profound revelations. Bad preaching is pedantic, marked by fractured thinking and trifling concerns.

John Bunyan's philosophy of preaching was encompassed in his desire that others might see, as he saw, what sin, death, hell, and the curse of God mean, and also that they might discover, as he had discovered, what grace, mercy, forgiveness, and the love of God can do for men and women. Too much modern preaching occupies itself with minor details of obscure texts instead of with such themes. Oratorical excellence or scholarly brilliance never make up for basic irrelevancy. The preacher's business is to seize important, timeless, biblical truth and bring it to bear upon the drama of life.

The temptation to substitute catchy contemporary topics for dominant scriptural themes seduces many modern preachers. Some pastors have capitulated to superficial sermonic fads in the name of relevance. Growth produced by superficial or sensational preaching will be characterized by nothing more than spiritually anemic crowds.

Inspirational Preaching

Effective preaching inspires. Many preachers assume that if the listener learns information found in scholarly books or commentaries they will be better people and more Christ-like, but rarely do erudite and factual essays make much difference in human lives. Explanation of subjects or texts serves extraordinarily limited purposes and is not the main business of preaching. Many suffering parishioners sit through tedious presentations of minutiae without ever recognizing anything of vital concern to them because the preacher has merely played trivial pursuit with biblical texts.

Every good sermon helps the listener to understand the Bible better, but the real business of preaching is to bring about change in human lives. For that to happen, the springs of human motives must be touched. A good sermon animates, quickens, persuades, elevates, and impels. Only truth made alive in the preacher and empowered by the Spirit transforms people.

Good preaching does not whip, it encourages. People come to church to find forgiveness, comfort, and healing, not more guilt. They desperately need a message of salvation, grace, and hope. Paul wrote: "For you know that we dealt with each of you as a father deals with his own children, encouraging, comforting and urging you to live lives worthy of God, who calls you into his kingdom and glory" (1 Thess. 2:11–12). Much more preaching should encompass such a philosophy. Such preaching stimulates growth.

Passionate Preaching

Has fear of emotionalism contributed to a cold, dead formality in preaching? Hardly anything engenders revulsion so much as dispassionate objectivity. Charles Spurgeon declared: "Even fanaticism is to be preferred to indifference. I had sooner risk the dangers of a tornado of religious excitement than to see the air grow stagnant with a dead formality. A lukewarm sermon sickens every healthy mind. It is dreadful work to listen to a sermon, and feel all the while as if you were sitting out in a snowstorm or dwelling in a house of ice, clear but cold, orderly but killing."[17] Or, as John Stott reminds us: "More to be feared than emotion is cold professionalism—the dry, detached utterance of a lecture which has neither heart nor soul in it."[18] Listeners hunger for evidence that preachers believe their own message. Perhaps our greatest pulpit need is for the warmth of spiritual fire. Carefully crafted sermons help, but spiritual preachers aflame with truth make the real difference in people's lives.

Truthful Preaching

Preachers sometimes compromise truth with expediency by taking texts out of context, twisting interpretation to fit prejudice, and citing authorities to buttress fallacy. No dividends achieved by such tactics justify the contamination or dilution of truth. Most listeners cannot be deceived by oratory for long. Deluded people become disillusioned people, and then absent people. Preachers cannot escape the necessity of a rigorous integrity in the handling of Scripture.

---

17. Charles Spurgeon, *All-Round Ministry* (reprint ed., Carlisle, Penn.: Banner of Truth, 1972), 173.
18. John R. W. Stott, *The Preacher's Portrait* (Grand Rapids: Eerdmans, 1961), 58.

"This is what we speak, not in words taught us by human wisdom, but in words taught by the Spirit, expressing spiritual truths in spiritual words" (1 Cor. 2:13).

Sometimes pastors preach what they do not believe, but wish they did. Some things sound great in sermons and make profound impressions, but simply are not true. Some sermons are attractive, even elegant, but play fast and loose with reality. After listening to one eloquent presentation, an unmoved listener responded: "That's a bunch of sentimental slop." Unfortunately, he was right. Much of our religion, hymnody, and preaching is sentimentally magnificent, but theologically weak. Rhetoric and passion that conflict with spiritual truth is contemptible and self-defeating.

Major in Evangelism

Many authors identify three kinds of numerical growth in churches: biological, transfer, and conversion growth. Biological growth is the addition of the children of church members to the church population, a process that tends to be slow. Transfer growth refers to the increase in membership of Christians who leave one church and join another. Conversion growth is membership increase resulting from the effective evangelism of the unchurched, the lost, and the vast number of nominal, nonpracticing professing Christians (one hundred million Americans, by some estimates).

A number of megachurches have been produced from transfer growth and their presiding pastors often become celebrities and "experts" on church growth.[19] In expanding suburbia, transfer growth is natural and the absence of it is abnormal, but transfer growth may mask evangelistic indifference and inertia. Many churches lack genuine leadership in producing conversion growth, and their leaders spend no time equipping people to share their faith.

Spiritual maturation precedes evangelistic efforts. Nevertheless, healthy church growth means effective evangelism. The church growth movement, heavily criticized in its early years for stressing numerical growth, has properly shifted its emphasis to evangelistic

19. Charles Colson, "We must forsake the worship of Christian megamen," *Christianity Today,* 5 Feb. 1990, 96.

growth. Donald McGavran, the father of the church growth movement, "admitted shortly before he died last year [1990] that because the term *church growth* had become so loaded with unfavorable baggage, he had not used it for two years, preferring instead to speak of 'effective evangelism.'"[20] Pastoral leadership includes mobilizing, equipping, and commissioning people to win their neighbors and friends to Christ.

What actions produce the most spiritual fruit? No generic answer can be applied to all situations. Pastors and their spiritual leaders must look carefully at a variety of approaches, experiment, and decide where to devote their efforts. In all cases, aggressive pastoral leadership is necessary.

Prepackaged Programs

Pastoral leaders may consider a number of evangelistic programs that have worked in other churches with varying degrees of success. These include Campus Crusade (religious surveys and the Four Spiritual Laws), Evangelism Explosion (D. James Kennedy, Coral Ridge Presbyterian Church in Fort Lauderdale, Florida[21]), the Navigators Bible studies (Colorado Springs, Colorado), Friendship Evangelism (Joe Aldrich), and others. One of these approaches may be productive, depending upon a number of factors. None of them, however, seem to be practical and effectual everywhere, and all need some adaptations for most communities. Pastoral modeling seems to be an integral part of any program's success.

The Willow Creek Model

In recent years a number of churches have adopted the strategy of the Willow Creek Community Church in South Barrington, Illinois. This church has embraced a philosophy of ministry distinctly different from that of traditional churches (see chap. 4). Evangelism centers on Sunday services geared to non-Christians, an innovative approach that includes drama, need-oriented sermons (as opposed to expository teaching directed mainly to Christians), and contemporary music (as opposed to traditional hymns). Members

20. "Church Growth Fine Tunes Its Formulas," *Christianity Today*, 24 June 1991, 47.
21. This church grew from seventeen members to twenty-five hundred in twelve years with about 10 percent of its members involved with Evangelism Explosion.

are encouraged to make friends with unbelievers and invite them to a Sunday service where the gospel message is presented in nonthreatening terms. Other weekday services are directed to Christians. Pastor Bill Hybels and his staff speak the language of the yuppie culture, dominant in the local community.

Undeniably, the design and tactics of Willow Creek have been evangelistically effective and the church breathes an excitement found only in churches that regularly see conversions. Perhaps enough testing of the model has not yet been done to determine its suitability for different types of communities. It seems apparent that significant modification would have to be made for nonyuppie, rural, small-town, or inner-city ministry. A few have been outspokenly critical of this philosophy.

Home Bible Studies

Many churches focus their evangelistic efforts on home Bible studies conducted by church members in their own communities. Generally, such groups number ten to fourteen people and meet weekly. Enduring relationships often come out of such regular gatherings. Christian bookstores feature abundant and excellent study materials.

This approach to evangelism has considerable merit. Growth tends to be slow, but if leaders do their job well, the church may be characterized by solid disciples rather than by shallow converts. Training leaders takes a significant amount of time, but pays handsome dividends. However, certain pitfalls must be avoided. Unhealthy relationships sometimes develop unless leaders exercise competent oversight. False doctrine finds fertile soil in small groups that lack well-trained leaders. Evangelistic orientation frequently gives way to mere cliquishness, hobnobbing with friends—what Stott calls "a good gossipy get-together over a hot cup of tea." Despite the obstacles, neighborhood Bible studies represent a firmly grounded, scriptural methodology.

Special Programs

Many churches experience evangelistic results from a wide assortment of special services or efforts. Children and youth programs, including Vacation Bible School, under competent leadership, pay rich dividends. Churches with excellent youth ministries often sustain considerable transfer growth in addition to the fruit of the ministry itself. Many parents, concerned about their children, choose churches almost solely on the basis of the quality of youth programs. Men's evangelistic breakfasts or women's luncheons with the best speakers obtainable prove effective in many churches. The atmosphere in such events usually is low-key; high-pressure tactics to get quick decisions usually backfire. Most churches have abandoned the evangelist-led, two-week services each spring or fall, but participation in citywide crusades like those held by Billy Graham produce results. The prolonged prophecy conferences that were so popular a generation ago have fallen into disfavor in most places, possibly because so many widely heralded prophetic interpretations already have been proven conspicuously wrong.

Competent pastoral leadership means creative and active effort to reach the community. Pastors have the responsibility to evaluate the community and help the church tailor an evangelistic ministry accordingly. In major medical centers (e.g., Rochester, Minn.) this could include an intensive hospital ministry. In places where young people gather for spring breaks (e.g., Fort Lauderdale, Fla.) a beach ministry might be appropriate. In some communities populated with retired people (e.g., Sun City, Ariz.) special activities and programs for senior citizens can be very fruitful. A prison, if the community has one, can be fertile soil for the gospel. Some churches have a coffee house in the inner city, staffed by those trained in personal evangelism. Some churches staff an unwed mothers' home. Drug or alcohol ministries bear fruit in major cities. Other churches find success with recreational activities or community social events that include a simple presentation of the gospel. Seminars oriented to a great variety of needs can be of exceptional value. Probably most of today's successful evangelistic efforts are those conducted outside the confines of a church building, though the Sunday school and various youth programs bear fruit.

All evangelistic efforts should be given careful thought and preparation. No program is better than a distasteful one. Shabby efforts frequently drive people away from the church. It is important that pastors pay attention not merely to the evangelistic effort itself, but also to a qualitative follow-up plan, remembering that the goal is not decisions, but disciples.

Ineffective Efforts

Evangelistic tactics that seem to be largely ineffective include media ministry (high costs in time and money), telemarketing (impersonal, time-consuming),[22] and direct mail (high costs, low value of unsolicited mail), though a few churches seem to succeed in these efforts. Most churches do not have the resources to do any of these things well and all of them lack one essential ingredient of successful evangelism: the building of quality relationships. Few people respond to button-holing tactics where no prior friendship has been established.

Personalize Spiritual Care

Obviously, dramatic changes in the way people live and the changing nature of the pastoral role have radically altered visitation and spiritual care ministry. Gone are the days when pastors routinely visited and provided pastoral care in the homes of all church members (the famous Southern Baptist preacher, Robert Greene Lee [1886–1978], reportedly made seventy-five calls a week).

Nevertheless, this bold assertion shocks us: "A successful pastor does not need the pastoral gift. The fact is, very few senior ministers of large, growing churches do have the gift of pastor. . . . The point is that not everyone who has the *office* of pastor needs the *gift* of pastor."[23] How can pastors equip others if they lack the requisite skills themselves? Can one have a shepherd's heart without a shepherd's gift? Can pastors preach relevantly and effectively if they remove themselves totally from pastoral care? Perhaps much of our trouble—particularly the secularization of the church—stems from the fact that many hold pastoral offices without pastoral gifts.

Of course, as a church becomes larger, direct attention to every parishioner from the senior pastor ceases to be practical; indeed, it soon becomes impossible! Routine care calls must be delegated to

---

22. The inadequacies of "Here's Life: America" are well-documented. See "A Church Growth Look at Here's Life: America," Win Arn, ed., *The Pastor's Church Growth Handbook* (Pasadena, Calif.: The Church Growth Press, 1979), 44.

23. Arn, *The Pastor's Church Growth Handbook*, 156–57.

staff members, lay elders, or others trained to do this visitation. Contemporary pastors generally have no time for survey calls, door-to-door canvassing, or social calls. Yet, even the busiest pastors must aggressively institute, supervise, and participate in pastoral care to ensure healthy church growth.

The church's visitation and care ministry depends on many factors: the size of the church, the abilities and size of the pastoral staff, the number of trained and active lay elders, the demographics of the congregation (number of shut-ins, elderly, hospitalized), the number of weekly visitors, the opportunities of the community, other pastoral responsibilities, and so forth—the list is almost endless. In large congregations, the senior pastor may be involved only in some crisis calls, hospital calls, or one-to-one visitation with people during a lunch hour meeting or at a parishioner's place of business. Busy pastors also make judicious use of the telephone. Sometimes the personal attention of the senior pastor may be limited to the pastoral staff, elders and/or deacons, and the seriously ill or deeply troubled, but in these situations the pastor must be competent to provide spiritual care.

The important point is not the degree of personal care rendered by senior pastors in megachurches, but rather the fact that in all healthy churches, regardless of size, pastoral care and one-to-one ministry takes place. Healthy and continuing growth greatly depends on how well spiritual care is provided. The current trend toward producing quantitative growth while neglecting spiritual care is a truly ominous development as we approach a new century. Yet, "the pastoral office is by definition a shepherding task that involves not just a single meeting with the flock, but continuing oversight and feeding. . . . Shepherding cannot be done at a sterile distance, with automated telephone answering services, computerized messages, and impersonal form letters. By definition there cannot be an absentee shepherd. There can be no mail-order or mechanized pastoral service, because pastoring is personal. It is not just public talk, but interpersonal meeting where richer self-disclosures are possible."[24]

The greatest problem created by numerical growth is how to adequately provide personal, spiritual care to so many people. Few

24. Thomas C. Oden, *Pastoral Theology* (San Francisco: Harper and Row, 1983), 171–72.

megachurches excel in this critical task; some have completely given up the attempt, to the harm of many needy people.

Steps to Stimulating Growth

Several factors contribute to church growth and form a foundation for the blessing of God.

Evaluate the church's commitment to growth, especially such ingredients as the maturity of lay leadership, compassion for the lost, respect and affection for pastoral leadership, a clear mission statement that focuses upon reaching the community, clarification of church values, development of a strategic plan, specific goals, organizational structures, and congregational education about the desirability and principles of growth. If the church commitment to growth is weak, pastors must concentrate their efforts upon these foundational stones of ministry before healthy growth can be expected.

Clarify personal and church philosophy of growth. Be certain that growth is desired as the by-product of effective ministry, that nurturing and equipping people takes precedence over the courting of crowds, that quiet dependency upon God and diligent hard work go hand in hand, and that leadership does not degenerate into manipulation.

Concentrate efforts on enhancing the atmosphere of the church, thereby creating a climate conducive to church growth. Work hard to achieve authentic preaching, preaching that majors on biblical themes relevant to people's lives. Evaluate various evangelistic methods and programs; decide where to focus church efforts. Some experimentation may need to be done. Stress excellence in personal, spiritual care, and especially in the identification, development, and use of spiritual gifts.

10

PERSON-TO-PERSON PASTORS

The power of a life, where Christ is exalted,
would arrest and subdue those who are bored to tears
by our thin version of Christianity.

Albert Edward Day

At the end of the twentieth century, shepherds are being axed by their flocks in record numbers. A 1988 study among Southern Baptists found that more than 2,100 pastors were fired by their churches during an eighteen-month period, 116 each month, a 31 percent increase over the rate found in a 1984 study.[1] About half of the ousted pastors leave the ministry and go into other kinds of work. Other groups reveal similarly tragic statistics. The top reason cited for forced terminations in pastoral ministry is relational problems between the pastor and lay leaders.

1. *Savannah News-Press,* 10 Feb. 1990.

In the secular world, 80 percent of people who fail at work do so because they do not relate well to other people. In business, the loss of customers relates directly to customer satisfaction—which is a relational issue. "No matter what anyone tells you, when you lose business, it's almost *always* a relationship problem."[2] Similarly, in pastoral ministry, the most basic cause of ineffectiveness and failure is an inability to build and sustain meaningful collegial relationships with the church's lay leaders. Many pastors simply do not realize the pivotal importance of relationships.

Healthy relationships precede effective ministry. Certain kinds of ministry may take place outside the church without vital relationships, but pastors cannot experience continuing effectiveness in their churches without developing and sustaining significant, friendly relationships. Strained or shattered relationships with alienated people thwart meaningful ministry.

The most fundamental responsibility of all pastors is to relate to people in such a way that the authentic Christian message becomes incarnated. Such relationships must be established, nurtured, and maintained. Pastors who earn respect and love become living letters, known and read by their congregations, as the apostle Paul knew so well.

Scriptural Emphasis on Relationships

God created us in his own image, as relational beings. God intends for us to relate to him: "For none of us lives to himself alone and none of us dies to himself alone. If we live, we live to the Lord; and if we die, we die to the Lord. So whether we live or die, we belong to the Lord" (Rom. 14:7–8). Sin alienated us from God. Scripture records the effort and sacrifice of God to restore the relationship he originally intended. The Old Testament laws were given to regulate and strengthen relationships with God and neighbor.

Christ founded the church to be an organic fellowship, a community of people who relate vertically to God in worship and obedience and horizontally to one another in interdependence and

2. James A. Autry, *Love and Profit, the Art of Caring Leadership* (New York: Morrow, 1991), 40.

unity—with all relationships characterized by the love of Christ. God's people relate to one another as indispensable parts of a body (1 Cor. 12:12–16). The church should be in "one accord," presided over by those who "set an example for the believers in speech, in life, in love, in faith and in purity" (1 Tim. 4:12). The communion of the saints includes the relational activities of sharing and carrying each other's burdens (Gal. 6:2), encouraging one another daily (Heb. 3:13), meeting together regularly (Heb. 10:25), breaking bread together (Acts 2:42), and laboring together in God's vineyard (1 Cor. 15:58). All Scripture pertains to relationships with God and neighbor.

Pastoral Productivity and Relationships

The productivity of ministers depends heavily on being surrounded by persons who are accepting, loving, encouraging, and reproving. Believing in God's best for us, supportive people stimulate us to godliness, mend our shattered egos, forgive our trespasses, tolerate our inconsistencies, and model God's grace for us. We seldom rise above the expectations and quality of care provided by friends. Lone rangers suffer a lingering, painful, and ignominious ministerial death.

Those in Christian ministry can never accomplish much of significance without an Onesiphorus who refreshes (2 Tim. 1:16), a Phoebe who helps (Rom. 16:1), a Priscilla and Aquila who risk their lives (Rom. 16:3), a Barnabas who encourages (Acts 4:36), and scores of others like them who seldom receive the credit they deserve. Wise pastors cultivate such relationships. Spiritual health and a fruitful ministry depend upon quality relationships with those who join with us as co-laborers in God's work. "As iron sharpens iron, so one man sharpens another" (Prov. 27:17).

Some clergy protest that they are too busy for such in-depth relationships. The only necessary reply to this objection is that neither Jesus nor the apostle Paul was too busy to spend quality time developing meaningful relationships. Do we have more urgent responsibilities? Without relational skills and healthy relationships, pastors set themselves up for failure in ministry. Pastors must learn to build and sustain sound relationships.

The Foundation of Relationships

The admonition "know thyself" dates more than six hundred years before Christ.[3] Obedience to this sage advice forms a necessary foundation for all relational skills. Failure to know and understand oneself prevents one from knowing and understanding others, or from self-disclosing to others—qualities that are indispensable and beneficial to relationships. Before excellence in ministry is possible spiritual leaders must diagnose their own inner world to discover traits that block the development of meaningful relationships.

A penetrating look at oneself and a candid appraisal of strengths and weaknesses in personality and character can be threatening. Furthermore, we like to be around people who reinforce our good characteristics, and we avoid people that draw attention to our dark side. Early in life when we learn that we cannot talk openly about certain inner realities, we erect walls and wear masks to screen our worst traits from public view, and eventually we may come to repress the truth about ourselves. Worthwhile interpersonal relationships depend on the mutual sharing of internal realities—what a person thinks, feels, values, loves, honors, hates, fears, desires, believes in, and is committed to. Unless we truly understand these things about ourselves we cannot communicate meaningfully or build valuable friendships.

Successful ministers have the courage to examine their own blind spots and character flaws. Self-examination enhances a person's competence, identity, and relational skills, and reduces susceptibility to problems of ego and power.

Scapegoating Forbidden

Effective pastors know something that ineffective pastors do not: it is the "in-here" problems rather than "out-there" problems that thwart meaningful relationships and productive ministry. Unsuccessful pastors often practice scapegoating, the projection of internal problems onto other people or circumstances.

Scapegoating enables people to see themselves as blameless and virtuous, sometimes because facing the truth about themselves is

3. Inscription at the Delphic Oracle, from Plutarch *Morals*. However, the phrase is most frequently associated with Socrates.

too painful. Denying or rationalizing away responsibility for their own problems, they fantasize about different circumstances (a new location or building) or different associates (better deacons), which they think would propel them to success.

Somehow it never occurs to many people in ministry that their barrenness or their conspicuous difficulties are the end product of their own personality defects. "The complex psychological forces that go to make up the leader's personality provide the real key to his or her behavior. Thus, core themes in a leader's 'inner theater' cause him or her to choose certain courses of action, and these themes hold the key to success or failure as a leader."[4]

Scapegoaters fail, though they may be sincere, hard workers and practice their denial in ignorance. Pastors must come to grips with their own personality, correct glaring flaws, and seek to become whole persons.

Character Flaws That Handicap Ministry

Other traits also hinder effectiveness in Christian ministry. Only a few of the most common disabling traits are identified here.

Low Self-worth

Research demonstrates a significant correlation between passivity and high scores on the Ministry Scale of the Strong Vocational Interest Test.[5] Apparently, the idealized image of the ministry attracts passive, insecure people with low self-esteem. These people may subconsciously see the nurturing, highly visible, and authoritative positions in ministry as opportunities to bolster their faltering sense of self-worth. Fragile egos often prompt people to seek the limelight, or positions of power, or high academic degrees to convince themselves and others that they are worthwhile persons. Many Christian ministers unwittingly seek this false pedestal of prestige and authority.

Efforts to prove self-worth may drive many people but seldom do they serve a beneficial purpose in ministry. People in ministry with low self-esteem are particularly susceptible to self-deception. They

4. Manfred F. R. Kets de Vries, *Prisoners of Leadership* (New York: Wiley, 1989), 9.
5. Donald Smith, *Clergy in the Cross-fire* (Philadelphia: Westminster, 1978), 109.

may try to prop up their feeble psyche, cover their desperate feelings of inadequacy, or atone for their subconscious sense of deficiency.

Weakness, compromise, and behavior dictated by the will of other people may be the result of low self-esteem. Paradoxically, many of the opposites of these traits may be traced to a minister's attempts to compensate for low self-esteem: an unwillingness or inability to compromise when necessary, uncooperative or stubborn behavior. Low self-esteem breeds an abnormal desire for both affection and control, dangerous for those in ministry. Some pastors flee from church to church throughout their lifetime without ever realizing their problem.

Egocentricity

An egocentric person is perennially concerned with the self—with one's own thoughts, feelings, plans, and environment—rather than with others or with God. Such a person is introverted in a truly negative sense, that is, "to concentrate one's interests upon oneself."[6] Confirmed egotists display an inordinate sense of self-importance, but deep inside they often feel inadequate—a crippling limitation. Pastoral ministry requires meaningful relationships with many people, something difficult for an egocentric person to achieve, or to think worthwhile.

Egocentric people generally desire to avoid deep, substantial, and lasting relationships or, if they desire them, they are unable to develop and sustain them. Such relationships threaten their sense of internal security. Sometimes they subconsciously reason: "To know me—to really know me—would be to reject me." Ludicrous as it sounds, many pastors would love their jobs if only they didn't have to face the terrifying prospect of relating to people.

In addition, sometimes those who are preoccupied with themselves are given to excessive introspection, moodiness, and melancholy. A certain amount of self-analysis is healthy and necessary for self-understanding, but an excessive self-preoccupation is crippling. Not only are such people incapable of proper concern for others, they are often also discouraged, depressed, and even morbid in their outlook on life.

6. Introvert (v), *The American Heritage Dictionary*, 2d college ed.

The Guru Mentality

Many pastors discover that the intoxicating power of organizational control and the domination of people's lives bolsters their sense of self-worth. Frequently, the prerogatives of leadership seduce and defile, according to Lord Acton's famous dictum: "Power tends to corrupt and absolute power corrupts absolutely." History offers many examples: King Saul, Napoleon, Hitler, Idi Amin, and James Jones to name a few. Such people cease to be leaders; they become gurus, dictators, and power wielders.[7] Tyrants desire to subjugate so that they may dominate. Control is the breath of life to a guru.

Power wielders often suffer from paranoia, particularly fear of the loss of control. For these people, every idea is tied inseparably to their ego. To reject the guru's ideas, plans, or goals is synonymous with rejecting the person, a bitter blow to individual pride and a threat to the much-coveted pedestal and ability to control. This intensifies adversarial relationships and the leader becomes increasingly determined to win. Authoritarian behavior accelerates dramatically in these circumstances because a failure to overpower pains the psyche of those afflicted with the guru syndrome.[8] "It's no wonder that paranoia is considered to be one of the major diseases of leadership."[9] Those determined to lord it over (Greek *katakyrieúō*, 1 Pet. 5:3) constituents cannot excel in Christian ministry. A fall from this elevated position is inevitable.

Autocratic personalities crave success, especially statistical, measurable success. Materialistic goals tend to shove more intangible, spiritual goals to the sidelines. All perspective about a humble position of service to God is lost. Autocratic personalities often come to believe that they are superior supersaints—gurus. "Too much admiration [and power] can have dire consequences for the leader's mind: he or she may eventually believe it all to be true—that he or she really is as perfect, as intelligent, or as powerful as others think is the case—and act accordingly."[10] Unfortunately, many of

---

7. See the classic book on leadership by James Burns, *Leadership* (New York: Harper and Row, 1979) for an excellent discussion of the difference between leaders and power wielders.

8. James Jones, who led 913 people to their deaths in Guyana, is a tragic case in point.

9. Kets de Vries, *Prisoners of Leadership*, 39.

10. Ibid., 37.

their undiscerning followers also come to believe in their infallibility, promoting still further the guru syndrome which obstructs ministry.

In their drive to succeed, win, and control, autocratic ministers become manipulative and exploitative. However, once constituents realize they are being manipulated and exploited, the tyrant's days are often numbered, except among exceptionally weak and submissive people. Authoritarian behavior often provokes a spirit of rebellion or hostility in constituents. Only the feeble and compliant will allow a demagogue to prevail for long.

The scathing words of Jesus call us to account for this attitude: "Woe to you Pharisees, because you love the most important seats in the synagogues and greetings in the marketplaces" (Luke 11:43). Those who covet authority and power over people surrender all hope of excellence in ministry. They settle for the shabby adulation of helpless and acquiescent people. Outwardly, autocrats may appear self-sufficient, but inwardly they feel deprived, empty, and alienated. Power, advancement, and prestige take precedence over people, servanthood, and ministry. Gurus run roughshod over people in pursuit of their own interests. They attract sycophants. Their ambition, manipulation, exploitation, and intolerance make meaningful ministry impossible.

Unresolved Guilt

For some, Christian ministry may be an unconscious means to atone for weakness or inadequacy and win God's approval, whose unconditional love they cannot otherwise accept. Inwardly they may feel, "If I give my life to Christian ministry I will make up for the bad person I really am." Past sins or a sense of unworthiness often impair a pastor's usefulness. For these people, ministry becomes an attempt at self-atonement.

Many pastors attempt to motivate laity by making them feel guilty, often because the pastors themselves feel guilty about their unconquered sins or underlying inadequacies.[11] Many sermons

---

11. See *No Condemnation: Rethinking Guilt Motivation in Counseling, Preaching, and Parenting*, by S. Bruce Narramore (Grand Rapids: Zondervan, 1984). Narramore makes a distinction between objective guilt, guilt feelings, and godly sorrow. The appendix "Guilt in Preaching" is particularly helpful.

major in scolding people; frequently these tongue-lashings are no more than projections of the preacher's own guilt.

Novices in ministry often have a tragically unrealistic outlook on themselves and the church. They typically think that they can and must measure up to the superhuman pastors of megachurches who have achieved phenomenal success and who seem to be able to do everything well. Rather than stimulating effective ministry, modelling these pastors erects a pseudo standard and provokes a false guilt and a despair in those who idolize them.

The apostle Paul is habitually thought of as assured, confident, and almost infallible—an omnicompetent supersaint—despite Paul's many protestations to the contrary. When ministers discover that they cannot live up to such a spurious archetype, they wallow in guilt and depression. Their unresolved guilt over their perceived lack of success dulls their sensitivity and eventually devours any opportunity for excellence. Unresolved guilt leads not to ministry, but to self-pity and despair.

False Expectations

Many young pastors have grandiose expectations of the kind of church they will be able to produce—with God's help, of course. Preoccupations with delusions of grandeur induce many leaders to become intolerant of criticism and callous about the needs or failings of their constituents. These pastors awaken one day to discover that the megachurch has not been built, will not be built, and the people have remained mostly the same as they have always been. As Eugene Peterson observes: "Much in pastoral work is glorious, but the congregation, as such, is not glorious. The congregation is like Nineveh: a site for hard work without a great deal of hope for success, at least not as I want it measured. . . . People who glamorize congregations do us grave disservice . . . there are no wonderful congregations. . . . Parish glamorization is ecclesiastical pornography."[12]

Most of the magnificent but unrealistic expectations of youth will never be fulfilled. Insecure pastors then feel they have failed, and their ministry erodes into humdrum routine. Shattered expecta-

12. Eugene Peterson, "The Jonah Syndrome," *Leadership* (Summer 1990).

tions and perceived failure have destroyed many a minister who fails to understand that God's standard of success is faithfulness, not the creation of "the ultimate church."[13]

Keys to Meaningful Relationships

Many factors govern the quality of interpersonal relationships, not all of which can be controlled. Sometimes despite our best efforts, people fail each other and even friends become estranged. Certain people are so obstinate no one can get along with them. Paul wrote: "If it is possible, as far as it depends on you, live at peace with everyone" (Rom. 12:18). Harmony is not always possible. Sometimes pastors must shake off the dust and go on with ministry to others. The apostle Paul did not succeed relationally with everyone. Demas deserted Paul when Paul needed him most (2 Tim. 4:10), and "Alexander the metalworker did [Paul] a great deal of harm" (2 Tim. 4:14). Paul and Barnabas "had such a sharp disagreement that they parted company" (Acts 15:39). These realities form an unpleasant but inevitable part of Christian ministry. Pastors who cannot tolerate some interpersonal dissonance will be unhappy in their ministries.

Nevertheless, our sacred responsibility includes "bearing with one another in love" (Eph. 4:2) and forgiving "whatever grievances you may have against one another" (Col. 3:13) "not [merely] seven times, but seventy-seven times" (Matt. 18:22). We are exhorted to love one another and "make every effort to keep the unity of the Spirit through the bond of peace" (Eph. 4:3). Strained or severed relationships hurt the entire body of Christ (e.g., Phil. 4:2–3) and the church's testimony to the world, for "by this all men will know that you are my disciples, if you love one another" (John 13:35). Everything possible should be done by pastors to preserve healthy relationships—short of compromising fundamental biblical convictions.

While a pastor may not always be able to maintain harmony with everyone, certain attitudes and approaches to ministry can best preserve the "one accord."

13. See *The Ultimate Church: An Irreverent Look at Church Growth, Megachurches, and Ecclesiastical "Show-Biz"* by Tom Raabe (Grand Rapids: Zondervan, 1991) and *Liberating Ministry from the Success Syndrome* by Kent and Barbara Hughes (Wheaton: Tyndale, 1987).

A Nonconfrontational Style

Pastors who have a confrontational style of leadership often have an exaggerated sense of their own importance and succeed only in developing adversarial rather than collegial relationships. "Bishops (1 Tim. 3:3), and indeed all Christians (Tit. 3:2), are not to be quarrelsome (*ámachos*). Where there is strife, it is due to passions."[14]

Such pastors tend to take firm, unyielding positions on matters of monumental insignificance, thus repeatedly reducing meetings to win-lose propositions. Some ministers make every issue a "right-wrong" decision (as opposed to "better-worse") and cannot admit the possibility that they themselves could be wrong. Sometimes leaders delude themselves into thinking that they alone possess the mind of God on every issue. Their psyches are too fragile to suffer the defeat of their opinions and, therefore, they fight to the bitter end. Failure dogs their ministries all of their days. Their churches eventually reject them as leaders, and rightly so.

Occasionally, leaders need to take a firm stand on an issue before the church or board. Usually such an uncompromising conviction should be reserved for truly important matters such as moral or doctrinal matters having unequivocal biblical support. Even then, a confrontational style is counterproductive. "Let your conversation be always full of grace, seasoned with salt, so that you may know how to answer everyone" (Col. 4:6; cf. Prov. 17:27; Titus 2:8; James 3:2). A bullying rudeness or dogmatism never achieves anything of value.

Excessive passion leads to overstating the case and losing a grip on facts. Many who defend positions because of pride can never admit defeat or error. They often impugn the motives of other people and speak dogmatically outside their area of competence. Relationships erode rapidly in these scenarios and tragically, some pastors never realize their transgression.

An Attentive Heart

"He who answers before listening—that is his folly and his shame" (Prov. 18:13). The value of leaders who listen was discussed in chapter 6, "Values—the Measure of a Ministry." Listening

14. Gerhard Kittel and Gerhard Friedrich, eds., *Theological Dictionary of the New Testament,* abridged (Grand Rapids: Eerdmans, 1985), 573.

includes sensing, attending, understanding, and remembering. Merely receiving information is insufficient. Rather, the receiver must attend to that information, filter out the irrelevant and the inconsequential, and understand the real message, which sometimes lies hidden. "Understanding . . . is the interpretation and evaluation of what you are able to sense. Understanding involves more than merely paying attention to what is heard; it implies that you assign a meaning that is close to what the speaker intended."[15] What pastor would deny the value of listening to and understanding the likes and dislikes, the concerns and fears, and the hopes and dreams of individuals in their congregations? But each pastor must ask himself if he really listens with an attentive heart.

Development of an attentive heart requires enormous self-discipline. Such listening necessitates withholding judgment (Matt. 7:1–2; Rom. 14:4). Closed-mindedness causes us to filter every message through our personal attitudes and beliefs, accepting those that agree and rejecting those that disagree. Judgmental attitudes and closed minds cause relationships to dissolve, fail to develop, or remain strained.

"A fool finds no pleasure in understanding but delights in airing his own opinions" (Prov. 18:2). Pastors who are far too opinionated, who either hold their opinions too deeply or venture to offer their opinions far too quickly, shut themselves off from the beliefs, values, and attitudes of the other people.

"Shallow relationships or relationships that know an early death result when people do not listen to each other . . . Our relationships with one another can only deepen to the extent that we truly listen to all of the verbal and nonverbal messages that the other person is attempting to communicate to us."[16]

A Transparent Manner

Mutual transparency is essential to meaningful relationships. "*Self-disclosure* is defined as communication in which a person voluntarily and intentionally tells another person accurate information

15. Gerald L. Wilson, Alan M. Hantz, and Michael S. Hanna, *Interpersonal Growth Through Communication* (Dubuque, Ia.: Wm. C. Brown, 1989), 90.

16. Judy Cornelia Pearson and Brian H. Spitzberg, *Interpersonal Communication* (Dubuque, Ia.: Wm. C. Brown, 1990), 203.

about himself or herself that the other person is unlikely to know or to find out from another source."[17]

It is not surprising to find that today's most popular and effective preachers are uncommonly transparent human beings. Great pastors of the past, such as Charles Spurgeon, were similarly open about themselves.[18] "Sharing that careful blend of humanness without false humility, victories sans pride, presents an authentic picture of God's work in a life. And that's one of the most important roles a sermon can play. Such illustrations demonstrate a pastor's willingness to own up to failures and work to improve them. They also set a tone that allows people to admit they need help, too."[19] Paul shared not merely share the gospel, but his own life as well (1 Thess. 2:8).

The self-disclosure of the apostle Paul offers an excellent model. He testified to being under pressure "far beyond our ability to endure, so that we despaired even of life. Indeed, in our hearts we felt the sentence of death" (2 Cor. 1:8–9). He wrote "out of great distress and anguish of heart and with many tears" (2 Cor. 2:4). On one occasion, he had "no peace of mind" (2 Cor. 2:13) and there were "conflicts on the outside, fears within" (2 Cor. 7:5). He begged his hearers "to put up with a little of my foolishness" (2 Cor. 11:1), after which he launched into a defense of his apostleship, admitting that he was not a "trained speaker" (2 Cor. 11:6). He talked about his thorn in the flesh and how he "pleaded with the Lord to take it away" (2 Cor. 12:8). He confessed that he was "less than the least of all God's people" (Eph. 3:8), had been "a blasphemer and a persecutor and a violent man" (1 Tim. 1:13), and felt himself to be "the worst of sinners" (1 Tim. 1:16). By contrast, some of today's preachers can hardly admit that they hate cauliflower, have arthritis, struggle with temptation, or enjoy golf.

Obviously, common sense must govern transparency or survival in ministry is unlikely. Appropriate pastoral transparency does not

17. Ibid., 142.
18. For example, Spurgeon suffered intensely from depression and often spoke about it: "I, of all men, am perhaps the subject of the deepest depression at times" and "I am the subject of depression so fearful that I hope none of you ever get to such extremes of wretchedness as I go to" (Metropolitan Tabernacle Pulpit, vol. 10, 352 and vol. 12, 298). Many other sermons testify to Spurgeon's extraordinary transparency.
19. Marshall Shelley, *Helping People Who Don't Want Help* (Waco: Word, 1986), 66.

mean indiscriminate baring of every thought, sin, habit, prejudice, attitude, opinion, or any other internal reality. A few pastors simply do not have enough discernment to know this; they do not last long in ministry. Information divulged about one's true self depends greatly upon the level of maturity of the person or persons to whom we communicate. To dump information on people who lack the maturity to handle it ensures catastrophe. Hence, there are appropriate levels of transparency. Normally, the level of self-disclosure is greatest with a spouse, competent counselor, or trusted friend, somewhat less with a group of elders, and less still with the church at large. Over time, as trust develops, transparency may increase. Trust and maturity determine the appropriate amount of transparency.

Despite the dangers of overzealous self-disclosure, the more common error is that pastors are too closed about themselves. Bruce Larson said the following when he came to his church in Seattle: "Let me describe myself. I have an extraordinary measure of the gift of faith; I believe *anything* is possible with God. I also have a great gift of hope; I really believe tomorrow is going to be the dawn of the Christian era. But where I got shortchanged is in the area of love. I'm insecure, I'm touchy, I'm critical, I'm fault-finding—help me! I'm not a very good lover at all."[20] Such communication reveals a human being, the kind of a person with whom congregations identify as a fellow struggler. Some ministers falsely believe that self-disclosure is dangerous, but as Larson says: "The more vulnerable you become, the safer you are"[21] — within limits, of course. Worthwhile relationships demand the revelation of humanness.

Nondefensiveness

Easily offended people gain few friends and make poor pastors. People in ministry soon learn that they cannot possibly meet everybody's expectations—and some people let them know it. No one in ministry altogether escapes criticisms, bruises, injustices, or worse. How we act when mud flies greatly determines the quality of our

20. "An Interview with Bruce Larson," *Leadership* (Fall 1984): 15.
21. Ibid., 21.

relationships, and ultimately our ministerial effectiveness. Mud brushes off better after it dries.

Nondefensiveness means that a pastor has achieved the grace of overlooking: "A fool shows his annoyance at once, but a prudent man overlooks an insult" (Prov. 12:16). Indeed, "even a fool is thought wise if he keeps silent, and discerning if he holds his tongue" (Prov. 17:28). Pastors who cannot hold their tongue and overlook the inequities perpetrated against them seldom gain much esteem or fruit in ministry. "Often the greatest damage is not done by the dragons [critics or dissidents] themselves but by the overre-actions they provoke in others. When attacked by dragons, our nor-mal response is to become upset or defensive, and when we feel threatened, we usually wind up dousing the fire with gasoline."[22] Some unfair criticism comes from chronic complainers, perennial dissidents; the best advice is to ignore it. Retaliation is fatal. If a per-son becomes disruptive to the entire church by continuing vicious attacks, church discipline may be necessary.

Few American presidents have been subjected to such unfair and bitter personal criticism as that heaped upon Abraham Lincoln, who simply responded: "If I tried to read, much less answer, all the criticisms made of me and all the attacks leveled against me, this office would be closed for all other business. I do the very best I know how, the very best I can. I mean to keep on doing this down to the very end. If the end brings me out all wrong, then ten angels swearing I was right would make no difference. If the end brings me out all right, then what is said against me now will not amount to anything." Pastors could profit greatly by adopting such a philoso-phy. "A man of knowledge uses words with restraint, and a man of understanding is even-tempered" (Prov 17:27).

Wise pastors evaluate the source of complaints in deciding how much attention to give to them. Most criticism should be evaluated carefully for whatever constructive value might be there, but a proper attitude means that we don't take any criticism too seriously, for "am I now trying to win the approval of men, or of God? Or am

22. Marshall Shelley, *Well-Intentioned Dragons: Ministering to Problem People in the Church* (Waco: Word, 1985), 120.

I trying to please men? If I were still trying to please men, I would not be a servant of Christ" (Gal. 1:10).

Diplomacy

"Politics" seems like a pejorative expression in our day, but pastors must be intelligent politicians—in the best sense of the word. Pastors must use sound judgment and diplomacy in working with people. Ours is an extraordinarily pluralistic society. Pastors who do not understand how to get along with many different kinds of people invariably fail in ministry.

This huge category could only be fleshed out adequately in a book devoted to the subject. A discretionary wisdom in interpersonal relationships includes the following elementary principles.

Accept limited responsibility. Pastors who suffer from the "junior messiah" complex accept responsibility for too many things, or the wrong things, and often interject themselves into the disputes of others. Some egotistical pastors truly believe that they can remedy everything that needs correcting. To their chagrin, they soon find they cannot and they are burned in the process. Many a pastor has suffered as a "busybody in other men's matters" (1 Pet. 4:15 KJV). Those determined to be fix-it-all pastors usually fix little but their date of departure.

Protect confidential information. People entrust pastors with a great deal of private information, and sometimes pastors discover more than they want or ought to know about people. Betrayal of trust destroys relationships far quicker than they can be established. Every good pastor holds many secrets that forever remain secret.

Give perceptive counsel. Many pastors find themselves in counseling situations far beyond their training, experience, or wisdom and, as a result, often give bad advice. Giving counsel outside of one's area of expertise jeopardizes one's ministry. Intelligent pastors know their limitations and often refer parishioners to competent counselors. Unwise pastors hand out advice indiscriminately and often suffer the just desserts of their inappropriate guidance. In addition, a new wrinkle has appeared in America: bad counsel may provoke a lawsuit! Liability insurance is no longer an option in pastoral ministry. Wise pastors master the art of referral. Counseling may be the most hazardous of all ministerial functions.

Avoid censure. Many pastors cannot seem to obey the Lord's words: "Do not judge, or you too will be judged" (Matt. 7:1). They say disparaging things about their constituents, usually in the belief that their words will not become known to the target of their remarks. Harsh and judgmental comments have an uncanny way of getting back to the one criticized. One of a pastor's most uncomfortable moments is when a parishioner asks: "Pastor, did you really say that about me?" Many a relationship ends at that point. Apologies rarely help. A few influential people who become alienated by thoughtless comments can effectively destroy a pastor's ministry.

Play no favorites. Many pastors give much attention to some and ignore others. To do so is unscriptural (James 2:2; 1 Tim. 5:21) and political suicide. Obviously, pastors cannot give each congregant an equal amount of time, but pastors must make an extra effort with those who seem alienated (Rom. 12:17); they must minister to the truly needy and care for the unlovely. Hobnobbing with socially desirable people while slighting the needy soon creates suspicion and undermines credibility.

Demonstrate patience. Most inexperienced pastors have far too idealistic expectations of their parishioners. Expressions of intolerance with people's grief, weakness, inconsistencies, or failures sabotages relationships. Pastors must clothe themselves with "compassion, kindness, humility, gentleness, and patience (Greek *makrothymía*)" and "bear (Greek *anéchō*) with each other and forgive whatever grievances . . ." (Col. 3:12–13). Exhibitions of anger and a peevish attitude never contribute to healthy relationships or enduring ministry. Some pastors verbalize their irritation in their preaching; they never enjoy long tenures. Effective pastors constantly encourage their congregants. "Don't forget encouragement. It's the salve for the bruised ego, the vitamin for the tired committee member, and the elixir for continuing success in business [ministry]."[23]

23. Jacqueline Dunckel and Brian Taylor, *Keeping Customers Happy* (North Vancouver, B.C.: International Self-Counsel Press, 1990), 68.

Conflict Management

Internal bickering scandalizes the gospel and makes the church the butt of community jokes. Most intrachurch conflicts may be traced to poor leadership. Wise leaders take preventive action to avert the squabbles that characterize so many congregations. Probably 90 percent of the internal wrangling of most congregations could be avoided if their spiritual leaders simply understood the dynamics of interpersonal relationships and acted according to a few elementary principles. A few of the most rudimentary of these precepts are mentioned here.

Deal with small conflicts immediately and directly, before they become massive and out-of-control. Many pastors make the fatal mistake of believing that little problems will just go away and time will take care of everything. It is "the little foxes that ruin the vineyards" (Song of Songs 2:15), but "how good is a timely word" (Prov. 15:23). More often than not, little problems become big problems and small conflicts that could be easily rectified grow into major controversies. "Consider what a great forest is set on fire by a small spark" (James 3:5). Good leaders take the pulse of the congregation, they have their ears to the ground, they identify potential sources of conflict, and they give attention to problems before positions harden and crises emerge. Bad leaders never recognize conflicts until they threaten to split the fellowship. Seldom do major conflicts emerge without warning signs.

Involve people impacted by decisions in the resolution of issues. Those who unilaterally make decisions that affect the quality of other people's lives place themselves in jeopardy. Most people resent domination by those who do not care enough to ask for their opinions. Wise leaders delegate decision-making power to those people most directly affected by the decision. Antagonists generally are nonparticipants in decision-making. Disfranchisement of church members epitomizes major leadership error and ensures eventual serious conflict.

Insist on open and honest communication at all times. Suspicion breeds conflict, and closed, clandestine channels of communication engender suspicion. In many churches, too many matters of great importance take place behind closed doors. Leaders frequently make virtually no effort to inform people what is going on, except when their participation or money is needed. Effective pastors make use of many different channels of communication: forums, newsletters, announcements, business meetings, telephones, and so forth, so that parishioners might know and participate in decision-making. More important actions demand more extensive communication.

Maintain leadership dignity. A leadership vacuum creates followership distrust and jockeying for power. Sometimes pastors become obsequious, apparently in the false belief that fawning and servile behavior equates with humility and servanthood. A wag has dramatized the error of some clergy:

> Here I stand, without one plea,
> Come wipe your muddy boots on me.

Such pastors soon find themselves in the center of a whirlwind of controversy. Worthy pastoral leaders are never manipulative or domineering, but neither do they allow effrontery and impudence to undermine their position as elders who "are worthy of double honor" (1 Tim. 5:17). They do not and cannot demand respect, but by their dignity, spiritual maturity, and ethical behavior they elicit esteem and deference.

Avoid no-win situations. Pastors who learn the skills of interpersonal relationships do not allow themselves to be caught in no-win situations. Novices frequently find themselves in a position where they feel forced to choose sides with part of a congregation against another part, thereby offending and alienating many. Fence-sitting sometimes is ridiculous and not always possible, but on the other hand, too many pastors engender conflict by taking sides unnecessarily and allowing themselves to be pressed into a no-win stance, a position sure to offend a sizable portion of the congregation.

Preserve church discipline. High-conflict churches go hand in hand with low-discipline churches. When elders wink at gossip, ignore false teaching, condone immorality, and tolerate the sowers of dissension, they invariably face the prospect of spending an exorbitant amount of time on conflict management. Churches that maintain high expectations of their members usually have minimal problems of controversy. Many leaders thumb their noses at scriptural admonitions about discipline, but they usually pay a high price down the road.

Admittedly, discipline is one of the toughest and most delicate of all leadership actions, especially with the threat of lawsuits in our society. Our purpose must always be the restoration of offenders, along with the protection of the church. The honor of God and the testimony of the church depend on discipline. Lack of discipline leads to an unhealthy church.

The extreme form of discipline—excommunication—should probably be reserved for persistent disruptors of church unity, unrepentant moral delinquents, and doctrinal heretics. Most matters should be handled discreetly, confidentially, and with a minimum of embarrassment to all parties. Discipline is a sign of love (Heb. 12:6; Rev. 3:19; Prov. 25:12; 29:17; Ps. 119:75), and it must be administered only in the spirit of genuine Christ-like love, humility, and gentleness (Gal. 6:1).

Effective church discipline is impossible if a biblical pattern of life has not been established in the church. The biblical norm for the church is that of a family committed to loving fellowship and mutual care. Just as in a normal family where there is continual care and the guidance of children, so in the church there must be continual exhortation, encouragement, admonishment, and discipline. Effective discipline is impossible unless the proper atmosphere and climate of a loving family has been previously established.

Dietrich Bonhoeffer deserves the final word: "Where defection from God's Word in doctrine or life imperils the family fellowship and with it the whole congregation, the word of admonition and rebuke must be ventured. Nothing can be more cruel than the tenderness that consigns another to his sin. Nothing can be more compassionate than the severe rebuke that calls a brother back from the path of sin."[24]

Expressions of Simple Kindness

Many clergy fail to understand the enormous power of little acts of kindness and caring, which reap rich dividends in relationships

24. Dietrich Bonhoeffer, *Life Together* (New York: Harper, 1954), 107.

disproportionate to the time or effort expended. A smile, a thank-you note, a telephone call, a meal, a visit, or a book make an enormous difference when given at just the right time. Insensitivity to these small necessities of relationship building and maintenance cost pastors dearly. A reminder from the business world is appropriate: "Doing business with people means . . . attention to the human things: illness, death, marriage, childbirth. It means notes, calls, and visits."[25]

Some of today's pastors delude themselves into thinking that they have no time for the little things that communicate concern and caring to individuals. If squeaky wheels squeeze out acts of kindness that say to people "you are important to me and to God," we have lost orientation to the meaning of ministry. Pastors sometimes boast of their position, power, and celebrity status, but they lack the authenticity of humble representatives of Christ who had time for lepers, sinful women, tax collectors, Pharisees, crippled men, and little children.

Relationships in Groups

Delicate and important human relationships exist between pastoral leaders and groups, including boards and committees. Every group reveals a complex network of interpersonal reactions and responses. These relationships and interactions influence the psychological and spiritual climate of the whole church. The method of making group decisions is often as important as the decisions themselves. In decision-making, the means cannot be divorced from the ends. The attitudes and actions of pastors in small groups greatly determines the quality of interpersonal relationships both for themselves, others in the groups, and the church as a whole. Many of the points previously mentioned relate to this subject and to them we add the following elements.

Invest Authority

Relationships suffer immeasurably when pastors attempt to do what people should do for themselves. Pastors must respect the fact that groups normally make better decisions than individuals.

25. Autry, *Love and Profit, the Art of Caring Leadership*, 42.

Groups must be entrusted with responsibility, treated with proper respect, and invested with sufficient authority so that members feel important and productive. The legitimate authority exercised by pastors depends on the degree to which they are accepted as leaders and liked as persons by the rest of the group. Failure in these important tasks undermines relationships and pastoral effectiveness.

Facilitate Participation

Group members must work together to resolve issues, make decisions, form policies, and advance the work of Christ and the church. The only circumstances people fully understand are those they themselves have experienced and the only ideas they fully grasp are those in whose formulation they have participated. In their work with groups, effective pastors conceive their responsibility as that of facilitators, ensuring every member's contribution and enabling the group to form proper agendas, utilize appropriate procedures, gather critical facts, analyze data intelligently, and resolve issues biblically and profitably to the cause of Christ. Defection of an individual is a symptom of the failure of group process and pastoral leadership. In accomplishing the crucial task of facilitator, pastors both draw upon their previously established relationships and build new, more secure ones.

Encourage and Utilize Diversity

Diversity contributes to group discussion and the forming of worthy solutions. Opposing ideas are assets, not liabilities, and as such they should be solicited, not discouraged. Leadership in groups encourages the free exchange of ideas and keeps personal friction from destroying group productivity. Members must be encouraged to participate in open brainstorming and debate without confusing or identifying their egos with their ideas. Decisions that emerge as a synthesis of a group's own efforts and their differing concepts elicit more solid and enduring support.

An emphasis on relationship building enables pastors to create a proper group climate, one that helps the group focus on concepts without judging motives or impugning character. When pastors behave in effective ways in groups, relationships of solidarity emerge and these relationships propel the church forward. It is not until a group—and, ultimately, the whole church—develops a cohesiveness that the church becomes a significant force in its community, a we-ness in which individuals take pride and satisfaction in their identification with the body.

Cohesiveness is not a matter of agreement, but of healthy interaction among group members who respect differing viewpoints, capabilities, and personalities. The description of a healthy church is not "an aggregate of contented cows," but a dynamic group of gifted and functioning Christians who respect and utilize individual differences. Complete unanimity may handicap rather than facilitate a group because a too-easy agreement leads to overconfidence and complacency, rather than to creative thinking.[26]

Steps to Healthy Relationships

Healthy relationships between pastors and parishioners form the sine qua non of ministry. Ministers desiring excellence and productivity must learn relational skills, develop collegial alliances, and maintain friendships throughout their tenures as pastors. A few crucial steps achieve sound relationships.

Study and preach on biblical texts stressing relationships with God and one another, particularly emphasizing the community of believers, responsibilities to the body, and pastoral servanthood in the church. Ask God for friends who will hold you accountable, refresh, nourish, rebuke, and encourage you in your ministry.

Identify your personality traits, especially those characteristics that may handicap your ministry. You may need help to overcome those idiosyncrasies that form barriers to meaningful relationships and ministry.

Examine your leadership style. Be sure you are not confrontational or defensive. Learn the skills of interpersonal diplomacy. It may be necessary to take graduate work in

26. The author's book *Leadership in Christian Ministry* (Grand Rapids: Baker, 1989) gives more detailed treatment of leadership in groups and group decision-making procedures.

communication, group process, group dynamics, and conflict management.

Begin now to do the little acts of kindness that pay disproportionate dividends in relationships.

Give special attention to your responsibility in groups. Invest authority, facilitate cooperative interaction, and utilize diversity advantageously.

CONCLUSION: MISSION POSSIBLE

There has never yet been a man
in our history who led a life of ease
whose name is worth remembering.

Theodore Roosevelt

A few years ago there was a television series entitled "Mission: Impossible!" However, each week the "impossible" task was accomplished, the good guys prevailed, and the formidable foes were overthrown. Thus, the production was mistitled; what seemed impossible was executed successfully—and in only one hour!

For those who have persevered in reading this book, it may seem that the pastoral commission exceeds the limits of both capability and reason, and that "Mission: Impossible!" would be suitable terminology to describe Paul's "noble task." Indeed, the forces against us appear overwhelming; the church's needs seem greater than our resources.

Since God has no superhuman, omnicompetent, clerical Tarzans running around in America's jungles, maybe we might as well forget

223

about pastoral ministry and go fishing (for real fish), as did Simon Peter and the other disciples—or, perhaps, give ourselves to some other line of work? No! We lay claim to Elisha's ancient words: "Don't be afraid. Those who are with us are more than those who are with them" (2 Kings 6:16). Our weapons "have divine power to demolish strongholds" (2 Cor. 10:4). With angelic hosts, the Spirit of power, and dynamic spiritual weapons, how shall we not succeed?

The strongholds of the world's evil and the church's lethargy intimidate those not properly equipped for battle, but we take courage in the admonition to "be strong in the Lord and in his mighty power" (Eph. 6:10) and the reminder that "the one who is in you is greater than the one who is in the world" (1 John 4:4). As in the television drama, what seems impossible can be done—but not without some sweat, great faith, and dogged determination. So let us refuse to be average, refuse to be discouraged, refuse to be defeated. Ultimately, the victory is ours, for the gates of hell will not prevail against the church!

Uncompromised integrity, spiritual authenticity, and unequivocal commitment to scriptural authority outweigh the strength of any enemy. As the great Bostonian clergyman and author Phillips Brooks suggested: "A man [or woman] who lives right, and is right, has more power in his silence than another has by his words." Let the mantle of Elijah fall upon our spiritual leaders; let those called to dream worthy dreams and lead the body of Christ in our day "make our lives sublime, and departing, leave behind us footprints in the sand of time." May those "footprints" be a revitalized American church. Let future generations—if the Lord tarries—take note of the great awakening that invigorated Christianity at the turn of the century, the beginning of the third millennium since Christ left his footprints upon the earth.

One of my favorite passages from *The Pilgrim's Progress* describes Christian struggling through the Valley of the Shadow, where he was threatened with hobgoblins, satyrs, and dragons of the pit. With that scary experience behind him, Bunyan writes: "Now, morning being come, he [Christian] looked back, not out of desire to return, but to see, by the light of day, what hazards he had gone through in the dark. So he saw more perfectly the ditch that was on the one hand, and the quag that was on the other; also how narrow the way was which led betwixt them both." Pastoral ministry seems like a menacing proposition, but there is grandeur on this road, nobility in this task, and unimaginable glory at the end, when we shall see by the light of day what hazards we have gone through in the dark.

The way to glory and spiritual effectiveness in ministry necessitates threading a precarious path, but as Shakespeare observes: "All glory comes from daring to begin." So begin! Begin with unwavering confidence in a great God who has entrusted us with a noble task.

BIBLIOGRAPHY

Aeschliman, Gordon. *Global Trends*. Downers Grove, Il.: InterVarsity, 1990.

Alcorn, Randy. *Christians in the Wake of the Sexual Revolution*. Portland, Ore.: Multnomah, 1987.

Allen, C. Leonard, Richard T. Hughes, and Michael R. Weed. *The Worldly Church: A Call for Biblical Renewal*. Abilene, Tex.: Abilene Christian University Press, 1991.

Ambler, Rex. *Global Theology*. Philadelphia: Trinity Press International, 1990.

Arn, Win, ed. *The Pastor's Church Growth Handbook*. Pasadena, Calif.: The Church Growth Press, 1979.

Arn, Win, and Charles Arn. *The Master Plan for Making Disciples*. Pasadena, Calif.: Church Growth Press, 1982.

Autry, James. *Love and Profit, The Art of Caring Leadership*. New York: Morrow, 1991.

Balswick, Jack O., and J. Kenneth Morland. *Social Problems*. Grand Rapids: Baker, 1990.

Barclay, William. *The Promise of the Spirit*. Philadelphia: Westminster, 1960.

Barna, George. *The Frog in the Kettle*. Ventura, Calif.: Regal, 1990.

———. *Marketing the Church*. Colorado Springs, Colo.: NavPress, 1988.

Barnette, Henlee H. *The Church and the Ecological Crisis*. Grand Rapids: Eerdmans, 1972.

Baxter, Richard. *The Reformed Pastor*. Portland, Ore: Multnomah, 1982.

Bellah, Robert N., et al. *Habits of the Heart: Individualism and Commitment in American Life*. New York: Harper and Row, 1985.

Bennis, Warren, and Burt Nanus. *Leaders: The Strategies for Taking Charge*. New York: Harper and Row, 1985.

Bloesch, Donald. *Crumbling Foundations*. Grand Rapids: Zondervan, 1984.

Bonar, Andrew. *Robert Murray McCheyne, Memoirs and Remains*. London: Banner of Truth, 1966.

Bonhoeffer, Dietrich. *The Cost of Discipleship*. New York: Macmillan, 1963.

———. *Life Together*. New York: Harper, 1954.

Bradley, Ian. *God Is Green: Ecology for Christians*. New York: Image Books, 1992.

Brown, Lester R., ed. *State of the World*. New York: Norton, 1990.

Burns, James. *Leadership*. New York: Harper and Row, 1979.

Calian, Carnegie Samuel. *Today's Pastor in Tomorrow's World*. New York: Hawthorn, 1977.

Callahan, Kennon L. *Effective Church Leadership*. San Francisco, Calif.: Harper and Row, 1990.

———. *Twelve Keys to An Effective Church*. New York: Harper and Row, 1983.

Clapp, Steve. *Ministerial Competency Report*. Champaign, Ill.: Crouse Printing, 1982.

Colson, Charles. *Kingdoms in Conflict*. Grand Rapids: Zondervan, 1987.

Cousins, Don, Leith Anderson, and Arthur DeKruyter. *Mastering Church Management*. Portland, Ore.: Multnomah, 1990.

Covey, Stephen. *The Seven Habits of Highly Effective People*. New York: Simon and Schuster, 1989.

DeWitt, Calvin. *The Environment and the Christian: What Can We Learn from the New Testament?* Grand Rapids: Baker, 1991.

Dietterich, Inagrace. *An Evaluation of Approaches to Church Transformation*. Chicago: The Center for Parish Development, 1991.

Dunckel, Jacqueline, and Brian Taylor. *Keeping Customers Happy*. North Vancouver, B.C.: International Self-Counsel Press, 1990.

Edwards, David L. *The Futures of Christianity*. Suffolk, England: Richard Clay Ltd., 1987.

Engstrom, Ted W., and Howard R. Dayton. *The Art of Management for Christian Leaders*. Waco: Word, 1982.

Exman, Gary. *Get Ready...Get Set...Grow!: Church Growth for Town and Country Congregations*. Lima, Ohio: The C.S.S. Publishing Co., 1987.

Frazier, Claude A. *Should Preachers Play God?* Independence, Mo.: Independence, 1973.

Gardner, John W. *The Heart of the Matter: Leader-Constituent Interaction*. Washington, D.C.: Independent Sector, 1986.

George, Carl. *Prepare Your Church for the Future*. Tarrytown, N.Y.: Revell, 1991.

Gibbs, Eddie. *I Believe in Church Growth*. Grand Rapids: Eerdmans, 1981.

Glasse, James D. *Profession: Minister*. Nashville: Abingdon, 1968.

Greenleaf, Robert. *Servant Leadership*. New York: Paulist, 1957.

Guinness, Os, and John Seel, eds. *No God But God.* Chicago: Moody, 1992.

Hanna, David P. *Designing Organizations for High Performance.* Reading, Mass.: Addison-Wesley, 1988.

Harmon, Frederick G. *The Executive Odyssey.* New York: John Wiley, 1989.

Harris, John. *Stress, Power and Ministry.* Washington, D.C.: Alban Institute, 1979.

Harris, Philip R. *High Performance Leadership.* Glenview, Ill.: Scott, Foresman and Co., 1989.

Hassinger, Edward, John S. Holik, and J. Kenneth Benson. *The Rural Church.* Nashville: Abingdon, 1988.

Heilbroner, Robert L. *An Inquiry Into the Human Prospect.* New York: Norton, 1974.

Henry, Carl F. H. *Twilight of a Great Civilization.* Westchester, Ill.: Crossway, 1988.

Horton, Michael, ed. *Power Religion.* Chicago: Moody, 1992.

Hull, Bill. *The Disciple Making Pastor.* Old Tappan, N.J.: Revell, 1988.

Hughes, Kent, and Barbara Hughes. *Liberating Ministry from the Success Syndrome.* Wheaton: Tyndale, 1987.

Hunter, James Davison. *American Evangelicalism.* New Brunswick, N.J.: Rutgers University Press, 1983.

Jansen, Frank Kaleb. *Target Earth.* Kailua-Kona, Hawaii: University of the Nations, 1989.

Jenson, Ron, and Jim Stevens. *Dynamics of Church Growth.* Grand Rapids: Baker, 1981.

Johnston, Jon. *Will Evangelicalism Survive Its Own Popularity?* Grand Rapids: Zondervan, 1980.

Jones, Bruce W. *Ministerial Leadership in a Managerial World.* Wheaton: Tyndale, 1988.

Kets de Vries, F. R. Manfred. *Prisoners of Leadership.* New York: Wiley, 1989.

Kilmann, Ralph H., Teresa Joyce Covin, and Associates. *Corporate Transformation: Revitalizing Organizations for a Competitive World.* San Francisco: Jossey-Bass, 1988.

Kittel, Gerhard, and Gerhard Friedrich, eds.. *Theological Dictionary of the New Testament,* abridged. Grand Rapids: Eerdmans, 1985.

Lewis, C. S., ed. *George MacDonald, An Anthology.* New York: Macmillan, 1947.

Lewis, Hunter. *A Question of Values.* New York: Harper and Row, 1990.

Longnecker, Harold L. *Building Town and Country Churches.* Chicago: Moody, 1973.

Luecke, David S., and Samuel Southard. *Pastoral Administration: Integrating Ministry and Management.* Waco: Word, 1986.

Lutzer, Erwin. *Failure: The Back Door to Success*. Chicago: Moody, 1976.

Manske, Fred A., Jr. *Secrets of Effective Leadership*. Memphis, Tenn.: Leadership Education and Development, Inc., 1987.

Maxwell, John C. *Be a People Person*. Wheaton: Victor, 1989.

McGavran, Donald A. *Effective Evangelism: A Theological Mandate*. Phillipsburg, N.J.: Presbyterian and Reformed, 1988.

————. *Understanding Church Growth*. Grand Rapids,: Eerdmans, 1970.

McGavran, Donald A., ed. *Church Growth and Christian Mission*. New York: Harper and Row, 1965.

McGavran, Donald A., and Win Arn. *Back to Basics in Church Growth*. Wheaton: Tyndale, 1981.

McGinnis, Alan Loy. *The Friendship Factor*. Minneapolis: Augsburg, 1979.

Means, James E. *Leadership in Christian Ministry*. Grand Rapids: Baker, 1989.

Molnar, Thomas. *The Pagan Temptation*. Grand Rapids: Eerdmans, 1987.

Myers, Kenneth A. *All God's Children and Blue Suede Shoes*. Westchester, Ill.: Crossway Books, 1989.

Naisbitt, John, and Patricia Aburdene. *Megatrends 2000*. New York: Morrow, 1990.

Nanus, Burt. *The Leader's Edge*. Chicago: Contemporary Books, 1989.

Narramore, S. Bruce. *No Condemnation: Rethinking Guilt Motivation in Counseling, Preaching, and Parenting*. Grand Rapids: Zondervan, 1984.

Niebuhr, H. Richard. *The Purpose of the Church and Its Ministry*. New York: Harper and Brothers, 1956.

Niebuhr, H. Richard, and Daniel D. Williams. *The Ministry in Historical Perspectives*. New York: Harper and Brothers, 1956.

Nouwen, Henri. *The Way of the Heart*. New York: Ballantine, 1981.

Oden, Thomas. *Pastoral Theology*. San Francisco: Harper and Row, 1983.

Oostdyk, Harv. *Step One: The Gospel and the Ghetto*. Basking Ridge, N.J.: SonLife International, 1983.

Packer, J. I. *The Quest for Godliness*. Wheaton: Crossway, 1990.

Pappas, Anthony G. *Entering the World of the Small Church*. New York: The Alban Institute, 1988.

Pavin, Earl. *Missions USA*. Chicago: Moody, 1985.

Pearson, Judy Cornelia, and Brian H. Spitzberg. *Interpersonal Communication*. Dubuque, Ia.: Wm. C. Brown, 1990.

Peters, Tom, and Nancy Austin. *A Passion for Excellence*. New York: Warner, 1985.

Quebedeaux, Richard. *The Worldly Evangelicals*. San Francisco: Harper and Row, 1978.

Raabe, Tom. *The Ultimate Church*. Grand Rapids: Zondervan, 1991.

Regenstein, Lewis. *Replenish the Earth*. New York: Crossroad, 1991.

Richards, Lawrence O., and Clyde Hoeldtke, *A Theology of Church Leadership.* Grand Rapids: Zondervan, 1980.

Robinson, Haddon. *Biblical Preaching.* Grand Rapids: Baker, 1980.

Robinson, Jackie. *Baseball Has Done It.* Philadelphia: Lippincott, 1964.

Rose, Larry L., and C. Kirk Hadaway, eds. *The Urban Challenge.* Nashville: Broadman, 1982.

———. *An Urban World: Churches Face the Future.* Nashville: Broadman, 1984.

Schaeffer, Francis. *No Little People.* Downers Grove, Ill.: InterVarsity, 1974.

Schaller, Lyle E. *The Multiple Staff and the Larger Church.* Nashville: Abingdon, 1980.

Schaller, Lyle E., ed. *The Rural Church.* Nashville: Abingdon, 1988.

Scherer, James A. *Global Living Here and Now.* New York: Friendship Press, 1974.

Schuller, David S., ed. *Ministry in America.* New York: Harper and Row, 1980.

Shawchuck, Norman. *What It Means to Be a Church Leader.* Indianapolis, Ind.: Spiritual Growth Resources, 1984.

Shelley, Bruce, and Marshall Shelley. *The Consumer Church.* Downers Grove, Ill.: InterVarsity, 1992.

Shelley, Marshall. *Helping People Who Don't Want Help.* Waco: Word, 1986.

———. *Well-Intentioned Dragons: Ministering to Problem People in the Church.* Waco: Word, 1985.

Smith, Donald. *Clergy in the Cross-Fire.* Philadelphia: Westminster, 1973.

Spurgeon, Charles. *All-Round Ministry.* Carlisle, Penn.: Banner of Truth, 1972.

———. *Metropolitan Tabernacle Pulpit,* vol. 20. Pasadena, Tex.: Pilgrim Publications.

———. *Metropolitan Tabernacle Pulpit,* vol. 59. Pasadena, Tex.: Pilgrim Publications.

Stott, John R. W. *The Preacher's Portrait.* Grand Rapids: Eerdmans, 1961.

Strachan, R. Kenneth. *The Inescapable Calling.* Grand Rapids: Eerdmans, 1968.

Surrey, Peter J. *The Small Town Church.* Nashville: Abingdon, 1981.

Taylor, Richard S. *Principles of Pastoral Success.* Grand Rapids: Francis Asbury Press, 1989.

Telushkin, Joseph. *Jewish Literacy.* New York: Morrow, 1991.

Thielicke, Helmut. *The Trouble with the Church.* Grand Rapids: Baker, 1965.

Thomas, Cal. *The Death of Ethics in America.* Waco: Word, 1988.

Todaro, Michael P. *Economic Development in the Third World.* New York: Longman, 1989.

Torney, George A., ed. *Toward Creative Urban Strategy.* Waco: Word, 1970.

Tozer, A. W. *Man: The Dwelling Place of God.* Harrisburg, Penn.: Christian Publications, 1966.

———. *The Root of the Righteous.* Harrisburg, Penn.: Christian Publications, 1955.

Tregoe, Benjamin, John Zimmerman, Ronald Smith, and Peter Tobia. *Vision in Action: Putting a Winning Strategy to Work.* New York: Simon and Schuster, 1989.

Wagner, C. Peter. *Leading Your Church to Growth.* Ventura, Calif.: Regal, 1984.

———. *Your Church Can Grow.* Ventura, Calif.: Regal, 1984.

Walrath, Douglas. *Finding Options for Ministry in Small Churches.* New York: National Council of Churches, 1981.

Waterman, Robert H., Jr. *The Renewal Factor.* New York: Bantam, 1988.

Wiersbe, Warren. *The Integrity Crisis.* Nashville: Oliver-Nelson, 1988.

Wilkinson, Loren, ed. *Earthkeeping in the '90s.* Grand Rapids: Eerdmans, 1991.

Wilson, Gerald L., Alan M. Hantz, and Michael S. Hanna. *Interpersonal Growth Through Communication.* Dubuque, Ia.: Wm. C. Brown, 1989.

INDEX

Calvary Community
   Church (Westlake Vil-
   lage, CA), 169
Calvin, John, 23
Calvinism, 62
Campus Crusade, 115, 193
Caring, 218–19
Carlzon, Jan, 132
Casals, Pablo, 150
Cell groups, 153, 154, 170
Censure, 215
Center for Creative Leader-
   ship, 107, 108, 112, 155
Center for Parish Develop-
   ment, 161
Change, 35, 104, 115, 143,
   145–46, 161, 174, 176,
   181 See also Transfor-
   mation
Character, 15, 19
Charismatic churches, 118,
   119
Cheap grace, 68
Chief executive officer
   (CEO), 87–92
Child abuse, 49
Chrysostom, 81
Church activities, 145
Church atmosphere,
   187–88, 198
Church discipline, 175,
   217–18
Church government, 111,
   181
Church growth, 56n,
   69–70, 89, 111, 160,
   169, 178–89, 192–93,
   197–201
Church renewal, 115
Civil rights movement, 54
Clergy failure, 20, 199
Cohesiveness, 221
Collegiality, 143–44, 170,
   173
Colson, Charles, 18, 50n,
   192n
Commitment to growth,
   179–80, 182, 198
Common sense, 19, 23–25

Communication, 27,
   31–32, 95, 216–17
Community, 50, 51, 117,
   200
Community Baptist Church
   (Alta Loma, CA), 134,
   153
Community values, 165
Compassion, 25–26
Competence, 18, 19
Competitiveness, 144
Competitor, 92
Complacency, 179
Compromise, 73, 204
Conflict management,
   216–17
Confrontational style, 209
Congeniality, 188
Congregational identity,
   165
Consensus, 109, 110, 111,
   113, 181
Consistency, 186
Consultants, 160
Consumerism, 92, 138–39
Contemporary music, 116,
   193
Contextualization, 14,
   57–58, 145, 166
Control, 24, 25, 205
Conversion, 63–64, 66
Conversion growth, 192
Counseling. See Pastoral
   counseling
Cousins, Dan, 90n, 126n
Covey, Stephen R., 129n,
   146n
Covin, Teresa Joyce, 143n,
   161n
Crane, George, 189
Creativity, 195
Critical thinking, 33
Criticism, 212–13
Cross-cultural ministry, 58,
   156
Cultural exegesis, 156, 162,
   164–65
Cultural pluralism, 58

Cultural sensitivity, 14, 27,
   28–29
Cultural upheaval, 36
Culture, 28–29, 57

Day, Albert Edward, 199
Dayton, Howard R., 89n
Deception, 114
Decision-making, 111, 216,
   219
DeKruyter, Arthur, 90n,
   126n
Delegation, 25, 98, 127,
   216
Demographics, 144, 164
Depersonalization, 56
Depression, 204, 207
Details, 131
Diettrich, Inagrace, 161n,
   168
Dignity, 217
Diplomacy, 186, 214
Direct mail, 196
Discernment, 24
Disciple-making, 15, 34,
   83, 105, 125, 180, 182,
   183, 184
Discipleship, 14, 63, 66, 67,
   68, 69–70, 71, 75, 78,
   94, 109, 117, 118, 119,
   120, 133, 134, 159,
   168–71, 194
Discipline, 13, 14, 34, 95,
   150–51
Discontentment, 128–29
Disenfranchisement of
   members, 181, 216
Diversity, 14, 220
Divorce, 41–42, 46, 49
Dobson, James, 46
Dogma, 14
Drucker, Peter, 51
Dunckel, Jacqueline, 215n

Easy-believism, 63–64
Ecological crisis, 42–43
Economics, 37–39, 144
Edification, 108
Edifice complex, 40
Edwards, David L., 47n

Needs, 120, 124, 125, 130, 184
Needy people, 125–26
Negativism, 189
Neopaganism, 60, 64, 78, 169
Networking, 144
New Age philosophy, 92
New Song Church (Walnut, CA), 134, 135, 145, 170
Nicklaus, Jack, 132
Niebuhr, H. Richard, 81n, 82n, 84, 87–89, 94
Nietzsche, Friedrich, 47
"No-win" situations, 217
Nonconfrontational style, 209
Nondefensiveness, 212–13
Nouwen, Henri, 70, 79
Numerical growth, 197

Obedience, 22
Oden, Thomas C., 67n, 197n
One-to-one ministry, 197
Onesiphorus, 134, 201
Oostdyk, Harv, 55n, 57
Optimism, 167, 188–89
Organizational skills, 33
Orthodoxy, 61, 158, 163, 174
Orthopraxy, 61, 158, 172
Our Savior's Lutheran Church (Denver, CO), 172
Overseer, oversight, 94–95, 134, 184

Packer, J. I., 59, 67, 68n, 74n, 76n, 77n, 158
Paganism, 62, 65
Pappas, Anthony G., 54
Parachurch ministries, 159, 173
Parson, 83
Participative management, 153
Passion for ministry 19, 25–26, 32, 77
Passivity, 186, 203

Past, 166
Pastoral care, 125, 126, 171, 196–97
Pastoral counseling, 86–87, 105, 214–15
Pastoral gifts, 196
Pastoral role, 79–87, 88, 90, 92–94, 99, 105
Patience, 215
Paul, 102, 113, 114, 134, 186, 201, 207, 208
  discipline, 151
  passion for ministry, 124–25
  philosophy of ministry, 102–3
  self-disclosure, 211
  vision, 150, 154
Pavin, Earl, 182n
Pearson, Judy Cornelia, 210n
Perkins, William, 23
Persistence, 151
Personality traits, 221
Peters, Tom, 130n, 132n, 148, 149, 153
Peterson, Eugene, 207
Pharisees, 18
Philosophy of ministry, 100–107, 110, 112, 114, 116–21, 198
Phoebe of Cenchrea, 134, 201
Pilgrim's Progress, 22, 27n, 224
Pius XI, 81
Pluralism, 28, 29, 36, 41, 50
Politics, 144
Popular culture, 48, 57
Popularity, 21
Population growth, 40
Pornography, 44
Poverty, 37–40, 54
Power, Grant, 38n
Practicality, 148
Pragmatism, 20, 21, 25, 73, 139, 163, 167–68

Prayer, 15, 22, 74, 77, 78, 118, 138, 186
Preaching, 15, 32, 81–83, 104–5, 169, 184, 189–92, 198
Priest, 81, 83
Priesthood of believers, 170
Priorities, 71, 110, 121
Priscilla, 134, 201
Prison Fellowship, 18
Privatization, 50
Problem analysis, 33
Programs, 125, 160
Prophet, 81
Prosperity theology, 21
Prudence, 176
Psychology, 86, 162
Public relations, 88
Puritans, 113

Quebedeaux, Richard, 65n

Raabe, Tom, 56n, 208n
Racism, 54
Rationalism, 60
Reductionism, 137
Referral, 215
Reformation, 82, 113
Regenstein, Lewis, 43
Relational aptitude, 27, 29–31, 202
Relational problems, 199–200
Relationships, 24, 30, 103–4, 133–34, 194, 196, 200–3, 204, 205, 208–10, 215, 216, 217, 218, 220, 221
Relativism, 28, 60
Relevance, 14, 72, 158
Renaissance, 60
Renewal, 177
Repentance, 63
Resistance, 147, 181, 182
Respect, 24
Retraining of ministers, 154–55
Revitalization, 13
Richards, Lawrence O., 91n
Rickey, Branch, 148